STREET FRENCH 2

To order the accompanying cassette for

STREET FRENCH 2

See the coupon on the last page for details

STREET FRENCH 2

The Best of French Idioms

David Burke

John Wiley & Sons, Inc.

New York • Chichester • Brisbane • Toronto • Singapore

Design and Production: Optima PrePress
Copy Editor: Nicolas Caron
Front Cover Illustration: Ty Semaka
Inside Illustrations: Ty Semaka

This publication is designed to provide accurate and authoritative information in regard to the subject matter covered. It is sold with the understanding that the publisher is not engaged in rendering legal, accounting, or other professional services. If legal advice or other expert assistance is required, the services of a competent professional person should be sought.

Library of Congress Cataloging-in-Publication Data
Burke, David
    Street French 2 : the best of French idioms / David Burke.
      p. cm.
    Includes index.
    ISBN 0-471-13899-2 (paper : alk. paper)
    1. French language—Idioms.   2. French language—Slang.   3. French language—Textbooks for foreign speakers—English.   I. Title.
    PC2460.B856   1996
    447'.09—dc20   96-15950

Printed in the United States of America
10 9 8 7 6 5 4 3 2 1

This book is dedicated to my mother.

ACKNOWLEDGMENTS

My special thanks to Nicolas Caron for all his hard work and significant contribution to this book. His insight into the *real* French language was indispensable. I feel extremely fortunate for having the opportunity to work with him and especially thankful for his wonderful friendship.

There's no doubt about it. It's hard to mention Ty Semaka's name without using adjectives like "amazing," "hilarious," "remarkably talented." As with all of the books in this series, Ty's illustrations never cease to astound me with their penetrating wit and unique style.

Once again, I'm grateful for having such a wonderful senior editor in PJ Dempsey of John Wiley & Sons. Her upbeat attitude, enthusiasm, and downright charm made every step of this project an absolute delight. PJ's affability seems to be a running theme throughout her department. Chris Jackson, Assistant Editor, and Elaine O'Neal, Editorial Assistant, always seem to go beyond the call of duty to be helpful, prompt, attentive, and congenial.

My associate managing editor and fellow Francophile, Benjamin Hamilton of John Wiley & Sons, is undoubedtly one of the most professional, meticulous, and affable people I've ever had the fortune to work with. His zeal for the French language was absolutely contagious and made the production phrase of this project an absolute joy. To Benjamin, I say a big *"Merci du fond de mon palpitant*, mon pote†!"*

---

*palpitant *m.* heart • (lit); palpitater.
†pote *m.* friend, chum.

CONTENTS

Lesson 1 — 1

Qu'est-ce qu'il chante-là?

(What's he talking about?)

Lesson 2 — 27

Nancy est une vraie fée du logis!

(Nancy's a real wiz around the house!)

Lesson 3 — 47

Georges semble avoir le cafard.

(George seems depressed.)

INTRODUCTION

To the outsider, idioms seem like a confusing secret code reserved only for the native speaker of English. Idioms are certainly tricky beasts, because it is the *sum* of all the words in the phrase that must be interpreted, not each word by itself. In other words, the listener must never confuse the literal translation of an idiom with the underlying meaning of what is really being expressed or symbolized. In English, if you are told *"Get me a pizza... and step on it!"* you are not being instructed to go trample on a round piece of cheesy bread. You are simply being told to hurry, since *"step on it"* refers to "pressing down on" the accelerator of a car. The same applies to French. For example, the popular idiom *"avoir le cafard"* literally "to have the cockroach," actually has nothing to do with slimy insects or cleanliness . It simply means "to be very depressed."

In short, idioms are simply an imaginative and expressive way to communicate an idea or thought. In order to be considered truly proficient in French, idioms must be learned, since they are consistently used in books, magazines, television, movies, songs, French homes, etc.

For the nonnative speaker, learning the information in **STREET FRENCH 2** will equal years of living in France and reduce the usual time it takes to absorb the intricacies of slang and colloquialisms.

STREET FRENCH 2 is a self-teaching guide made up of ten chapters, each divided into four primary parts:

■ DIALOGUE

Twenty to thirty popular French idioms (including some key slang terms) are presented as they may be heard in an actual conversation. A translation of the dialogue in standard English is always given on the opposite page, followed by an important phonetic version of the dialogue as it would actually be spoken by a French native. This page will prove vital to any nonnative, since the French tend to rely heavily on contractions, reductions, and other shortcuts in pronunciation.

■ VOCABULARY

This section spotlights all of the slang terms that were used in the dialogue and offers:

1. An example of usage for each entry.

2. Another look at the example, this time written as it may *actually* be spoken by a native speaker. Here you will encounter two symbols:

(1) ____ an underline indicating:

    a. where a contraction/reduction would be commonly made when spoken; or

    b. where a personal pronoun has been added.
SEE: *STREET FRENCH 1, Popular Usage of Objective Case Personal Pronouns & Ça, p. 102.*

(2) ~ a squiggle indicating where *ne* has been dropped.

3. An English translation of the example.

4. In addition, synonyms, antonyms, variations, or special notes are offered to give you a complete sense of the word or expression:

---

caler le bide (se) *exp.* to eat • (lit); to stablize one's stomach

    example: J'ai faim. Je vais *me caler le bide.*

    as pronounced: J'ai faim. J'vais m'caler l'bide.

    translation: I'm hungry. I'm going *to eat something.*

    NOTE: The masculine noun *bide* is a shortened version of *bidon,* meaning "belly" • (lit); can or drum.

■ PRACTICE THE VOCABULARY

These word games include all of the slang terms and idioms previously learned and will help you test yourself on your comprehension. *IMPORTANT:* All exercises will be presented using contractions and reductions as learned in lesson one in order to get you used to thinking like a native. *(The pages providing the answers to all the drills are indicated at the beginning of this section.)*

■ A CLOSER LOOK SECTION

This section introduces unconventional "rules" and insights regarding the usage of idioms and colloquialisms in a clear, concise, and easy-to-understand style. In addition, you will explore common idioms pertaining to a specific category such as idioms containing numbers, colors, fruits and vegetables, animals, etc.

■ EXERCISES

Helpful drills are presented in this section to help test you on the previous A CLOSER LOOK section.

■ DICTATION (Test your oral comprehension)

Using an optional audio cassette *(see coupon on back page),* the student will hear a paragraph containing many of the idioms from opening dialogue. The paragraph will be read *as it would actually be heard* in a conversation, using frequent contractions and reductions.

■ REVIEW

Following each sequence of five chapters is a summary review encompassing all the words and expressions learned up to that point.

The secret to learning **STREET FRENCH 2** is by following this simple checklist:

■ Make sure that you have a good grasp on each section before proceeding to the drills. If you've made more than two errors in a particular drill, simply go back and review...then try again! *Remember:* This is a self-paced book, so take your time. You're not fighting the clock!

■ It's very important that you feel comfortable with each chapter before proceeding to the next. Words learned along the way may crop up in the following dialogues. So feel comfortable before moving on!

■ Make sure that you read the dialogues and drills aloud. This is an excellent way to become comfortable speaking colloquially and begin thinking like a native.

At the end of each five chapters is a review exam encompassing all of the words and expressions learned up to that point.

If you have always prided yourself on being fluent in French, you will undoubtedly be surprised and amused to encounter a whole new world of phrases usually hidden away in the French language and usually reserved only for the native speaker...*until now!*

IMPORTANT

The dialogues and exercises in **Street French 2** have been entirely written using contractions and reductions. Their use is perhaps the single most critical element when speaking like a native. Make sure you have a good grasp on these before moving on!

The following is an abridged list of the shortcuts and contracts that you will find throughout this book. For a more detailed explanation, refer to **Street French 1**.

Contraction	Example	Note
celui = **c'ui**	Tu connais celui-là? *Tu connais **c'ui**-là?*	Contraction occurs only when *celui* is followed by **-ci** (pronounced *sui-si*) or **-là** (pronouned *sui-la*).
c'est un(e) = **c't'un(e)**	C'est un(e) bon(ne) ami(e). ***C't'un(e)*** *bon(ne) ami(e).*	
elle(s) = **è**	Elle m'énerve! **È** *m'énerve!* Elles sont belles. **È** *sont belles.*	This reduction is only used when followed by a consonant. However, in certain rural parts of France, *elle* is changed to **l'** when followed by a vowel: Elle est bizarre. **L'***est bizarre.* *Note:* This rural style was used in *Street French 1*, but will not be used in this book.
elles = **è'z'**	Elles écoutent la radio. **È'z'***écoutent la radio.*	This contraction is used only when followed by a vowel.

Contraction	Example	Note
il faut = **faut**	Il faut que je parte. 1. **Faut** qu'je parte. 2. **Faut** que j'parte.	**il** may be dropped in all tenses: **faudrait** (que), **fallait** (que), etc.
il y a = **y a**	Il y a du monde ici! **Y a** du monde ici!	Also, **y aurait**, **y avait**, **y a eu**, etc. *Note:* When used as an abbreviation of **il y a**, **y a** is articulated as one syllable: **ya**.

il(s) = **y**	Il va venir m'aider.
	Y va v'nir m'aider.
	
	Ils vont au magasin.
	Y vont au magasin.
		This reduction is only used when followed by a consonant. However, in certain rural parts of France, il (as well as *elle*) is changed to **l'** when followed by a vowel:
		    Il est très intelligent.
		    L'est très intelligent.

ils = **y z' (or z')**	Ils ont de la chance. 1. **Y z'**ont d'la chance. 2. **Z'**ont d'la chance.	This contraction is used only when followed by a vowel.
lui = **'ui**	Je lui ai dit de partir. J'**ui** ai dit de partir.	
parce que = **pasque** (and **parc'que**)	Il sourit parce qu'il est content. Il sourit **pasqu'**il est content.	
petit(e) = **p'tit(e)**	Il est petit. Il est **p'tit**. Elle est petite. Elle est **p'tite**.	

Contraction	Example	Note
peut-être = **p't'êt'**	Peut-être qu'il est malade. *P't'êt'qu'il est malade.*	
quelque = **quèque**	Tu veux quelque chose à boire? *Tu veux quèque chose à boire?*	This contraction is commonly used with *quelque chose (kèk chose)* and *quelque part (kèk part).*
qui = **qu'**	Aujourd'hui, j'ai rencontré une dame qui a cent ans! *Aujourd'hui, j'ai rencontré une dame qu'a cent ans!*	This contraction occurs when *qui* is followed by a verb beginning with a vowel. **Note:** Contraction does not occur when *qui* begins a sentence.
s'il te plaît = **s'te plaît**	Passe-moi le beurre, s'il te plaît. *Passe-moi l'beurre, s'te plaît.*	

Legend

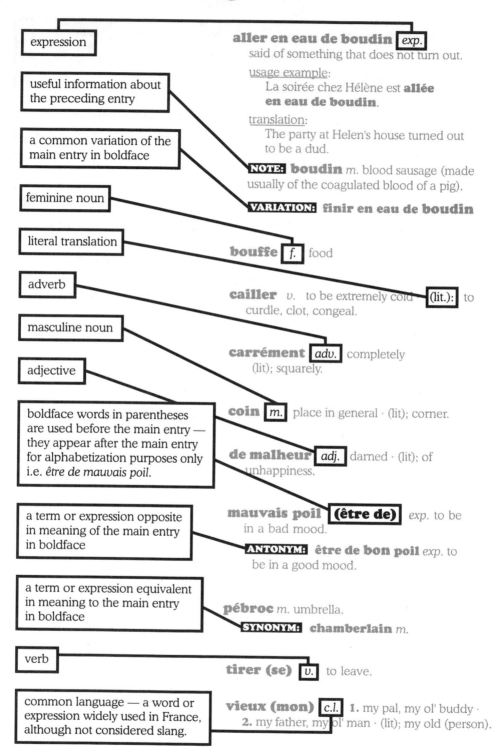

expression

aller en eau de boudin *exp.*
said of something that does not turn out.

useful information about the preceding entry

usage example:
La soirée chez Hélène est **allée en eau de boudin**.

translation:
The party at Helen's house turned out to be a dud.

a common variation of the main entry in boldface

NOTE: **boudin** *m.* blood sausage (made usually of the coagulated blood of a pig).

VARIATION: **finir en eau de boudin**

feminine noun

literal translation

bouffe *f.* food

adverb

cailler *v.* to be extremely cold · *(lit.):* to curdle, clot, congeal.

masculine noun

carrément *adv.* completely (lit; squarely).

adjective

coin *m.* place in general · (lit; corner).

boldface words in parentheses are used before the main entry — they appear after the main entry for alphabetization purposes only i.e. *être de mauvais poil.*

de malheur *adj.* darned · (lit; of unhappiness.

mauvais poil **(être de)** *exp.* to be in a bad mood.

a term or expression opposite in meaning of the main entry in boldface

ANTONYM: **être de bon poil** *exp.* to be in a good mood.

a term or expression equivalent in meaning to the main entry in boldface

pébroc *m.* umbrella.

SYNONYM: **chamberlain** *m.*

verb

tirer (se) *v.* to leave.

common language — a word or expression widely used in France, although not considered slang.

vieux (mon) *c.l.* **1.** my pal, my ol' buddy · **2.** my father, my ol' man · (lit; my old (person).

Qu'est-ce qu'il chante-là?!

(trans.): What's he talking about?
(lit.): What's he singing about?

Dialogue in Slang

Qu'est-ce qu'il chante-là?!

Martine: Tiens! Voilà Marie DuBois. Mais, c'est qui à son bras? Ce n'est pas son mari, ça!

Sylvie: Tu n'es pas **au jus**? **Ça a fait les infos de vingt heures**! Elle a **plaqué** son **tendre et cher** après avoir su qu'il avait pris un **petit à côté**. Et **pour comble de malheur**, c'était avec la meilleure amie de Marie!

Martine: Mais, qu'est-ce que tu me **chantes**-là?! Tu **colportes des cancans**, toi!

Sylvie: Mais non, je t'assure! Hier, je suis allée **boire un pot** avec Marie et elle **m'a déballé toutes ses salades**. Je pensais qu'elle allait **piquer une crise** et **au beau milieu** du bar. Quand **il lui a craché le morceau**, elle est **sortie de ses gonds** et **lui a poché un œil au beurre noir**! Elle **ne s'est pas gênée pour** lui montrer exactement ce qu'elle en pensait! Elle est **haute comme trois pommes**, mais elle **l'a passé à tabac**.

Martine: **Oh, là, là**! Moi qui croyais qu'ils **s'entendaient comme cul et chemise**! **Les bras m'en tombent**!

Sylvie: **Au tout début**, c'était **tout feu tout flamme**... **la vie en rose**, quoi. Ils étaient **sur la même longueur d'ondes**. Et puis **petit à petit**, ils **se sont cherchés noise**. C'est allé **de mal en pis** jusqu'à la rupture.

Martine: C'est **sidérant** qu'**ils en soient arrivés là**. **Bon**, je lui souhaite **de filer le parfait amour** la prochaine fois et que cela ne finisse pas en **feu de paille**!

Leçon Une

Translation in English

What's he talking about?!

Martine: Hey! There's Marie DuBois. Gee, who's that on her arm? That's not her husband!

Sylvie: You're not **up on what's going on**? **Everyone's talking about it**! She **dumped** her **husband** after finding out that he was having an **affair**. And **to make matters worse**, it was with Marie's best friend!

Martine: What are you **handing** me?! You're **spreading rumors**!

Sylvie: No, honest! Yesterday, I went and **had drinks** with Marie and she **told me all the details**. I thought she was going **to flip out** and **right in the middle** of the bar. When **he fessed up**, she **became unglued** and **gave him a black eye**! She **made no bones about** showing him exactly how she felt about it! She's **small**, but she **totally clobbered him**.

Martine: **Wow**! And I thought they **got along great**! **I'm stunned**!

Sylvie: **Right off the bat**, it was **all fireworks and passion**... **the perfect life**. They were **on the same wave length**. And then **little by little**, they **started picking at each other**. It went **from bad to worse** up until the breakup.

Martine: It's **astonishing** that **it had to come to this**. **Well**, I hope **she finds the perfect match** next time and that it doesn't end up being a **flash in the pan**!

Dialogue in slang as it would be spoken

Qu'est-c'qu'y chante-là?!

Martine: Tiens! Voilà Marie DuBois. Mais, c'est qui à son bras? C'est pas son mari, ça!

Sylvie: T'es pas **au jus**? **Ça a fait les infos d'vingt heures**! Elle a **plaqué** son **tendre et cher** après avoir su qu'il avait pris un **p'tit à côté**. Et **pour comble d'malheur**, c'était avec la meilleure amie d'Marie!

Martine: Mais, qu'est-c'que tu m'**chantes**-là?! Tu **colportes des cancans**, toi!

Sylvie: Mais non, j'tassure! Hier, j'suis allée **boire un pot** avec Marie et è **m'a déballé toutes ses salades**. J'pensais qu'elle allait **piquer une crise** et **au beau milieu** du bar. Quand **il lui a craché l'morceau**, elle est **sortie d'ses gonds** et **lui a poché un œil au beurre noir**! È **s'est pas gênée pour** lui montrer exactement c'qu'elle en pensait! Elle est **haute comme trois pommes**, mais è **l'a passé à tabac**.

Martine: **Oh, là, là**! Moi qui croyais qu'y **s'entendaient comme cul et ch'mise**! **Les bras m'en tombent**!

Sylvie: **Au tout début**, c'était **tout feu tout flamme... la vie en rose**, quoi. Y z'étaient **sur la même longueur d'ondes**. Et puis **p'tit à p'tit**, y **s'sont cherchés noise**. C'est allé **d'mal en pis** jusqu'à la rupture.

Martine: C'est **sidérant** qu'**y z'en soient arrivés là**. **Bon**, j'lui souhaite **de filer l'parfait amour** la prochaine fois et qu'ça finisse pas en **feu d'paille**!

Literal Translation

What's he singing there?!

Martine: Hey! There's Marie DuBois. But, who's that at her arm? That's not her husband!

Sylvie: You're not **in the juice**? **It made the eight o'clock news**! She **dumped** her **tender and dear** after having known that he took a **little on the side**. And **for culmination of misfortune**, it was with Marie's best friend!

Martine: What are you **singing** to me?! You're **peddling rumors**!

Sylvie: But no, I assure you! Yesterday, I went **to drink a pot** with Marie and she **reeled off all her salads to me**. I thought she was going **to take a crisis** and **in the handsome middle** of the bar. When **he spit up the morcel to her**, she **came out of her hinges** and **poached him an eye of black butter**! She **didn't strain herself for** showing him exactly what she thought about it! She is **high like three apples**, but she **put him through like tobacco**.

Martine: **Ooo, la, la**! And I thought that they **heard each other like buttocks and shirt**! **My arms are falling off because of it**!

Sylvie: **At the complete beginning**, it was **all fire all flame... life like a rose**. They were **on the same wave length**. And then **little to little**, they **looked for quarrel in each other**. It went **from bad to worse** up until the rupture.

Martine: It's **astonishing** that **they be arrived there over it**. **Good**, I wish her **to spin the perfect love** the next time and may it not finish in a **straw fire**!

Vocabulary

arriver là (en) *exp.* to come to this • (lit.): to arrive there from it.

    example: Laurent et Jeanne ont divorcé la semaine dernière parce qu'ils ne faisaient que se disputer. C'est dommage que leur marriage *en soit arrivé là.*

    as spoken: Laurent et Jeanne, <u>y z</u>'ont divorcé la <u>s</u>'maine dernière <u>pasqu'y</u> n'faisaient que <u>s</u>'disputer. C'est dommage que leur marriage, <u>y</u> *en soit arrivé là.*

    translation: Laurent et Jeanne got divorced last week because all they did was argue. It's a shame that their marriage has *come to this.*

beau milieu (au) *exp.* right in the middle • (lit.): in the handsome middle.

    example: J'ai trouvé un portefeuille *au beau milieu* de la rue!

    as spoken: J'ai trouvé un portefeuille *au beau milieu* <u>d</u>'la rue!

    translation: I found a wallet *in the middle* of the street!

boire un pot *exp.* to have a drink • (lit.): to drink a pot.

    example: Tu veux aller *boire un pot* après le boulot?

    as spoken: Tu veux aller *boire un pot* après <u>l</u>'boulot?

    translation: Wanna go *drink a jar* after work?

    NOTE: **boulot** *n.* (*very popular*) work.

        SUB-NOTE: **boulonner** *v.* to work.

    SYNONYM: **boire un coup** *exp.* • (lit.): to drink a shot.

bon *adj.* well (used to begin a new thought).

    example: *Bon*, je vais rentrer. Je te verrai demain.

    as spoken: *Bon*, <u>j</u>'vais rentrer. <u>J</u>'te verrai <u>d</u>'main.

    translation: *Well*, I'm going home. I'll see you tomorrow.

NOTE: **Ah, bon?** *exclam.* Really?

example: "Guy va passer tout l'été à Paris!"
"*Ah, bon?*"

as spoken: "Guy, y̱ va passer tout l'été à Paris!"
"*Ah, bon?*"

translation: "Guy is going to spend the entire summer in Paris!"
"*Really?*"

SUB-NOTE: Although the expression *Ah, bon* is literally translated as "Ah, good," it is used to mean "Really" in any context and can, therefore, be used upon hearing bad news as well:

example: "Mon chien est mort ce matin."
"*Ah, bon?* Qu'est-ce qui s'est passé?"

as spoken: "Mon chien, y̱ est mort c̱'matin."
"*Ah, bon?* Qu'est-c̱'qui s'est passé?"

translation: "My dog died this morning."
"*Really?* What happened?"

chanter *v.* to talk nonsense, to hand someone a line • (lit.): to sing.

example: Marie-Chantal est une princesse? *Qu'est-ce que tu me chantes-là?!*

as spoken: Marie-Chantal, c̱'ṯ'une princesse? *Qu'est-c̱'que tu m'chantes-là?!*

translation: Marie-Chantal is a princess? *What are you handing me?!*

SYNONYM: **balancer** *v.* • (lit.): to throw.

chercher noise à quelqu'un *exp.* to look for a fight.

example: Arrête de me critiquer! Tu essaies de *me chercher noise* ou quoi?

as spoken: Arrête ḏ'me critiquer! Ṯ'essaies ḏ'me chercher noise ou quoi?

translation: Stop picking on me! Are you trying *to start a fight with me* or what?

colporter des cancans *exp.* to spread rumors.

> example: Voilà Léon! Je ne veux pas *colporter des cancans*, mais j'ai entendu dire qu'il vient de perdre toute sa fortune à Monte Carle!

> as spoken: V'là Léon! J'veux pas *colporter des cancans*, mais j'ai entendu dire qu'y a perdu toute sa fortune à Monte Carle!

> translation: There's Léon! I don't want *to spread rumors* but I heard that he lost his entire fortune in Monte Carlo!

> **NOTE:** As seen in the previous example, the expression "to hear that" is translated in French as *"entendre dire que"* ("to hear said that").

cracher le morceau *exp.* to fess up • (lit.): to spit up the morsel (of truth).

> example: Enfin, le voleur a *craché le morceau*. C'était lui qui avait braqué la banque.

> as spoken: Enfin, l'voleur, y a *craché l'morceau*. C'était lui qui avait braqué la banque.

> translation: Finally, the thief *fessed up*. He was the one who pulled the bank job.

> **NOTE:** **braquer** *v.* to pull an armed robber • (lit.): to aim.

de mal en pis (être) *exp.*

> example: Ils ont des problèmes chez eux. *Ça va de mal en pis*!

> as spoken: Y z'ont des problèmes chez eux. *Ça va d'mal en pis*!

> translation: There are problems at their house. *Things are getting worse and worse*!

déballer ses salades *exp.* to reel off one's problems • (lit.): to uncrate one's salads.

> example: Je regrette d'être en retard, mais je suis tombé sur Marcel Clément qui m'a *déballé ses salades* pendant toute une heure!

as spoken: J'regrette d'êtr'en r'tard, mais j'suis tombé sur Marcel Clément qui m'a *déballé ses salades* pendant toute une heure!

translation: I'm sorry to be late, but I ran into Marcel Clément who *went on and on about his problems* for an entire hour!

NOTE: **tomber sur quelqu'un** *exp.* to run into someone • (lit.): to fall on someone.

entendre comme cul et chemise (s') *exp.* to get along extremely well (with someone) • (lit.): to get along like one's buttocks and shirt.

example: Marius et Rémy étaient ennemis depuis longtemps, mais maintenant ils *s'entendent comme cul et chemise.*

as spoken: Marius et Rémy, y z'étaient ennemis depuis longtemps, mais maintenant y *s'entendent comme cul et ch'mise.*

translation: Marius and Rémy were enemies for a long time, but now they *get along famously.*

faire les infos de vingt heures *exp.* everyone is talking about it • (lit.): it made the eight o'clock news (which is the time of the most popular news broadcast in France).

example: Tu ne sais pas ce qui s'est passé hier soir? *Ça a fait les infos de vingt heures!*

as spoken: Tu ~ sais pas c'qui s'est passé hier soir? *Ça a fait les infos d'vingt heures!*

translation: You don't know what happened last night? *Everyone's been talking about it!*

NOTE: In this expression, the term *"infos"* is a popular abbreviation of *"informations"* meaning "the news." In addition, in France the 24-hour clock is typically used. Therefore, *"vingt heures"* (commonly written "20h") is 8:00pm.

feu de paille *exp.* a flash in the pan • (lit.): a straw fire.

>   example: Son succès est *un feu de paille*.

>   as spoken: Son succès, <u>c't'</u>*un feu d'paille*.

>   translation: His success is *a flash in the pan*.

filer le parfait amour *exp.* to get the perfect relationship • (lit.): to spin the perfect love.

>   example: Ça fait longtemps que Carole essaie de *filer le parfait amour* mais elle reste toujours seule.

>   as spoken: Ça fait longtemps <u>qu'</u>Carole, <u>elle</u> essaie d'*filer l'parfait amour* mais <u>è</u> reste toujours seule.

>   translation: For a long time now Carole's been trying to *get the perfect relationship* but she's still single.

gêner pour (ne pas se) *exp.* to make no bones about • (lit.): not to restrain oneself.

>   example: Elle était fachée avec moi et *ne s'est pas gênée pour* me le dire!

>   as spoken: Elle était fachée avec moi et ~ *s'est pas gênée pour* me <u>l'</u>dire!

>   translation: She was angry with me and *made no bones about* telling me!

haut(e) comme trois pommes (être) *exp.* to be very short • (lit.): to be as high as three apples.

>   example: David a beaucoup grandi! L'année dernière, il était *haut comme trois pommes!*

>   as spoken: David, <u>il</u> a beaucoup grandi! L'année dernière, il était *haut comme trois pommes!*

>   translation: David has really grown! Last year, he was *really short!*

jus (être au) *exp.* to be up-to-date, current • (lit.): to be in the (electric) juice.

> example: Emile a déménagé! Tu *n'est pas au jus?*
>
> as spoken: Emile, i̲l a déménagé! T̲'es pas au jus?
>
> translation: Emile moved out of town! You *didn't hear about it?*
>
> **NOTE:** The expression *être au jus,* literally meaning "to be in the (electrical) juice," is a humorous play-on-words on the popular expression *être au courant,* literally "to be in the current." In French and English, *courant* ("current") can be used to mean both "up-to-date" as well as "electrical current."
>
> **SYNONYM:** **hauteur (être à la)** *exp.* • (lit.): to be at the height.

les bras m'en tombent *exp.* I'm dumbfounded • (lit): my arms are falling off me.

> example: On a volé ta voiture? *Les bras m'en tombent!*
>
> as spoken: [no change]
>
> translation: Your car was stolen? *I'm stunned!*
>
> **SYNONYM:** **rester baba (en)** *exp.* to be so stunned that the sound *baba* is all that can be uttered.

oh, là, là *exclam.* wow (used to signify surprise or disbelief).

> example: *Oh, là, là!* Qu'est-ce qu'il est bizarre, lui!
>
> as spoken: *Oh, là, là!* Qu'est-c̲'qu'il est bizarre, lui!
>
> translation: *Wow!* Is he ever strange!
>
> **NOTE (1):** Many Americans mistakenly pronounce this exclamation as "*Oooooo, là, là!*"
>
> **NOTE (2):** In the previous example, "*qu'est-ce que*" was used before the phrase "*il est bizarre, lui.*" This is an extremely common formula used to add emphasis to a statement. For example: **Qu'est-ce qu**'elle est grande!; Is she ever tall! • **Qu'est-ce qu**'il pleut aujourd'hui!; Is it ever raining today!

passer quelqu'un à tabac *exp.* to beat someone up, to give someone a thrashing • (lit.): to pass someone like tobacco.

    example: Ma mère m'a *passé à tabac* pour être rentré trop tard.

    as spoken: Ma mère, <u>è</u> m'a *passé à tabac* pour êt'rentré trop tard.

    translation: My mother *give me a thrashing* for coming home too late.

        SYNONYM: **battre comme plâtre** *exp.* to beat to a pulp • (lit.): to beat up like plaster.

petit à côté *exp.* a sexual fling • (lit.): a little on the side.

    example: Le patron n'est jamais dans son bureau à midi. Tu crois qu'il a un *petit à côté* quelque part?

    as spoken: Le patron, <u>il</u> est jamais dans son bureau à midi. Tu crois qu'<u>il</u> a un *p'tit à côté* <u>quèque</u> part?

    translation: The boss is never in his office at noon. You think he's having a *little fling* somewhere?

        ALSO: **jeter un vite fait (s'en)** *exp.* to have a quickie • (lit.): to throw oneself a quickly-done.

petit à petit *exp.* little by little • (lit.): little to little.

    example: J'ai été malade pendant deux semaines, mais *petit à petit* je vais mieux.

    as spoken: J'ai été malade pendant deux <u>s'</u>maines, mais *<u>p</u>'tit à <u>p</u>'tit* <u>j'</u>vais mieux.

    translation: I've been sick for two weeks, but *little by little* I'm doing better.

piquer une crise *exp.* to have (to throw) a fit • (lit.): to take a crisis.

    example: J'ai *piqué une crise* quand j'ai appris que mon frère a emprunté ma voiture sans permission.

    as spoken: J'ai *piqué une crise* quand j'ai appris <u>qu'</u>mon frère, <u>il</u> a emprunté ma voiture sans permission.

translation: I *threw a fit* when I found out that my brother borrowed my car without permission.

NOTE: The verb *piquer*, literally meaning "to prick or sting," is used in slang to mean "to take or steal."

plaquer quelqu'un *v.* to jilt someone.

example: Henri a *plaqué* sa femme après avoir été mariés quinze ans.

as spoken: Henri, <u>il</u> a *plaqué* sa femme après avoir été mariés quinze ans.

translation: Henry *dumped* his wife after having been married fifteen years.

pocher un œil au beurre noir à quelqu'un *exp.* to give someone a black eye • (lit.): to poach someone an eye of black butter.

example: Quand je l'ai insulté, il m'a *poché un œil au beurre noir*.

as spoken: Quand <u>j'</u>l'ai insulté, <u>y</u> m'a *poché un œil au beurre noir*.

translation: When I insulted him, he *gave me a black eye*.

ALSO: **coquelicot** *n.* black eye • (lit.): poppy.

pour comble de malheur *exp.* to top it all • (lit.): for an overflowing of misfortune.

example: J'ai eu une crevaison en pleine autoroute. Et *pour comble de malheur*, il a commencé à pleuvoir.

as spoken: J'ai eu une crevaison en pleine autoroute. Et *pour comble <u>d'</u>malheur*, <u>il</u> a commencé à pleuvoir.

translation: I got a flat tire on the highway. And *to top it all off*, it started to rain.

sidérant(e) (être) *adj.* to be astonishing, incredible.

example: Je viens d'apprendre que mon neveu est devenu président de la plus grande companie à Paris. C'est *sidérant*! Il n'a que vingt-huit ans!

as spoken: J'viens d'apprend' que mon neveu, il est dev'nu
              président d'la plus grande companie à Paris. C'est
              sidérant! Il a qu'vingt-huit ans!

translation: I just found out that my nephew became president of
              the biggest company in Paris. It's *incredible*! He's only
              twenty-eight years old!

sortir de ses gonds *exp.* to fly off the handle • (lit.): to exit one's hinges.

example: Si ton père voit ce que tu as fait de sa voiture, il va *sortir
              de ses gonds*!

as spoken: Si ton père, y voit c'que t'as fait d'sa voiture, y va *sortir
              d'ses gonds*!

translation: If your father sees what you did to his car, he's gonna *fly
              off the handle*!

NOTE: As seen above, in spoken French, it is much more
              common to use the progressive future (*va sortir*) than
              the simple future (*sortira*).

SYNONYM: **mettre en boule (se)** *exp.* • (lit.): to put oneself in a
              ball (since every muscle is cramping from anger).

sur la même longueur d'ondes (être) *exp.* to be on the same wave length • (lit.): same.

example: Je ne suis pas du tout d'accord avec toi. Normalement,
              nous sommes *sur la même longeur d'ondes* mais pas cette
              fois-ci.

as spoken: J'suis pas du tout d'accord avec toi. Normalement, nous
              sommes *sur la même longeur d'ondes* mais pas cette
              fois-ci.

translation: I don't agree with you at all. Usually, we're *on the same
              wave length* but not this time.

tendre et cher/chère *exp.* an affectionate term for one's husband or wife • (lit.): tender and dear.

example: Je te présente mon *tendre et cher*. Ça fait quinze ans que
              nous sommes mariés.

as spoken: J'te présente mon *tendre et cher*. Ça fait quinze ans qu'nous sommes mariés.

translation: I'd like you to meet my *husband*. We've been married for fifteen years.

SYNONYM (1): **son cinquante pour cent** *exp.* • (lit.): one's fifty percent.

SYNONYM (2): **sa douce moitié** *exp.* • (lit.): one's sweet half.

tout début (au) *exp.* at the very beginning • (lit.): at the complete beginning.

example: *Au tout début de l'année scolaire, le professeur était sympatique, mais maintenant il est carrément ennuyant.*

as spoken: *Au tout début d'l'année scolaire, le prof, il était sympa, mais maintenant il est carrément ennuyant.*

translation: *At the very beginning* of the school year, the teach was very nice, but now he's downright annoying.

tout feu tout flamme (être) *exp.* to be enthusiastic, gung-ho • (lit.): to be all fire all flame.

example: Quand Antoine a commencé à lui faire la cour, il était *tout feu tout flamme*. Mais maintenant qu'ils sont mariés, il ne fait que lire son journal.

as spoken: Quand Antoine il a commencé à lui faire la cour, il était *tout feu tout flamme*. Mais maintenant qu'y sont mariés, y fait qu'lire son journal.

translation: When Antoine started courting her, he was *all gung-ho*. But now that they're married, he just reads his paper.

vie en rose (la) *exp.* said of a wonderful life, life through rose-colored glasses • life like a rose.

example: J'ai été pauvre toute ma vie. Mais après avoir gagné au lotto, c'est *la vie en rose*.

as spoken: J'ai été pauv' toute ma vie. Mais après avoir gagné au lotto, c'est *la vie en rose*.

translation: I've been poor all my life. But after having won in the lottery, *life is wonderful*.

Practice The Vocabulary

(Answers to Lesson 1, p. 251)

A. CROSSWORD PUZZLE
Complete the sentences by using the list below. Write your answer in the crossword puzzle on the opposite page.

beau	cancans	comble	gonds	paille
beurre	chantes	côté	infos	pot
bras	chemise	crise	jus	tabac

ACROSS

8. Lise, elle a quitté son mari après avoir su qu'il avait pris un p'tit à _____ .

13. J'dois sortir ce soir mais j'suis malade. Et pour _____ d'malheur, y pleut!

20. J'peux pas l'croire! Les _____ m'en tombent!

22. Jean et Martin, y s'entendent comme cul et _____ .

28. Quoi?! Qu'est-c'que tu m' _____ -là?!

34. Son succès, c'est qu'un feu d' _____ .

40. Elle a réprimandé son fils au _____ milieu du supermarché!

45. Quand il a ruiné mon tricot, j'suis sorti d'mes _____ .

DOWN

10. Elle est p'tite, mais elle l'a passé à _____ .

13. J'veux pas colporter des _____ mais Suzanne habite avec Georges!

20. Michel, y m'a poché un œil au _____ noir!

28. En apprenant la nouvelle, j'pensais qu'elle allait piquer une _____ .

34. J'ai soif, moi. Tu veux aller boire un _____ ?

35. Tu sais pas c'qui s'est passé? Ça a fait les _____ d'vingt heures!

38. Qu'est-c'qui s'est passé? J'suis pas au _____ .

CROSSWORD PUZZLE

B. CONTEXT EXERCISE
Underline the words that best complete the phrase.

1. J'suis pas (**au livre**, **au jus**, **à la brochure**). Qu'est-c'qui s'est passé?

2. Son succès, il a pas duré longtemps. C'était qu'un feu d'(**foin**, **paille**, **ciment**).

3. Marie, elle a quitté son mari après avoir su qu'il avait pris un p'tit à (**tabac**, **cancan**, **côté**).

4. Quand je l'ai insultée, è m'a poché un œil au (**sel**, **poivre**, **beurre**) noir.

5. J'peux pas l'croire! Les (**bras**, **jambes**, **doigts**) m'en tombent!

6. Elle était tellement fâchée avec lui qu'è l'a passé à (**cigare**, **tabac**, **beurre noir**).

7. Tu sais pas c'qui s'est passé? Ça a fait les infos d'(**dix**, **quinze**, **vingt**) heures!

8. Quoi?! Mais, qu'est-c'que tu m'(**chantes**, **cries**, **chuchotes**)-là?

9. Au tout (**debout**, **bout**, **début**), y paraissaient très contents ensemble.

10. Sandra, elle est haute comme trois (**citrons**, **oranges**, **pommes**) tandis que son frère, c't'un géant!

C. Complete the dialogue using the appropriate idioms from the list below. Make all necessary changes.

à côté	**gonds**	**plaqué**
arrivés là	**jus**	**pot**
beau milieu	**malheur**	**rose**
beurre noir	**morceau**	**salades**
bon	**noise**	**sidérant**
cancans	**oh, là, là**	**tabac**
chantes	**ondes**	**tendre et cher**
chemise	**paille**	**tombent**
crise	**parfait amour**	**tout flamme**
début	**petit**	**trois pommes**
gênée pour	**pis**	**vingt heures**

Martine: Tiens! Voilà Marie DuBois. Mais, c'est qui à son bras? Ce n'est pas son mari, ça!

Sylvie: Tu n'es pas au **(1)**_____? Ça a fait les infos de **(2)**_____
_____! Elle a **(3)**_____ son
(4)_____ après avoir su qu'il avait pris
un petit **(5)**_____. Et pour comble de **(6)**_____,
c'était avec la meilleure amie de Marie!

Martine: Mais, qu'est-ce que tu me **(7)**_____-là?! Tu
colportes des **(8)**_____, toi!

Sylvie: Mais non, je t'assure! Hier, je suis allée boire un **(9)**_____ avec
Marie et elle m'a déballé toutes ses **(10)**_____. Je
pensais qu'elle allait piquer une **(11)**_____ et au
(12)_____ du bar. Quand il lui a craché le
(13)_____, elle est sortie de ses
(14)_____ et lui a poché un œil au
(15)_____! Elle ne s'est pas
(16)_____ lui montrer exactement ce qu'elle
en pensait! Elle est haute comme **(17)**_____,
mais elle l'a passé à **(18)**_____.

Martine: **(19)**_____! Moi qui croyais qu'ils
s'entendaient comme cul et **(20)**_____! Les
bras m'en **(21)**_____!

Sylvie: Au tout **(22)**_____, c'était tout feu **(23)**_____
...la vie en **(24)**_____. Ils étaient sur la même
longueur d'**(25)**_____. Et puis petit à
(26)_____, ils se sont cherchés **(27)**_____. C'est
allé de mal en **(28)**_____ jusqu'à la rupture.

Martine: C'est **(29)**_____ qu'ils en soient **(30)**_____.
(31)_____, je lui souhaite de filer le **(32)**_____ la
prochaine fois et que cela ne finisse pas en feu de **(33)**_____!

DICTATION
Test Your Aural Comprehension.

If you are following along with your cassette, you will now hear a paragraph containing many of the terms from this section. The paragraph will be read at normal conversational speed (which may actually seem fast to you at first). In addition, the words will be pronounced as you would actually hear them in a conversation, including many common reductions.

The first time the paragraph is presented, simply listen in order to get accustomed to the speed and heavy use of reductions. The paragraph will then be read again with a pause after each group of words to give you time to write down what you heard. The third time the paragraph is read, follow along with what you have written.

A CLOSER LOOK 1:
Colloquial Use of "On"
and Adjectives

A. Colloquial use of personal pronoun *"on"*

The personal pronoun *on* traditionally falls under the heading of third person singular and is translated as meaning "one" or "they":

> *On sait jamais.*
> One never knows.

> *On dit qu'il va pleuvoir.*
> They say it's going to rain.

However, in colloquial French, *on* is frequently used to replace the first person plural *nous*:

> *On y va?*
> Shall we go?

> *On devrait se dépêcher!*
> We should hurry!

NOTE 1: This is an extremely popular usage of *on* and may be used with everyone.

NOTE 2: *On y va?* is one of the most popular ways of saying, "Shall we go?"

PRACTICE USING THE PERSONAL PRONOUN *"ON"*

A. Rewrite the sentences using the personal pronoun *"on."*

1. Nous l'avons pas vu.

   _____ .

2. Nous devrions signaler l'accident à la police.

   _____ .

3. Si nous allions à la plage?

   _____ ?

4. Nous nous voyons tout l'temps.

   _____ .

5. J'crois qu'nous nous sommes rencontrés avant.

   _____ .

6. Nous arrivons!

   _____ !

7. Nous pourrons aller au cinéma si tu veux.

   _____ .

8. Nous nous amusons ici.

   _____ .

9. J'espère qu'nous trouverons une belle maison.

   _____ .

10. Nous y allons?

    _____ ?

A CLOSER LOOK 2:

Colloquial Use of Pronoun "En"

A. To add emphasis to the verb

It is commonly taught in French classes that the pronoun **en** (translated as "some" in this case) replaces the object of the phrase when preceded by a partitive artlce (**de**, **des**, **de la**, and **du**) or indefinite article (**un**, **une**):

> *Elle a des chaussures.* (She has some shoes.)
> *Ell* **en** *a.* (She has some.)

> *Je veux du vin.* (I want some wine.)
> J'**en** veux. (I want some.)

In colloquial French, the pronoun **en** and the subject may be used together to emphasize the verb. In this case, **en** is translated as "do." Note that in English the stress falls on the word "do," whereas in French it falls on the word just after **en**:

> *Elle* **en** *a, des chaussures!* (She *does* have shoes!)
> J'**en** *veux, du vin!* (I *do* want some wine!)

B. To emphasize quantity

The same construction is extremely popular when emphasizing the numbers of objects in question. Note that the stress is on the number (indicated by an arrow):

> *J'ai deux bagnoles = j'**en** ai deux = J'**en** ai deux, des bagnoles*
> *J'ai trois enfants = J'**en** ai trois = J'**en** ai trois, des enfants*

PRACTICE THE COLLOQUIAL USAGE OF "EN"

A. Answer each question using "*en*" to add emphasis to the phrase.

Example:

Tu veux pas d'vin?
Si! J'en veux, du vin!

Tu veux pas d'enfants?
Si! J'en veux, des enfants!

1. Tu veux pas d'gâteau?

   Si! _____

2. Il a pas d'lunettes de soleil, lui?

   Si! _____

3. Elle a pas d'sœurs?

   Si! _____

4. T'as pas vu d'oiseaux au parc?

    Si! _____

5. T'as pas d'idées sur le sujet?

    Si! _____

6. T'as jamais mangé d'chocolats belges?

    Si! _____

7. Il a jamais vu d'coucher d'soleil?

    Si! _____

8. Elle a pas d'chance?

    Si! _____

9. T'as pas d'argent sur toi?

    Si! _____

10. Y prend pas d'risques?

    Si! _____

B. Answer each question using *"en"* to emphasize the quantity.

Example:

T'en as combien, des enfants?
(deux) J'en ai deux, des enfants.

T'en as mangé combien, des sandwiches?
(trois) J'en ai mangé trois, des sandwiches.

1. T'en as combien, des chemises?

   (huit) _____

2. Elle en a combien, des enfants?

   (trois) _____

3. Il en a bu combien, des bières?

   (quatre) _____

4. T'en as ach'té combien, des pantalons?

   (six) _____

5. Elle en a pris combien, des aspirines?

   (cinq) _____

6. Il en a combien, des chaussures?

   (huit) _____

7. T'en as combien, des frères?

(cinq) _____

8. T'en comptes combien, des spectateurs?

(quarante) _____

9. T'en as rencontré combien, des vedettes?

(dix) _____

10. Elle en a brûlé combien, des dîners cette semaine?

(cinq) _____

11. T'en as trouvé combien, des erreurs?

(cinq) _____

12. T'en veux combien, des macarons au chocolat?

(un millier) _____

Nancy est une vraie fée du logis!

(trans.): Nancy's a real wiz around the house!
(lit.): Nancy is a true fairy of the domicile!

Leçon Deux

Dialogue in Slang

Une Fée du Logis

Carole: Salut mon Nico! Ça **fait une paye** qu'on ne s'est pas vu! Tu as l'air de **péter la forme**! Je savais que tu viendrais **à coup sûr**. La fête **bat son plein**! Ce soir, on va **s'en donner à cœur joie**. Je crois que cette fête va **avoir un succès fou**!

Nicolas: Comme tu dis. Mais il y a des ballons **à perte de vue**! Et regarde-moi tous ces desserts! **C'est Byzance**! Nancy est une pâtissière extra! Une vraie **fée du logis**! Je me demande comment elle est arrivée à tout faire toute seule.

Carole: Oh, **ce n'est pas la mer à boire**. Elle m'a dit qu'elle a commencé à tout préparer **de bon matin**. Quelquefois je pense que **tu n'as d'yeux que pour elle**.

Nicolas: Mais non, **voyons**! Tu sais très bien que **j'en pince pour toi**. Tiens! Regarde qui vient d'**arriver en trombe**...cette **bêcheuse de** Cécile Daudé. Mais quelle **Madame Sans Gène**! Cette robe **épouse la forme de** son corps et **lui arrive au ras des fesses**.

Carole: Je **ne peux pas la voir en peinture**. Elle m'a **fait une vacherie** l'année dernière, **que je ne te raconte pas**.

Nicolas: Mais pourquoi pas aller **dissiper le malentendu** au lieu de **la battre froid**? Il est temps de **faire peau neuve**!

Carole: Non, chaque fois que je veux **mettre les choses au point**, **c'est la galère**. Elle **ne recule jamais d'une semelle**. Elle m'insulte **à tout propos**. Je **lui en veux**, c'est tout. C'est une **sale histoire**.

Nicolas: Il est **grand temps** de **passer l'éponge là-dessus**. **Faites vous la bise!** Allez, va!

Carole: J'ai une meilleure idée. **Ne bouge pas d'un poil**. Je reviens.

Nicolas: Mais où vas-tu avec cette tarte à la crème? Carole! Carole!

Translation in English

A Wiz in the Home

Carole: Hi Nickie! It's **been a long time** since we've seen each other! You look like you're **in tip-top shape**! I knew that you would come **for sure**. The party is **in full swing**! Tonight, we're gonna **live it up**. I think this party's going **to be a huge success**!

Nicolas: You said it. Gee, there are balloons **as far as the eye can see**! And just look at all these desserts! **It's so abundant**! Nancy is a fantastic pastry chef! A real **wiz around the house**! I wonder how she managed to do everything all alone.

Carole: Oh, **it's not such a big deal**. She told me she started to prepare everything **early in the morning**. Sometimes I think **you only have eyes for her**.

Nicolas: Of course not, **for crying out loud**! You know very well that **I have a crush on you**. Hey! Look who just **stormed in**... **that little priss**, Cécile Daudé. What an **ill-mannered woman**! That dress **looks painted on** to her body and **hits her just below the cheeks of her buttocks**.

Carole: I **can't stand her**. She really did a **nasty number to me** last year. **I won't even go into it**.

Nicolas: Why not **clear the air** instead of **snubbing her**? It's time **to turn over a new leaf**!

Carole: No, every time I want **to set things straight**, it **blows up in my face**. She **won't give an inch**. She insults me **at every turn**. **I have a grudge against her**, period. It's a **sordid story**.

Nicolas: It's **high time** to **patch tings up**. **Kiss and make up**! **Come on**!

Carole: I have a better idea. **Don't move an inch**. I'll be right back.

Nicolas: Hey, where are you going with that cream pie? Carole! Carole!

Leçon Deux

Dialogue in slang as it would be spoken

Une Fée du Logis

Carole: Salut mon Nico! Ça **fait une paye** qu'on s'est pas vu! T'as l'air de **péter la forme**! J'savais qu'tu viendrais **à coup sûr**. La fête, è **bat son plein**! Ce soir, on va **s'en donner à cœur joie**. J'crois qu'cette fête, è va **avoir un succès fou**!

Nicolas: Comme tu dis. Mais y a des ballons **à perte de vue**! Et regarde-moi tous ces desserts! **C'est Byzance**! Nancy, c't'une pâtissière extra! Une vraie **fée du logis**! J'me d'mande comment elle est arrivée à tout faire toute seule.

Carole: Oh, **c'est pas la mer à boire**. È m'a dit qu'elle a commencé à tout préparer **d'bon matin**. Quèquefois, j'pense que **t'as d'yeux que pour elle**.

Nicolas: Mais non, **voyons**! Tu sais très bien qu'**j'en pince pour toi**. Tiens! Regarde qui vient d'**arriver en trombe**... **cette bêcheuse de** Cécile Daudé. Mais quelle **Madame Sans Gène**! C'te robe, elle **épouse la forme de** son corps et **lui arrive au ras des fesses**.

Carole: J'**peux pas la voir en peinture**. È m'a **fait une vach'rie** l'année dernière, **que j'te raconte pas**.

Nicolas: Mais pourquoi pas aller **dissiper le malentendu** au lieu d'**la battre froid**? L'est temps d'**faire peau neuve**!

Carole: Non, chaque fois qu'j'veux **mett' les choses au point, c'est la galère**. È r'cule jamais **d'une semelle**. È m'insulte **à tout propos**. J'**lui en veux**, c'est tout. C't'une **sale histoire**.

Nicolas: Il est **grand temps** d'**passer l'éponge là-d'ssus. Faites vous la bise**! **Allez, va**!

Carole: J'ai une meilleure idée. **Bouge pas d'un poil**. Je r'viens.

Nicolas: Mais où tu vas avec c'te tarte à la crème? Carole! Carole!

Literal Translation

A Fairy of the Home

Carole: Hi Nickie! It's **been a pay period** since we've seen each other! You look like you're **bursting with shape**! I knew that you would come **for sure**. The party is **beating its full capacity**! Tonight, we're going to **treat each other to a joyful heart**. I think this party is going **to be an insane success**!

Nicolas: You said it. Gee, there are balloons **until they are out of sight**! And just look at all these desserts! **It's so bountiful**! Nancy is a fantastic pastry chef! A real **fairy of the home**! I wonder how she managed to do everything all alone.

Carole: Oh, **it's not like drinking the ocean**. She told me she started to prepare everything **of good morning**. Sometimes I think **you only have eyes for her**.

Nicolas: Of course not, **let's see**! You know very well that **I'm pinching some of it for you**. Hey! Look who just **arrived like a tornado... that priss of** Cécile Daudé. What a **Madame without restraint**! That dress is **marrying the shape of her body** and **arrive just below the cheeks of her buttocks**.

Carole: I **can't see a painting of her**. She really did a **cow thing** to me last year **that I'm not telling you about**.

Nicolas: Why not **dissipate the misunderstanding** instead of **beating her cold**? It's time **to make new skin**!

Carole: No, every time I want **to put things in order**, it is **extremely difficult**. She **won't back up a sole's worth**. She insults me **at every opportunity**. **I want her from it**. It's a **dirty story**.

Nicolas: It's **big time** to **put the sponge on it. Make yourself the little kiss! Go, go**!

Carole: I have a better idea. **Don't move by a hair**, I'll be right back.

Nicolas: Hey, where are you going with that cream pie? Carole! Carole!

Vocabulary

allez, va *exp.* come on

example: *Allez, va!* Il fera meilleur la semaine prochaine et tu
pourras aller à la plage à ce moment-là.

as spoken: *Allez, va!* Y̲ f̲'ra meilleur la s̲'maine prochaine et tu
pourras aller à la plage à c̲'moment-là.

translation: *Oh, come on!* The weather will be better next week and
you'll be able to go to the beach then.

arriver au ras des fesses *exp.* to come just up to the cheeks of one's
buttocks.

example: Tu as vu la jupe que Mimi a porté aujourd'hui? Elle était
super courte. Sa jupe lui *arrivait au ras des fesses*!

as spoken: T̲'as vu la jupe que Mimi a porté aujourd'hui? Elle était
super courte. Sa jupe, è̲ lui *arrivait au ras des fesses*!

translation: Did you see the skirt Mimi wore today? It was super
short. Her skirt *came just up to the cheeks of her buttocks*!

arriver en trombe *exp.* to storm in • (lit.): to arrive like a tornado.

example: Regarde qui vient d'*arriver en trombe*... Amélie
Dupont-Durand. Elle est prétentieuse, elle!

as spoken: [no change]

translation: Look who just *stormed in*... Amélie Dupont-Durand.
She's so pretentious!

battre froid à *exp.* to be cool toward • (lit.): to beat coldly toward.

> example: Quand je suis tombé sur Hélène au supermarché aujourd'hui, elle m'a *battu froid*.
>
> as spoken: Quand j'suis tombé sur Hélène au supermarché aujourd'hui, è m'a *battu froid*.
>
> translation: When I ran into Hélène at the supermarket today, she was *cold to me*.
>
> **SNYONYM:** **recevoir quelqu'un comme un chien dans un jeu de quilles** *exp.* • (lit.): to receive someone like a dog in a lawn bowling game.

battre son plein *exp.* to be in full swing • (lit.): to beat one's full.

> example: La soirée devrait *battre son plein* d'ici une heure.
>
> as spoken: La soirée, è devrait *batt' son plein* d'ici une heure.
>
> translation: The party should *be in full swing* in an hour.

bêcheuse *f.* a priss, snob.

> example: Michelle se croit supérieure parce que son père est Ministre de la Culture. Quelle *bêcheuse*, celle-là!
>
> as spoken: Michelle, è s'croit supérieure pasque son père, il est Ministre d'la Culture. Quelle *bêcheuse*, celle-là!
>
> translation: Michelle thinks she's better than everyone because her father is Minister of Culture. What a *snob*!

bise (faire la) *f.* to kiss.

> example: N'oublie pas de *faire la bise* à ta maman avant de partir.
>
> as spoken: ~ Oublie pas d'*faire la bise* à ta maman avant d'partir.
>
> translation: Don't forget *to give a kiss* to your mom before leaving.
>
> **SYNONYM:** **bisou (faire un)** *exp.*

bon matin (de) *exp.* early in the morning • (lit.): from good morning.

> example: Je me suis levé *de bon matin* pour aller à l'école.
>
> as spoken: Je m'suis levé d'bon matin pour aller à l'école.
>
> translation: I got up *early* to go to school.

SYNONYM: **petit jour (au)** *exp.* dawn • (lit.): at the little day.

bouger d'un poil (ne pas) *exp.* not to budge an inch • (lit.): not to budge a hair.

> example: *Ne bouge pas d'un poil*! J'ai une surprise pour toi.
>
> as spoken: ~ *Bouge pas d'un poil*! J'ai une surprise pour toi.
>
> translation: *Don't budge an inch*! I have a surprise for you.

Byzance (être) *adj.* to be bountiful.

> example: Tu aurais dû voir le dîner qu'on a mangé chez Madelaine. C'était *Byzance*!
>
> as spoken: T'aurais dû voir le dîner qu'on a mangé chez Mad'leine. C'était *Byzance*!
>
> translation: You should have seen the dinner we ate at Madeleine's house. There was *tons of food*!

ce n'est pas la mer à boire *exp.* it's not such a big deal • (lit.): it's not like drinking the sea.

> example: Tu peux apprendre à faire de la planche à voile. *Ce n'est pas la mer à boire*!
>
> as spoken: Tu peux apprendre à faire d'la planche à voile. *C'est pas la mer à boire*!
>
> translation: You can learn how to windsurf. *It's not such a big deal*!

coup sûr (à) *exp.* for sure • (lit.): at sure blow.

> example: Cette fois-ci, je vais gagner le tiercé *à coup sûr*.
>
> as spoken: Cette fois-ci, j'vais gagner l'tiercé *à coup sûr*.
>
> translation: This time, I'm going to win at the races *for sure*.

SYNONYM: **sans faute** *exp.* • (lit.): without fail.

dissiper les malentendus *exp.* to clear the air • (lit.): to dissipate the misunderstandings.

> example: Je crois qu'il est temps de *dissiper les malentendus*.
>
> as spoken: J'crois qu'il est temps de *dissiper les malentendus*.
>
> translation: I think it's time *to clear the air*.

donner à cœur joie (s'en) *exp.* to treat oneself to one's heart's delight • (lit.): to give oneself some of it to joyful heart.

> example: On *s'en est donné à cœur joie* quand on a visité les caves du Bordelais.
>
> as spoken: [no change]
>
> translation: We *consumed to our heart's delight* when we visited the wine cellars in the Bordeaux region.

épouser la forme de *exp.* to cling • (lit.): to marry the form of.

> example: Ta chemise est trop serrée, non? Elle *épouse la forme de* ton corps!
>
> as spoken: Ta ch'mise, elle est trop serrée, non? Elle *épouse la forme de ton corps!*
>
> translation: Your shirt is too small, don't you think? It's *clinging to* your body!

fée du logis (être une) *exp.* to be a wiz around the house • (lit.): to be a fairy in the home.

> example: J'adore ta maison. Elle n'est jamais en désordre. Tu es une vraie *fée du logis*, toi.
>
> as spoken: J'adore ta maison. Elle est jamais en désordre. T'es une vraie *fée du logis*, toi.
>
> translation: I love your house. It's never messy. You're a real *wiz in the house.*

galère (être la) *f.* to be extremely difficult and unpleasant • (lit.): it's the galleys (as difficult as being a slave in the galleys).

>   example: Ça fait deux heures que j'essaie de réparer ma bagnole, mais c'est *la galère*!

>   as spoken: Ça fait deux heures que j'essaie d'réparer ma bagnole, mais c'est *la galère*!

>   translation: I've been trying to repare my car for the past two hours, but it's *too difficult*!

> **NOTE:**   **bagnole** *f. (extremely popular)* car.

grand temps (être) *exp.* to be high time • (lit.): to be big time.

>   example: Je sais que tu es fâché avec le curé mais je crois qu'il est *grand temps* que tu lui pardonnes.

>   as spoken: Je sais qu't'es fâché avec le curé mais j'crois qu'il est *grand temps* qu'tu lui pardonnes.

>   translation: I know you've been angry with the local priest but I think it's *high time* that you forgave him.

Madame Sans Gène *exp.* said of a woman with no manners or shame • (lit.): Madame Without Shame.

>   example: Louise s'est déshabillée en plein magasin au lieu d'entrer dans une cabine d'essayage. Quelle *Madame Sans Gène*!

>   as spoken: Louise, è s'est déshabillée en plein magasin au lieu d'entrer dans une cabine d'essayage. Quelle *Madame Sans Gène*!

>   translation: Louise took off her clothes in the middle of the store instead of using a dressing room. What a *shameless woman*!

> **NOTE:**   This expression comes from a character in French history who was known for being rude and shameless.

mettre les choses au point *exp.* to set the record straight • (lit.): to put things to the point.

> example: Michel m'a demandé de sortir avec lui ce soir. Alors, j'ai *mis les choses au point* et lui ai dit que j'étais mariée.

> as spoken: Michel, y m'a d'mandé d'sortir avec lui c'soir. Alors, j'ai *mis les choses au point* et lui ai dit qu'j'étais mariée.

> translation: Michel asked me to go out with his tonight. So, I *set the record straight* and told him I was married.

passer l'éponge là-dessus *exp.* to reconcile, to let bygones be bygones • (lit.): to pass the sponge (that "soaks up" our differences).

> example: Oublions notre querelle et *passons l'éponge là-dessus*.

> as spoken: Oublions not' querelle et *passons l'éponge là-d'ssus*.

> translation: Let's forget about our quarrel and *let bygones be bygones*.

paye (faire une) *exp.* to be a long time • (lit.): to be a pay period (a period of time, usually a month, between pay checks).

> example: Salut Robert! Ça *fait une paye* qu'on ne s'est pas vu!

> as spoken: Salut Robert! Ça *fait une paye* qu'on ~ s'est pas vu!

> translation: Hi Robert! It's *been a long time* since we've see each other!

> **SYNONYM:** **bail (faire un)** *exp.* • (lit.): to be a rent period (a period of time between when one's rent is due).

peau neuve (faire) *exp.* to turn over a new leaf • (lit.): to make new skin.

> example: J'ai décidé de *faire peau neuve*. A partir de demain, je vais renoncer à fumer.

> as spoken: J'ai décidé d'*faire peau neuve*. A partir de d'main, j'vais renoncer à fumer.

> translation: I decided to *turn over a new leaf*. Starting tomorrow, I'm going to give up smoking.

perte de vue (à) *exp.* as far as the eye can see • to the loss of the view.

> example: Quelle belle forêt! Il y a des arbres *à perte de vue*!
>
> as spoken: Quelle belle forêt! ~ Y a des arbres *à perte de vue*!
>
> translation: What a beautiful forest! There are trees *as far as the eye can see*!

péter la forme *exp.* to be in tip-top shape • (lit.): to burst with good shape.

> example: J'ai été malade pendant une semaine, mais maintenant je pète la forme!
>
> as spoken: J'ai été malade pendant une s'maine, mais maintenant j'pète la forme!
>
> translation: I was sick for a week, but now I'm *in tip-top shape*!

pincer pour quelqu'un (en) *exp.* to be attracted to someone • (lit.): to pinch for someone.

> example: Pourquoi est-ce que tu parles de Léonie tout le temps? Tu *en pinces pour elle* ou quoi?
>
> as spoken: Pourquoi tu parles de Léonie tout l'temps? T'*en pinces pour elle* ou quoi?
>
> translation: What do you speak about Léonie all the time? Do you *have a crush on her* or what?

pouvoir voir quelqu'un en peinture (ne pas) *exp.* to be unable to stand someone • (lit.): to be unable to see a painting of someone (since just the mere sight of him/her would be too much to bear).

> example: Voilà Bernard! Je *ne peux pas le voir en peinture*!
>
> as spoken: V'là Bernard! J'*peux pas l'voir en peinture*!
>
> translation: There's Bernard! I *can't stand him*!

> **SYNONYM:** **pouvoir blairer quelqu'un (ne pas)** *exp.* • (lit.): not to be able to smell someone.
>
> > **SUB-NOTE:** The verb *blairer* comes from the masculine noun *blair* meaning "nose" or "schnoz."

que je ne te raconte pas *exp.* I won't even go into it.

example: Je ne me suis pas du tout amusé en vacances. Elles étaient horribles, *que je ne te raconte pas!*

as spoken: Je m'suis pas du tout amusé en vacances. È z'étaient horribles, *que j'te raconte pas!*

translation: I didn't have a good time at all on vacation. It was horrible! *I won't even go into it!*

reculer d'une semelle (ne pas) *exp.* not to give an inch • (lit.): not to back up from a [shoe's] sole.

example: J'ai essayé de discuter le problème avec lui, mais il *ne recule pas d'une semelle.*

as spoken: J'ai essayé d'discuter l'problème avec lui, mais y r'cule pas d'une s'melle.

translation: I tried to discuss the problem with him, but he *wouldn't give an inch.*

sale histoire (une) *exp.* a sordid story.

example: "Mais qu'est-ce qui s'est passé avec ton œil? C'est tout gonflé!"
"Je me suis disputé avec mon boucher. Oh, c'est *une sale histoire.*"

as spoken: "Mais qu'est-c'qui s'est passé avec ton œil? C'est tout gonflé!"
"Je m'suis disputé avec mon boucher. Oh, c't'une sale histoire."

translation: "What happened to your eye? It's all swollen!"
"I got into a fight with my butcher. Oh, it's a *sordid story.*"

succès fou (avoir un) *exp.* to go over with big bang • (lit.): to have a crazy success.

example: Notre pièce de théâtre *a eu un succès fou!*

as spoken: Not' pièce de théâtre, elle *a eu un succès fou!*

translation: Our theater play *went over with a big bang!*

tout propos (à) *exp.* at every turn, opportunity • (lit.): at every subject.

      example: Etienne est extrêmement ennuyant! Il m'interrompt *à tout propos!*

      as spoken: Etienne, <u>il</u> est extrêmement ennuyant! <u>Y</u> m'interrompt *à tout propos!*

      translation: Steve is extremely annoying. He interrupts me *at every turn!*

vacherie à quelqu'un (faire une) *exp.* to do a dirty trick on someone.

      example: Je ne parle plus à Joseph. La semaine dernière, il m'a fait une *vacherie.*

      as spoken: <u>J'</u>parle <u>pu</u> à Joseph. La <u>s'</u>maine dernière, <u>y</u> m'a fait une *vach'rie.*

      translation: I don't speak to Joseph any more. Last week, he played a real *dirty trick* on me.

    SYNONYM: **cochonnerie à quelqu'un (faire une)** *exp.*

vouloir à (en) *exp.* to have a grudge against • (lit.): to want someone from it.

      example: C'est ton ami, ça? Moi, je *lui en veux* parce qu'il ment sans arrêt.

      as spoken: C'est ton ami, ça? Moi, <u>j'</u>ui *en veux* <u>pasqu'y</u> <u>m'</u>ment sans arrêt.

      translation: That's your friend? I *have a grudge against him* because he lies nonstop.

voyons *exp.* for crying out load • (lit.): let's see.

      example: "Ça, c'est ton mari?"
                       "Mais, non *voyons!* C'est mon fils!"

      as spoken: [no change]

      translation: "That's your husband, isn't it?"
                       "Of course not, *for crying out loud!* That's my son!"

Practice The Vocabulary

(Answers to Lesson 2, p. 253)

A. Fill in the blank with the corresponding letter of the word that best completes the phrase.

1. Mais regarde tous ces chocolats! C'est _____ !
   a. **la mer à boire**   b. **peau neuve**   c. **Byzance**

2. Ta robe, elle est trop p'tite. Elle épouse la _____ de ton corps.
   a. **forme**   b. **cochonnerie**   c. **semelle**

3. Ça fait une _____ qu'on s'est pas vu!
   a. **histoire**   b. **semelle**   c. **paye**

4. J'ai passé une journée difficile que j'te _____ !
   a. **fais peau neuve**   b. **raconte pas**   c. **fais la bise**

5. T'inquiète pas. Il arriv'ra à _____ sûr.
   a. **coup**   b. **loup**   c. **trou**

6. J'peux pas l'voir en _____ !
   a. **peinture**   b. **photo**   c. **dessin**

7. T'as l'air de péter la _____ aujourd'hui! Evidemment, t'es pu malade.
   a. **mer à boire**   b. **forme**   c. **paye**

8. J'ai beaucoup à faire demain. J'crois que j'vais m'lever d' _____ matin.
   a. **bon**   b. **mauvais**   c. **moyen**

9. Tu peux rien discuter avec elle. È r'cule pas d'une _____ .
   a. **semelle**   b. **chaussure**   c. **chaussette**

10. J'vais t'apporter une surprise. Bouge pas d'un _____ !
    a. **porc**   b. **poil**   c. **port**

B. Circle the letter which corresponds to the correct translation of the phrase in boldface.

1. **Y sont d'bons amis maintenant. Y z'ont passé l'éponge là-d'ssus**.
   a. They're good friends now. They do cleaning together.
   b. They're good friends now. They patched things up.

2. **V'là Jean! J'lui en veux.**
   a. There's John! I want him.
   b. There's John! I have a grudge against him.

3. **Suzanne, è m'bat froid.**
   a. Suzanne's giving me the cold shoulder.
   b. Suzanne beat me up badly.

4. **C'est pas la mer à boire!**
   a. It's very difficult!
   b. It's not very difficult!

5. **Je m'suis levé d'bon matin.**
   a. I got up early in the morning.
   b. I got up late this morning.

6. **La fête, è bat son plein.**
   a. The party's in full swing.
   b. The party's a bore.

7. **J'peux pas la voir en peinture.**
   a. I just love her.
   b. I can't stand her.

8. **Y r'cule pas d'une semelle.**
   a. He's a great dancer.
   b. He doesn't give an inch.

9. **Y viendra à coup sûr.**
   a. He'll never show up.
   b. He'll show up for sure.

10. **È m'a fait une vach'rie.**
    a. She did me a big favor.
    b. She did something really nasty to me.

C. Are the following idioms used correctly or incorrectly?

1. **Ce soir, on va s'en donner à cœur joie. Ça va êtr'une soirée horrible!**
   ☐ correct usage ☐ incorrect usage

2. **J'lui en veux. J'l'admire beaucoup.**
   ☐ correct usage ☐ incorrect usage

3. **Ma nouvelle companie, elle a un succès fou!**
   ☐ correct usage ☐ incorrect usage

4. **C'est évident que tu l'aimes pas. J'pense que tu n'as d'yeux que pour elle.**
   ☐ correct usage ☐ incorrect usage

5. **Mais non, voyons! T'as complètement tort!**
   ☐ correct usage ☐ incorrect usage

6. **Tu peux rien discuter avec lui. Y r'cule pas d'une semelle.**
   ☐ correct usage ☐ incorrect usage

7. **Cette robe, elle est trop grande. Elle épouse la forme de mon corps.**
   ☐ correct usage ☐ incorrect usage

8. **J'adore faire la cuisine. C'est la galère!**
   ☐ correct usage ☐ incorrect usage

9. **C't'une vraie bêcheuse. J'la trouve très gentille.**
   ☐ correct usage ☐ incorrect usage

10. **Tu peux certainement apprendre à jouer du piano. C'est pas la mer à boire!**
    ☐ correct usage ☐ incorrect usage

DICTATION
Test Your Aural Comprehension.

If you are following along with your cassette, you will now hear a paragraph containing many of the idioms from this section. The paragraph will be read at normal conversational speed (which may actually seem fast to you at first). In addition, the words will be pronounced as you would actually hear them in a conversation, including many common reductions.

The first time the paragraph is presented, simply listen in order to get accustomed to the speed and heavy use of reductions. The paragraph will then be read again with a pause after each group of words to give you time to write down what you heard. The third time the paragraph is read, follow along with what you have written.

A CLOSER LOOK:
Fruits and Vegetables Used
in Idiomatic Expressions

It's commonly known that the French do not eat to live but LIVE TO EAT! So it's only natural that food should creep into slang and make its own mark. For some reason, fruits and vegetables are among the most commonly used food groups in slang:

Asparagus (asperge)

> **asperge** *f.* tall, thin person •
> (lit.): asparagus.

Beet (betterave)

> **betterave** *f.* red nose •
> (lit.): beet.

Wheat (blé)

> **blé (du)** *m.* money •
> (lit.): wheat.

Salad (salade)

> **salades** *f.pl.* problems, gossip
> • (lit.): salades.

Cherry (cerise)

cerise *f.* face • (lit.): cherry.

Mushroom (champignon)

champignon *m.* gas pedal • (lit.): mushroom.

Lemon (citron)

citron *m.* head • (lit.): lemon.

Pumpkin (citrouille)

citrouille *f.* face • (lit.): pumpkin.

Pickle (cornichon)

cornichon *m.* telephone • (lit.): pickle.

Strawberry (fraise)

fraise *f.* face • (lit.): strawberry.

Vegetable (légume)

grosse légume *f.* executive, "bigwig" • (lit.): big vegetable.

Onion (oignon)

c'est pas tes oignons *exp.* "It's none of your business" • (lit.): "it's not your onions."

Sorrel (oseille)

oseille *f.* money • (lit.): sorrel.

Potato (patate)

patate *f.* big nose • (lit.): potato.

Peach (pêche)

pêche *f.* a blow to the face • (lit.): peach.

pêche (avoir la) *exp.* to be energetic • (lit.): to have the peach.

Pear (poire)

poire *f.* face • (lit.): pear.

Leek (poireau)

faire le poireau *exp.* to wait for a long period of time, to cool one's heels • (lit.): to do like a leek.

Apple (pomme)

pomme *f.* face • (lit.): apple.

Plum (prune)

pour des prunes *exp.* for nothing, "for zilch" • *(lit);* for plums.

Radish (radis)

n'avoir plus un radis *exp.* to be stone broke • (lit.): to be without a single radish.

PRACTICE THE USE OF FRUITS AND VEGETABLES IN SLANG

A. Match the two columns.

☐ 1. I don't have a red cent.

☐ 2. It's none of your business.

☐ 3. He's a bigwig.

☐ 4. You're wanted on the phone.

☐ 5. I feel great today!

☐ 6. She gave me zilch for my birthday!

☐ 7. He slugged me in the face!

☐ 8. What a fat nose!

☐ 9. I have a headache.

☐ 10. Step on the gas!

A. Y m'a filé une **pêche** en pleine **poire**!

B. J'ai **la pêche** aujourd'hui!

C. On te d'mande au **cornichon**.

D. J'ai mal au **citron**.

E. È m'a donné des **prunes** pour mon anniversaire!

F. Appuie sur le **champignon**!

G. J'ai plus un **radis**!

H. C't'une grosse **légume**, lui.

I. C'est pas tes **oignons**.

J. Quelle gross **patate**!

Georges semble avoir le cafard.

(trans.): George seems depressed.
(lit.): George seems to have the cockroach.

Leçon Trois

Georges semble avoir le cafard

Eric: Mais, **quelle mouche le pique**? Il semble **avoir le cafard**, Georges. **Cela ne cadre pas avec sa personnalité**!

David: **Il y a de fortes chances que** le patron l'**ait mis sur la sellette**. Après tout, tu sais que le rendement de Georges **est en baisse** depuis longtemps. Et **comme de juste**, il n'est plus **dans les petits papiers du** patron.

Eric: Je parie que Georges finira par **claquer la porte**. Il **tourne en rond** ici.

David: Franchement, j'ai l'impression que Georges est déjà **à deux doigts** de **se faire envoyer sur les roses**. C'est dommage parce qu'il a une vraie **assiette au beurre** avec de bons **à-côtés**.

Eric: C'est sûr qu'avec le patron, **on ne sait jamais sur quel pied danser**. On est tout le temps **à se gratter la tête** pour savoir ce qu'il **a derrière la tête**.

David: Oui, mais **toujours est-il que** Georges ne comprend pas que c'est le patron qui **tire les ficelles**, pas lui. Si Georges refuse d'**entrer dans le jeu**, il va **s'en mordre les doigts**.

Eric: Il n'y a pas de doute. Il faut **faire dans la dentelle** avec le patron.

David: **A qui le dis-tu**! L'épisode est **à suivre**. Bon. **Il se fait** tard et **on a bien donné** aujourd'hui. Si on **abandonnait la partie**?

Leçon Trois

Translation in English

George seems to be depressed

Eric: Gee, **what's gotten into him**? George seems **to be down in the dumps. That's out of character for him**.

David: **Chances are that** the boss **called him on the carpet**. After all, you now that George's productivity has been **going downhill** for some time now. And **as it might be expected**, he's no longer on the boss's **good side**.

Eric: I bet George ends up **quitting**. He **doesn't know what to do with himself** here.

David: Frankly, I get the impression that George is **on the brink** of **getting himself fired**. It's too bad because he has a real **cush job** with good **perks.**

Eric: With the boss **you never know where you stand**. You always have to **scratch your head** wondering **what's in the back of his mind**.

David: Yes, but **the fact remains that** George doesn't understand that the boss is the one who **calls the shots**, not him. If George refuses **to play ball**, he's going **to regret it**.

Eric: There's no doubt about it. You have **to wear kid gloves** with the boss.

David: **You're telling me**! The episode is **to be continued**. Okay. **It's getting** late and **we put in a hard day**. What do you say we **call it quits**?

Dialogue in slang as it would be spoken

Georges, y semble avoir le cafard

Eric: Mais, **quelle mouche le pique**? Y semble **avoir le cafard**, Georges. **Cela cadre pas avec sa personnalité**!

David: **Y a d'fortes chances que** l'patron, y l'**ait mis sur la sellette**. Après tout, tu sais que l'rendement d'Georges **est en baisse** depuis longtemps. Et **comme de juste**, il est pu **dans les p'tits papiers du** patron.

Eric: J'parie qu'Georges, y finira par **claquer la porte**. Y **tourne en rond** ici.

David: Franchement, j'ai l'impression qu'Georges, il est déjà **à deux doigts** d'**se faire envoyer sur les roses**. C'est dommage pasqu'il a une vraie **assiette au beurre** avec de bons **à-côtés**.

Eric: C'est sûr qu'avec le patron, **on sait jamais sur quel pied danser**. On est tout l'temps **à z'gratter la tête** pour savoir c'qu'il **a derrière la tête**.

David: Oui, mais **toujours est-il que** Georges, y comprend pas qu'c'est l'patron qui **tire les ficelles**, pas lui. Si Georges, y r'fuse d'**entrer dans l'jeu**, y va **s'en mordre les doigts**.

Eric: Y a pas d'doute. Faut **faire dans la dentelle** avec le patron.

David: **A qui l'dis-tu**! L'épisode, il est **à suivre**. Bon. **Y s'fait** tard et **on a bien donné** aujourd'hui. Si on **abandonnait la partie**?

Literal Translation

George seems to have the cockroach

Eric: Gee, **what fly's biting him**? George seems **to have the cockroach. That doesn't frame with his personality**.

David: **There are strong chances that** the boss **put him on the saddle**. After all, you now that George's productivity has been **going down** for some time now. And **in fairness**, he's no longer **in the little papers of** the boss.

Eric: I bet George ends up **slamming the door**. He **turns in circles** here.

David: Frankly, I get the impression that George is **two fingers away** from **getting himself thrown on the roses**. It's too bad because he has a real **plate of butter** with good **sides**.

Eric: With the boss **you never know where you stand**. You always have to **scratch your head** wondering **what he has behind his head**.

David: Yes, but **it is always that** George doesn't understand that the boss is the one who **pulls the strings**, not him. If George refuses **to enter in the game**, he's going **to bite his fingers over it**.

Eric: No doubt. You have **to do it in lace** with the boss.

David: **Who are you telling that to**! The episode is **to follow**. Good. **It's making itself** late and **we gave well** today. What do you say we **abandon the match**?

Vocabulary

à qui le dis-tu *exp.* you're telling me! • (lit.): to whom are you speaking?

      example: "Paul raconte toujours la même histoire!"
                "*A qui le dis-tu?*"

      as spoken: "Paul, <u>y</u> raconte toujours la même histoire!"
                "*A qui <u>l</u>'dis-tu?*"

      translation: "Paul's always telling the same story!"
                 "*You're telling me!*"

à suivre (être) *exp.* to be continued • (lit.): to be followed.

      example: "...Et le géant a capturé notre héro!" (*à suivre*).

      as spoken: "...Et <u>l</u>'géant, <u>il</u> a capturé notre héro!" (*à suivre*).

      translation: "...And the giant captured our hero!" (*to be continued*).

à-côtés *exp.* perks • (lit.): on-the-sides.

      example: Mon travail a de très bons *à-côtés*.

      as spoken: Mon travail, <u>il</u> a <u>d</u>'très bons *à-côtés*.

      translation: My work has very good *perks*.

abandonner la partie *exp.* to call it a day • (lit.): to abandon the match.

      example: Je suis fatigué. Je vais *abandonner la partie*.

      as spoken: <u>J</u>'suis fatigué. <u>J</u>'vais *abandonner la partie*.

      translation: I'm tired. I'm going *to call it a day*.

assiette au beurre *exp.* cush job • (lit.): plate of butter.

      example: J'adore mon travail. J'ai une vraie *assiette au beurre*.

      as spoken: [no change]

      translation: I love my work. I have a real *cush job*.

baisse (être en) *exp.* to be going downhill • (lit.): to be in a downward motion.

> example: Sa santé est *en baisse* et les docteurs ne savent pas quoi faire.
>
> as spoken: Sa santé, <u>elle</u> est *en baisse* et les docteurs, <u>y</u> ~ savent pas quoi faire.
>
> translation: His/her health is *slipping* and the doctors don't know what to do.

c'est moi qui te le dis *exp.* I'm telling you • (lit.): I'm the one who's telling you.

> example: Méfie-toi de lui. *C'est moi qui te le dis!*
>
> as spoken: Méfie-toi <u>d'</u>lui. *C'est moi qui <u>t'</u>le dis!*
>
> translation: Don't trust him! *I'll telling you!*
>
> **NOTE:** This expression has been used in this dialogue because of its frequency. If you go to France, you'll probably hear it within the first few hours of your visit!

cafard (avoir le) *exp.* to be depressed • (lit.): to have the cockroach.

> example: J'*ai le cafard* aujourd'hui. Je pense que je vais aller voir un film pour me remonter le moral.
>
> as spoken: J'*ai <u>l'</u>cafard* aujourd'hui. <u>J'</u>pense que <u>j'</u>vais aller voir un film pour me remonter <u>l'</u>moral.
>
> translation: I'm *feeling down* today. I think I'll go see a film to boost my spirits.

cela ne cadre pas avec sa personnalité *exp.* that's out of character (for him, for her, etc.) • (lit.): that doesn't frame with his/her personality.

> example: Grégoire m'a réprimandé parce que j'étais en retard de cinq minutes. *Cela ne cadre pas avec sa personnalité.*
>
> as spoken: Grégoire, <u>y</u> m'a réprimandé <u>pasque</u> j'étais en <u>r'</u>tard <u>d'</u>cinq minutes. *Cela ~ cadre pas avec sa personnalité.*

translation: Greg reprimanded me because I was five minutes late.
That's out of character for him.

VARIATION: **cela ne cadre pas avec son rôle** *exp.* • (lit.): that
doesn't frame with his/her role.

claquer la porte *exp.* to quit • (lit.): to slam the door (behind oneself).

example: Si le patron n'arrête pas de m'embêter, je vais finir par
claquer la porte!

as spoken: Si l'patron ~ arrête pas d'm'embêter, j'vais finir par
claquer la porte!

translation: If the boss doesn't stop bugging me, I'm going to end up
quitting!

comme de juste *exp.* as (it) might be expected • (lit.): as of just.

example: Au lieu d'étudier, je suis parti en ville. *Comme de juste,*
j'ai échoué à l'examen.

as spoken: Au lieu d'étudier, j'suis parti en ville. *Comme de juste,* j'ai
échoué à l'exam.

translation: Instead of studying, I went into town. *As might be
expected*, I flunked the exam.

derrière la tête (avoir quelque chose) *exp.* to have some-
thing in the back of one's mind • (lit.): to have something behind the head.

example: Je ne comprends pas ce qu'il veut, Laurent. On ne sait
jamais ce qu'il *a derrière la tête.*

as spoken: J'comprends pas c'qu'y veut, Laurent. On ~ sait jamais
c'qu'il *a derrière la tête.*

translation: I don't understand what Laurent wants. You never
know what's *in the back of his mind.*

deux doigts (être à) *exp.* on the brink • (lit.): to be at two fingers.

example: Ma mère était *à deux doigts* de hurler!

as spoken: Ma mère, elle était *à deux doigts* de hurler!

translation: My mother was *on the edge* of screaming!

donner v. to be productive, to put in a full day • (lit.): to give (it one's all).

    example: Enfin, il est temps de rentrer. On a *bien donné* aujourd'hui.

    as spoken: Enfin, il est temps d'rentrer. On a *bien donné* aujourd'hui.

    translation: Finally, it's time to go home. We really *put in a full day*.

entrer dans le jeu exp. to play by the rules, to "play ball" • (lit.): to enter in the game.

    example: S'il refuse d'*entrer dans le jeu*, sa vie dans cette companie sera très dure.

    as spoken: S'y r'fuse d'*entrer dans l'jeu*, sa vie dans cette companie, è s'ra très dure.

    translation: If he refuses *to play ball*, his life with this company will be very hard.

    VARIATION: **jouer le jeu** exp.

envoyer sur les roses (se faire) exp. • **1.** to get oneself fired • **2.** to get reprimanded.

    example (1): Régis *s'est fait envoyer sur les roses* parce qu'il est arrivé au boulot complètement saoûl pour la dixième fois!

    as spoken: Régis, y *s'est fait envoyer sur les roses* pasqu'il est arrivé (or: pasqu'y't'arrivé) au boulot complètement saoûl pour la dixième fois!

    translation: Régis *got himself fired* because he came to work completely drunk for the tenth time!

    example (2): Je *me suis fait envoyer sur les roses* pour être rentré à deux heures du matin. Mes parents en étaient furieux!

    as spoken: Je m'suis fait envoyer sur les roses pour êt'rentré à deux heures du mat'. Mes parents, y z'en étaient furieux!

    translation: I *got myself chewed out* for coming home at two o'clock in the morning. My parents were really furious!

faire (se) *exp.* to be getting • (lit.): to make itself.

    example: Il *se fait* sombre dehors.

    as spoken: <u>Y</u> *s'fait* sombre dehors.

    translation: It's *getting* dark outside.

faire dans la dentelle *exp.* to put on kid gloves • (lit.): to do in the lace (suggesting that with lace, as with certain people, one must be very careful).

    example: Quand tu lui parleras, ne manque pas de *faire dans la dentelle.* Elle est très sensible.

    as spoken: Quand tu lui parleras, ~ manque pas <u>d'</u>*faire dans la dentelle.* Elle est très sensible.

    translation: When you speak to her, make sure you *put on kid gloves.* She's very sensitive.

gratter la tete (se) *exp.* to try and figure out something • (lit.): to scratch one's head (trying to figure out something).

    example: Je *me gratte la tête* pour savoir ce qu'elle veut pour son anniversaire.

    as spoken: <u>J'</u>*me gratte la tête* pour savoir <u>c'</u>qu'<u>è</u> veut pour son anniversaire.

    translation: I *wonder what* she wants for her birthday.

il y a de fortes chances que *exp.* chances are that • (lit.): there are strong chances that.

    example: *Il y a de fortes chances que* tu vas recevoir ta promotion.

    as spoken: ~ <u>Y</u> a <u>d'</u>*fortes chances que* tu vas recevoir ta promotion.

    translation: *Chances are that* you're going to get your promotion.

mordre les doigts (s'en) *exp.* to regret something • (lit.): to bite one's fingers over something.

    example: Marie est toujours malpolie. Si elle ne change pas sa conduite, un de ces jours elle va *s'en mordre les doigts.*

as spoken: Marie, <u>elle</u> est toujours malpolie. Si <u>è</u> change pas sa conduite, un <u>d'</u>ces jours <u>è</u> va *s'en mord' les doigts.*

translation: Marie is always so rude. If she doesn't change her behavior, one of these days she's going *to regret it.*

petits papiers de quelqu'un (être dans les) *exp.* to be on someone's good side • (lit.): to be in someone's little papers.

example: J'ai complètement oublié l'anniversaire de mon père. Pour le moment, je *ne suis pas dans ses petits papiers.*

as spoken: J'ai complètement oublié l'anniversaire <u>d'</u>mon père. Pour <u>l'</u>moment, <u>i'</u>*suis pas dans ses p'tits papiers.*

translation: I completely forgot my father's birthday. At the moment, I'm *not on his good side.*

quelle mouche te/le/la/les pique? *exp.* what's gotten into you/him/her/them? • (lit.): what fly biting you/him/her/them?

example: *Quelle mouche te pique,* Charles?

as spoken: [no change]

translation: *What's eating you,* Charles?

savoir sur quel pied danser (ne pas) *exp.* not to know where you stand with someone • (lit.): not to know which foot to dance on.

example: Elle n'est pas facile à comprendre. On *ne sait jamais sur quel pied danser* avec elle.

as spoken: Elle ~ est pas facile à comprendre. On ~ *sait jamais sur quel pied danser* avec elle.

translation: She's hard to read. You *never know where you stand* with her.

sellette (mettre sur la) *exp.* to call on the carpet, to rake over the coals • (lit.): to put on the saddle.

example: Etienne! Le patron veut te voir dans son bureau. J'espère pour toi qu'il ne compte pas te *mettre sur la sellette* comme la semaine dernière!

as spoken: Etienne! Le patron, <u>y</u> veut <u>t'</u>voir dans son bureau. J'espère pour toi qu'<u>y</u> ~ compte pas <u>t'mett'</u> *sur la sellette* comme la <u>s'</u>maine dernière!

translation: Steve! The boss wants to see you in his office. I hope for your sake that he's not planning on *raking you over the coals* like last week!

tirer les ficelles *exp.* to run the show • (lit.): to pull the strings (of a theater curtain).

example: C'est moi qui *tire les ficelles*! Pas vous!

as spoken: [no change]

translation: I'm the one *running the show*! Not you!

SYNONYM: **commandes (être aux)** *exp.* to call the shots • (lit.): to be at the commands.

toujours est-il que *exp.* the fact remains that • (lit.): always is it that.

example: Je sais que c'est ton frère, mais *toujours est-il qu'*il m'énerve!

as spoken: Je sais <u>qu'</u>c'est ton frère, mais *toujours est-il qu'*<u>y</u> m'énerve!

translation: I know he's your brother, but *the fact remains that* he's bothering me!

tourner en rond *exp.* • **1.** to have nothing to do • **2.** to go around in circles.

example (1): Depuis que Lucien a quitté son travail, il *tourne en rond*.

as spoken: Depuis <u>qu'</u>Lucien, <u>il</u> a quitté son boulot, <u>y</u> *tourne en rond*.

translation: Ever since Lucien quit his job, he *has nothing to do*.

example (2): Je ne comprends pas ce problème de mathématiques. Je *tourne en rond*.

as spoken: <u>J'</u>comprends pas <u>c'</u>problème de <u>maths</u>. <u>J'</u>*tourne en rond*.

translation: I don't understand this math problem. I'm *going around in circles* (trying to figure it out).

NOTE: **maths** *m.pl.* a popular abbreviation for "*mathématiques*" meaning "mathematics."

Practice the Vocabulary

[Answers to Lesson 3, p. 253]

A. Complete the idiom by choosing the correct word below.

baisse	**mouche**
cadre	**papiers**
doigts	**pied**
fait	**porte**
gratte	**tête**

1. Quelle _____ le pique? Georges, il est d'mauvaise humeur c'matin.

2. Irène, è m'a réprimandé pour être arrivé deux minutes en r'tard! Ça _____ pas avec sa personnalité!

3. Avec le patron, on sait jamais sur quel _____ danser.

4. C'est vrai qu'Thomas, il a claqué la _____ hier? J'espère qu'y pourra trouver un autre emploi!

5. J'me _____ la tête pour savoir pourquoi elle est si malheureuse.

6. Le travail d'Marc, il est en _____ depuis longtemps. Si ça change pas, y risque de devoir trouver un autre emploi!

7. J'sais pas c'qu'y veut, lui. J'me d'mande c'qu'il a derrière la

   _____ .

8. Y s' _____ tard. J'vais rentrer. A d'main!

9. Si tu l'insultes, tu vas t'en mord' les _____ !

10. J'suis pas dans les p'tits _____ du patron pasque j'ai oublié son anniversaire.

B. WORD SEARCH
Circle the words in the grid (on the opposite page) that complete the idioms below. Words may be spelled up, down or diagonally. The first one has been done for you.

1. **à-**_____ *exp.* perks.

2. **abandonner la** _____ *exp.* to call it a day.

3. **assiette au** _____ *exp.* cush job.

4. _____ **(avoir le)** *exp.* to be depressed.

5. **comme de** _____ *exp.* as (it) might be expected.

6. **deux** _____ **(être à)** *exp.* on the brink.

7. **entrer dans le** _____ *exp.* to play ball, to participate in the game.

8. **faire dans la** _____ *exp.* to put on kid gloves.

9. _____ **(mettre sur la)** *exp.* to call on the carpet, to rake over the coals.

10. **tirer les** __·_____ *exp.* to run the show.

WORD SEARCH

```
A D O I G T S A T J W E T
F E F S I D R W O A A F A
P N J P S P S B M D S I N
A T O I C O T E S O S C N
R E B E N K T U N T E E A
T L I S G B I R D E R L U
I L R S I E A R H S C L G
E E E A T L J E U C A E E
B G L S C K E D P A F S N
A V U A K A A R H R A E K
L J L H T H N C H E R T E
I A S E L L E T T E D A W
S T I S C H N L N S T I L
```

C. Match the columns.

☐ 1. cush job

☐ 2. to call it a day

☐ 3. to play by the rules

☐ 4. to be depressed, down

☐ 5. to be on the verge of

☐ 6. the fact remains that

☐ 7. to be continued

☐ 8. to put on kid gloves with someone

☐ 9. to get fired

☐ 10. to be on someone's good side

A. **avoir le cafard**

B. **être dans les petits papiers de quelqu'un**

C. **entrer dans le jeu**

D. **être à deux doigts de**

E. **toujours est-il que**

F. **à suivre**

G. **abandonner la partie**

H. **se faire envoyer sur les roses**

I. **faire dans la dentelle avec quelqu'un**

J. **assiette au beurre**

DICTATION
Test Your Aural Comprehension.

If you are following along with your cassette, you will now hear a paragraph containing many of the idioms from this section. The paragraph will be read at normal conversational speed (which may actually seem fast to you at first). In addition, the words will be pronounced as you would actually hear them in a conversation, including many common reductions.

The first time the paragraph is presented, simply listen in order to get accustomed to the speed and heavy use of reductions. The paragraph will then be read again with a pause after each group of words to give you time to write down what you heard. The third time the paragraph is read, follow along with what you have written.

A CLOSER LOOK:
Professions in Slang

As learned in the opening dialogue at the beginning of this lesson, *toubib* is a slang term for "doctor." However, the following list demonstrates how slang has left virtually no vocation unmarked by its presence.

Artist

barbouilleur, euse *n.* bad artist • (lit.): one who makes a mess.

> **NOTE:** **barbouiller** *v.* to make a mess, to dirty.

croûtier *v.* bad artist.

> **NOTE:** This comes from the feminine noun *croûte* meaning "crust" which is also used to refer to a bad painting.

Butcher

louchébem *m.*

> **NOTE:** This is a largonji transformation of the masculine noun *boucher*. *See: A Closer Look — The Language of "Largonji,"* p. 216.

Butler

larbin *m.*

> **NOTE:** This term is a general term for "waiter" or "servant."

Dentist

quenottier *m.*

> **NOTE:** This comes from the feminine noun *quenotte* meaning "tooth."

Dermatologist

peaussier m.

> **NOTE:** This comes from the feminine noun *peau* meaning "skin."

Detective

bourrin *m.* • (lit.): horse, donkey.

Doctor

toubib *m.* (Arabic).

Door-to-door salesman

posticheur *m.*

> **NOTE:** **postiche** *f.* sales talk, sales spiel.

Female lavatory attendant

Madame-pipi *f.*

Fireman

pomplard *m.*

> **NOTE:** This comes from the verb *pomper* meaning "to pump (water, etc.)."

Hairdresser; Barber

coupe-tiffes *m.* •
(lit.): cut(ter of) hair.

> **NOTE:** **tiffes** *m.pl.* hair.

figaro *m.* (humorous).

> **NOTE:** This is from the Barber of Seville.

gratte-couenne *m.* •
(lit.): scratch(er of) skin.

> **NOTE:** **couenne** *f.* skin.

merlan *m.* • (lit.): whiting.

perruquemar *m.*

> **NOTE:** This comes from the feminine noun *perruque* meaning "wig."

pommadin *m.*

> **NOTE:** This comes from the feminine noun *pommade* meaning "skin ointment."

tiffier *m.*

> **NOTE:** This comes from the masculine noun *tiffe* meaning "hair."

Interpreter

inter *m.*

> **NOTE:** This is an abbreviation of *interprète* meaning "interpreter."

Laundress

briqueuse *f.*

> **NOTE:** **briquer** *v.* to clean well.

Lawyer

babillard *m.* •
(lit.): chatterbox, babbler.

> **NOTE:** This comes from the verb *babiller* meaning "to babble (of brook, person, etc.)."

blanchisseur *m.*

> **NOTE:** **blanchir** *v.* to clean (someone's criminal record).

débarbe or **débarbot** *m.* •
(lit.): cleaner.

> **NOTE:** **débarboter** *v.* to clean (someone's criminal record).

débarbotteur *m.* •
(lit.): cleaner (of someone's criminal record).

parrain *m.* • (lit.): godfather.

tabellion *m.* • (lit.): scrivener.

Mechanic

mécano *m.*

Nurse

artilleur de la pièce humide *m.* male nurse •
(lit.): artilleryman of the wet gun.
NOTE: pièce humide *f.*
syringe • (lit.): wet gun.

pique-fesse *f.* •
(lit.): prick-buttock.

tisanier *m.* • (lit.): one who infuses (drugs into someone).
NOTE: This comes from the feminine noun *tisane* meaning "infusion (of herbs, etc.)."

Obstetrician; Midwife

vise-au-trou *m.* • (lit.): one who "looks at the hole."
NOTE: viser *v.* to look, to see.

Orderly

canulard *m.*
NOTE: This comes from the feminine noun *canule* meaning "the nozzle of a syringe."

Paper pusher

gratte-papier *m.* •
(lit.): paper-scratcher.

Plumber

plombard *m.*
NOTE: This comes from the masculine noun *plomb* meaning "lead."

Policeman

cognard *m.* • (lit.): hitter.
NOTE: This comes from the verb *cogner* meaning "to hit."

cogne *m.* abbreviation of: *cognard.*

flic *m.* *(extremely popular)*

flicard *m.* variation of *flic.*

fliquette *f.* police woman.

fliqueuse *f.* police woman.

hirondelle *f.* cycle cop •
(lit.): swallow (bird).

pingouin *m.* • (lit.): penguin.

Priest

coincoin *m.* • (lit.): quacking sound of a duck.

Private investigator

privé *m.* • (lit.): private.

Professor

prof *m. & f.*

> **NOTE:** The term *professeur* is always masculine. However, in its abbreviated form *prof,* it is both masculine and feminine.

Psychiatrist

psi *m.* "shrink" •
1. psychiatrist • 2. psycho.

Sailor; Blue-collar worker

col bleu *m.* • (lit.): blue collar.

Taxi driver

loche *m. & f.*

Top surgeon

couteau *m.* • (lit.): knife.

> **ALSO:** **couteau** *m.* lead actor.

Veterinarian

véto *m.*

> **NOTE:** This is an abbreviation of the masculine noun *vétérinaire* meaning "veterinarian."

Waiter

louf(f)iat *m.*

larbin *m.*

> **NOTE:** This term is a general term for "waiter" or "servant."

White-collar worker

col blanc *m.* • (lit.): white collar.

Writer

buveur *m.* writer, journalist • (lit.): drinker (of ink).

scribouillard(e) *n.*

> **NOTE:** This comes from the verb *scribouiller* meaning "to scribble, to write."

scribouilleur, euse *n.* a variation of *scribouillard(e).*

PRACTICE USING PROFESSIONS IN SLANG

A. Match the colums by writing the correct letter in the box.

☐ 1. private investigator   A. **prof**

☐ 2. dentist   B. **scribouillard(e)**

☐ 3. police officer   C. **toubib**

☐ 4. butler   D. **mécano**

☐ 5. psychiatrist   E. **merlan**

☐ 6. professor   F. **blanchisseur**

☐ 7. doctor   G. **flicard**

☐ 8. lawyer   H. **couteau**

☐ 9. surgeon   I. **psi**

☐ 10. hairdresser   J. **privé**

☐ 11. writer   K. **larbin**

☐ 12. mechanic   L. **quenottier**

B. Underline the slang synonyms that match the vocation to the left.
Note: **There may be more than one answer in each case.**

1. **coiffeur**:
   a. pommadin
   c. plombard
   e. blanchisseur
   b. tiffier
   d. coupe-tiffes
   f. larbin

2. **agent de police**:
   a. merlan
   c. prof
   e. cognard
   b. flicard
   d. pingouin
   f. toubib

3. **écrivain**:
   a. psi
   c. loche
   e. flic
   b. scribouilleur
   d. scribouillard
   f. col bleu

4. **avocat**:
   a. blanchisseur
   c. parrain
   e. babillard
   b. hirondelle
   d. débarbotteur
   f. quenottier

5. **infirmière**:
   a. mécano
   c. tisanier
   e. pique-fesse
   b. posticheur
   d. plombard
   f. inter

6. **investigateur privé**:
   a. col blanc
   c. buveur
   e. cogne
   b. privé
   d. couteau
   f. posticheur

7. **artiste**:
   a. barbouilleur
   c. tisanier
   e. bourrin
   b. babillard
   d. croûtier
   f. figaro

Il est rond comme une bille!

(trans.): He's drunk as a skunk!
(lit.): He's as round as a billiard ball!

Dialogue in slang

Il est rond comme une bille!

Marc: J'ai **décroché le contrat**!

Jean: Bravo! **Ça s'arrose**, ça! C'est moi qui régale.

Marc: **Ce n'est pas de refus**. Je crois que j'ai bien besoin de **me rincer le sifflet**! J'avais tellement **les boules** pendant l'entretien que j'étais **en nage**!

Jean: Oh, **ne te frappe pas le biscuit**. Maintenant l'affaire est **dans le sac**. Je t'offre un whisky.

Marc: D'accord, mais **attention les dégats**! Si je bois avant de **me caler le bide**, j'**en ai vite dans le casque**. La dernière fois que j'ai bu **à jeun**, j'étais **rond comme une bille** et **en un rien de temps**! Le lendemain, j'**avais la G.D.B.** et au lieu de **me pointer** au boulot, j'ai **fait le tour du cadran**. Ce que j'**avais la tête en compote**! Je **m'en suis payé une tranche** mais **ça ne valait pas le coup**.

Jean: J'ai l'impression que tu n'aimes pas trop **écumer les bars**. Bon. On **s'enfile** quelques **amuse-gueules** pour commencer?

   (peu après...)

Marc: On **boit à ton succès, vieille branche**!

Jean: **Voilà ce qui s'appelle** une boisson délicieuse et **qui dégage**!

Marc: En ce cas-là, on **recharge les accus**!

Translation in English

He's drunk out of his mind!

Marc: I **landed the contract**!

Jean: Congratulations! **That calls for a drink**! It's on me.

Marc: **Don't mind if I do**. I think I need **to wet my whistle**! I was so **freaked out** during the meeting that I was **soaked in sweat**!

Jean: Oh, **don't get yourself all worked up**. Now the whole deal is **in the bag**. Let me treat you to a whisky.

Marc: Okay, but **watch out for any damage**. If I drink before **eating**, it **goes right to my head**. The last time I drank **on an empty stomach**, I got **drunk out of my mind** and **in no time flat**! The next day, I **had a hangover** and instead of **showing up** for work, I **slept the day away**. Did I ever have **a killer headache**! I **had a blast** but **it wasn't worth it**.

Jean: I get the feeling you're not really into **bar hopping**. Okay. What do you say we **down** a few **appetizers** to start?

   (a little later...)

Marc: Let's **drink to your success, old chum**!

Jean: **That's what I call** a delicious drink and one that **packs a wallop**!

Marc: In that case, let's **stack them up again**!

Leçon Quatre 📼

Dialogue in slang as it would be spoken

Y est rond comme une bille!

Marc: J'ai **décroché l'contrat**!

Jean: Bravo! **Ça s'arrose**, ça! C'est moi qui régale.

Marc: **C'est pas d'refus**. J'crois qu'j'ai bien besoin de **m'rincer l'sifflet**! J'avais tellement **les boules** pendant l'entretien qu'j'étais **en nage**!

Jean: Oh, **t'frappe pas l'biscuit**. Maintenant l'affaire, elle est **dans l'sac**. J't'offre un whisky.

Marc: D'accord, mais **attention les dégats**! Si j'bois avant d'**me caler l'bide**, j'**en ai vite dans l'casque**. La dernière fois qu'j'ai bu **à jeun**, j'étais **rond comme une bille** et **en un rien d'temps**! Le lend'main, j'**avais la G.D.B.** et au lieu d'**me pointer** au boulot, j'ai **fait l'tour du cadran**. C'que j'**avais la tête en compote**! J'**m'en suis payé une tranche** mais ça valait pas l'coup.

Jean: J'ai l'impression qu't'aimes pas trop **écumer les bars**. Bon. On **s'enfile** quèques **amuse-gueules** pour commencer?

   (peu après...)

Marc: On **boit à ton succès, vieille branche**!

Jean: **Voilà c'qui s'appelle** une boisson délicieuse et **qui dégage**!

Marc: En c'cas-là, on **r'charge les accus**!

Leçon Quatre

Literal Translation

He's as round as a marble!

Marc: I **unhooked the contract**!

Jean: Congratulations! **That waters itself**! It's on me.

Marc: **It's not refused**! I think I need **to rinse my whistle**! I had such **balls (in my throat)** during the meeting that I was **swimming (in sweat)**!

Jean: Oh, **don't hit your biscuit**. Now the whole deal **is in the bag**. I offer you a whisky.

Marc: Okay, but **watch out the damages**. If I drink before **regulating my tummy**, I **have it quickly in the helmet**. The last time I drank **on empty**, I was **as round as a marble** and **in a nothing of time**! The next day, I **had the wooden mouth** and instead of **punching the time clock** to work, I **did a tour of the face of the clock**. Did I ever have **the head of compote**! I **treated myself to a slice (of fun)** but **it wasn't worth the blow**!

Jean: I get the feeling you don't really like **foaming the bars**. Good. Shall we **thread** a few **mouth-amusers** to start?

(a little later...)

Marc: Let's **drink to your success, old branche**!

Jean: **Here's what's called** a delicious drink and one that **opens (the nostrils)**!

Marc: In that case, let's **recharge the batteries**!

Vocabulary

amuse-gueules *m.pl.* appetizers • (lit.): mouth amusers.

>   example: On va dîner dans une heure. Mais si tu as très faim, tu
>   peux toujours prendre quelques *amuse-gueules*
>   maintenant.

>   as spoken: On va dîner dans une heure. Mais si <u>t</u>'as très faim, tu
>   peux toujours pren<u>d</u>' <u>quèques</u> *amuse-gueules*
>   maintenant.

>   translation: We're going to have dinner in an hour. But if you are
>   really hungry, you can always have some *appetizers* now.

>   **NOTE (1):**   **gueule** *f.* derogatory for the "mouth" of a human being
>   • (lit.): mouth of an animal.

>   **NOTE (2):**   In the example above, the verb *"prendre"* was used to
>   mean "to have." This is an extremely popular usage of
>   *"prendre"* when used in connection with food. For
>   example:

>   example: Je *prends* toujours un croissant et un café pour mon petit
>   déjeuner.

>   as spoken: J'*prends* toujours un croissant et un café pour mon <u>p</u>'tit
>   <u>dèj</u>.

>   translation: I always *have* a croissant and a coffee for my breakfast.

arroser une affaire *exp.* to celebrate an event with a drink • (lit.): to
water an occasion.

>   example: Le patron vient de m'augmenter. *Ça s'arrose!*

>   as spoken: Le patron, <u>y</u> vient <u>d</u>'m'augmenter. *Ça s'arrose!*

>   translation: The boss just gave me a raise. *This calls for a drink!*

attention les dégats! *exp.* Beware of any damage (that I may cause by being out of control!) • (lit.): [same].

　　　　example: Essaie cette nouvelle recette de gâteau au chocolat mais alors *attention les dégats* question calories!

　　　　as spoken: [no change]

　　　　translation: Try this new chocolate cake recipe but *you better watch out* for the calories!

　　NOTE: In correct academic French, the previous expression should actually be *"Attention aux dégats."* The omission of the preposition *"à"* following *"Attention"* is common in everyday speech.

boire au succès de quelqu'un *exp.* to toast someone's success • (lit.): to drink to someone's success.

　　　　example: *Buvons au succès de* Marcel! Félicitations pour ton nouvel emploi!

　　　　as spoken: *Buvons au succès d'*Marcel! Félicitations pour ton nouvel emploi!

　　　　translation: *Let's drink to* Marcel's success. Congratulations on your new job!

　　ALSO: **boire à la santé de quelqu'un** *exp.* • (lit.): to drink to someone's health.

boules (avoir les) *exp.* to be extremely nervous • (lit.): to have balls (in one's throat).

　　　　example: J'ai eu *les boules* quand j'ai fait ma présentation devant les cadres.

　　　　as spoken: J'ai eu *les boules* quand j'ai fait ma présentation *d'*vant les cadres.

　　　　translation: I was *extremely nervous* when I did my presentation in front of the executives.

　　SYNONYM: **glandes (avoir les)** *exp.* • (lit.): to have glands (that are swollen).

caler le bide (se) *exp.* to eat • (lit.): to stabilize one's stomach.

> example: J'ai faim. Je dois *me caler le bide.*
>
> as spoken: J'ai faim. <u>J'</u>dois <u>m'caler l'</u>bide.
>
> translation: I'm hungry. I'm have to *eat something.*
>
> > **NOTE:**   The masculine noun *"bide"* is a shortened version of *"bidon,"* meaning "belly" • (lit.): can or drum.

ce n'est pas de refus *exp.* don't mind if I do • (lit.): it's not from refusal.

> example: Tu m'offres cette boisson? *Ce n'est pas de refus*, ça.
>
> as spoken: Tu m'offres cette boisson? <u>C'</u>est pas <u>d'</u>refus, ça.
>
> translation: You're offering me this drink? Don't mind if I do.

dans le sac (être) *exp.* to be a sure thing, to be in the bag • (lit.): to be in the sack.

> example: Je suis certain que le patron va t'augmenter. C'est *dans le sac.*
>
> as spoken: <u>J'</u>suis certain que <u>l'</u>patron, <u>y</u> va t'augmenter. C'est *dans l'*sac.
>
> translation: I'm sure the boss will give you a raise. It's *in the bag.*

décrocher un contrat *exp.* to land a contract • (lit.): to unhook a contract.

> example: Je viens de *décrocher un contrat* avec le distributeur du Brésil!
>
> as spoken: <u>J'</u>viens <u>d'</u>*décrocher un contrat* avec le distributeur du Brésil!
>
> translation: I just *landed a contract* with the distributor from Brazil!
>
> > **SYNONYM:**   **boucler une affaire** *exp.* to clinch a deal • (lit.): to tie up a deal.

dégager v. to pack a wallop • (lit.): to clear out (the nose).

> example: De boire de la vodka à sec, ça *dégage*!
>
> as spoken: De boire d'la vodka à sec, ça *dégage*!
>
> translation: Drinking vodka straight up *packs a kick*!

écumer les bars exp. to barhop • (lit.): to skim bars.

> example: Il aime passer le vendredi soir à *écumer les bars*.
>
> as spoken: Il aime passer l'vendredi soir à *écumer les bars*.
>
> translation: He likes to spend Friday nights *bar hopping*.

enfiler (s') v. to consume something quickly • (lit.): to thread (a needle, etc.).

> example: Je *me suis enfilé* trois glaces de suite hier.
>
> as spoken: Je *m'suis enfilé* trois glaces de suite hier.
>
> translation: I *downed* three ice cream cones one after the other yesterday.
>
> **NOTE:**   The verb *"enfiler"* (literally meaning "to thread a needle, etc.) is humorously used in French slang to mean "to stuff something down a narrow tube (i.e. one's throat)."

SYNONYM (3):   **avaler** v. • (lit.): to swallow.

SYNONYM (2):   **descendre** v. • (lit.): to down.

frapper le biscuit (se) exp. to get oneself all worked up • (lit.): to hit one's head (with both hands from worrying).

> example: *Ne te frappe pas le biscuit.* Je suis certain que ton entretien s'est bien passé.
>
> as spoken: ~ *Te frappe pas l'biscuit.* J'suis certain qu'ton entretien, y s'est bien passé.
>
> translation: *Don't get yourself all worked up.* I'm sure your interview went well.
>
> **NOTE:**   **biscuit** n. noggin, head • (lit.): cookie.

G.D.B. (avoir la) *exp.* to have a hangover • (lit.): to have the mouth of wood (since G.D.B. is an abbreviation for *"gueule de bois"* - See notes below).

example:	Si tu bois trop ce soir, tu risques d'avoir la *G.D.B.* demain!
as spoken:	Si tu bois trop <u>c'</u>soir, tu risques d'avoir la *G.D.B.* <u>d'</u>main!
translation:	If you drink too much tonight, you're asking for a *hangover* tomorrow!

NOTE (1): *G.D.B.* is pronounced *jé, dé, bé* and is an abbreviation for "gueule de bois."

NOTE (2): The feminine noun *"gueule,"* literally meaning the "mouth of an animal," is commonly used in French slang to mean "mouth" in general. This expression conjures up an image of someone who is so hungover, that he/she can barely move his/her mouth.

SYNONYM: **mal aux cheveux (avoir)** *exp.* • (lit.): to have a hairache.

jeun (à) *exp.* on an empty stomach • (lit.): after having fasted.

example:	Pour ma prise de sang demain matin, je dois arriver chez le médecin *à jeun*.
as spoken:	Pour ma prise de sang <u>d'</u>main matin, <u>j'</u>dois arriver chez <u>l'</u>médecin *à jeun*.
translation:	For my blood test tomorrow morning, I have to go to the doctor's office on an empty stomach.

nage (être en) *exp.* to be soaking wet from perspiraton • (lit.): to be wet as if one had been swimming.

example:	Quand j'ai finit mon footing ce matin, j'étais *en nage*!
as spoken:	Quand j'ai finit mon footing <u>c'</u>matin, j'étais *en nage*!
translation:	When I finished jogging this morning, I was *soaked in sweat*!

VARIATION: **tout en nage (être)** *exp.* to be completely soaking wet from perspiration.

pointer (se) *v.* to arrive, to show up • (lit.): to point oneself, to punch a time clock.

> example: Georges *s'est pointé* au boulot deux heures en retard! C'est la deuxième fois cette semaine!

> as spoken: Georges, y *s'est pointé* au boulot deux heures en r'tard! C'est la deuxième fois cette s'maine!

> translation: Geroges *showed up* to work two hours late! It's the second time this week!

> **SYNONYM:** **radiner (se)** *v.*

recharger les accus *exp.* to set 'em up (the glasses for another round of drinks) • (lit.): to recharge the batteries.

> example: Et maintenant, buvons à la santé de Louise! *Rechargeons les accus!*

> as spoken: Et maintenant, buvons à la santé d'Louise! *Rechargeons les accus!*

> translation: And now, let's drink to Louise! *Stack 'em up again!*

rien de temps (en un) *exp.* in no time flat • (lit.): in a nothing of time.

> example: Si tout va bien, je pourrai réparer ta voiture *en un rien de temps*.

> as spoken: Si tout va bien, J'pourrai réparer ta voiture *en un rien d'temps*.

> translation: If everything goes well, I'll be able to repare your car *in no time flat*.

rincer le sifflet (se) *exp.* to wet one's whistle • (lit.): to rinse one's whistle.

> example: J'ai soif. Je vais *me rincer le sifflet*.

> as spoken: J'ai soif. J'vais *m'rincer l'sifflet*.

> translation: I'm thirsty. I'm going *to wet my whistle*.

rond(e) comme une bille (être) *exp.* to be roaring drunk • (lit.):
to be as round as a marble.

> example: Mais tu ne peux pas conduire comme ça! Tu es *rond comme une bille!*
>
> as spoken: Mais tu ~ peux pas conduire comme ça! T'es *rond comme une bille!*
>
> translation: You can't drive like that! You're *bombed out of your skull!*
>
> > **NOTE:** This expression is a play on words since the adjective *rond(e)* (meaning "round") is commonly used to mean drunk. Therefore, *être rond(e) comme une bille* simply emphasises the subject's intoxicated condition.
> >
> > > **SUB-NOTE:** A common hand gesture made to indicate when someone is *rond* can be found in lesson 10, *A Closer Look — Surely You Gesture!*, p. 238.

tête en compote (avoir la) *exp.* to have a horrible headache •
(lit.): to feel like one's head has been turned to compote.

> example: Je ne peux pas me lever du lit. J'ai *la tête en compote!*
>
> as spoken: J'peux pas m'lever du lit. J'ai *la tête en compote!*
>
> translation: I can't get out of bed. I have a *monster headache!*

tour du cadran (faire le) *exp.* to sleep the day away • (lit.): to do
the tour of the clock's face.

> example: Quand je suis malade, je reste au lit et je *fais le tour du cadran.*
>
> as spoken: Quand j'suis malade, j'reste au lit et j'fais l'tour du cadran.
>
> translation: When I'm sick, I sleep around the clock.

tranche (s'en payer une) *exp.* to have a great time • (lit.): to treat
oneself to a slice (of fun).

> example: On *s'en est payé une tranche* à la fête du village.
>
> as spoken: [no change]

translation: We *had a blast* at the village festival.

> **NOTE:** **payer (se)** *v.* to treat oneself • (lit.): to pay oneself (something).
>
> example: Je *me suis payé* une glace.
>
> as spoken: Je *m'suis payé* une glace.
>
> translation: I *treated myself to* an ice cream.

valoir le coup *exp.* to be worth it • (lit.): to be worth the exploit.

example: Ça *ne vaut pas le coup* d'aller à Paris pour juste deux jours!

as spoken: Ça *vaut pas l'coup* d'aller à Paris pour juste deux jours!

translation: Its *not worth it* to go to Paris for just two days!

vieille branche *exp.* old pal, chum, buddy • (lit.): old branch.

example: Salut ma *vieille branche*! Comment vas-tu?

as spoken: Salut ma *vieille branche*! Comment tu vas?

translation: Hi my *old chum*! How are you?

vite dans le casque (en avoir) *exp.* to go quickly to one's head (said of alcohol) • (lit.): to have it quickly in the helmet.

example: Quand je bois du vin, j'*en ai vite dans le casque*.

as spoken: Quand j'bois du vin, j'*en ai vite dans l'casque*.

translation: When I drink wine, it *goes right to my head*.

> **NOTE:** **casque** *f.* head • (lit.): helmet.

voilà qui s'appelle... *exp.* that's what I call... • (lit.): that's what's called...

example: *Voilà qui s'appelle* bizarre!

as spoken: [no change]

translation: *That's what I call* strange!

Practice the Vocabulary

[Answers to Lesson 4, p. 254]

A. Choosing from the list below, complete the idiom by writing the correct word in the crossword puzzle on the opposite page.

accus	**boit**	**décroché**	**nage**
appelle	**boules**	**dégage**	**pointer**
arrose	**branche**	**dégats**	**refus**
bars	**cadran**	**enfile**	**sac**
bide	**casque**	**G.D.B.**	**sifflet**
bille	**compote**	**gueules**	**temps**
biscuit	**coup**	**jeun**	**tranche**

Marc: J'ai **(29A)** le contrat!

Jean: Bravo! Ça s' **(1A)** , ça! C'est moi qui régale.

Marc: Ce n'est pas de **(54D)** . Je crois que j'ai bien besoin de me rincer le **(5D)** ! J'avais tellement les **(42D)** pendant l'entretien que j'étais en **(78A)** !

Jean: Oh, ne te frappe pas le **(17D)** . Maintenant l'affaire est dans le **(22A)** . Je t'offre un whisky.

Marc: D'accord, mais attention les **(52D)** ! Si je bois avant de me caler le **(51A)** , j'en ai vite dans le **(58A)** . La dernière fois que j'ai bu à **(36A)** , j'étais rond comme une **(42A)** et en un rien de **(64A)** ! Le lendemain, j'avais la **(13A)** et au lieu de me **(30A)** au boulot, j'ai fait le tour du **(21D)** . Ce que j'avais la tête en **(58D)** ! Je m'en suis payé une **(75A)** mais ça ne valait pas le **(41D)** .

Jean: J'ai l'impression que tu n'aimes pas trop écumer les **(51D)** . Bon. On s'**(37D)** quelques amuse-**(48A)** pour commencer?

Marc: On **(24D)** à ton succès, vieille **(14D)** !

Jean: Voilà ce qui s'**(28D)** une boisson délicieuse et qui **(26D)** !

Marc: En ce cas-là, on recharge les **(70A)** !

CROSSWORD PUZZLE

B. Choose the phrase that best fits the idiom.

1. **J'veux prendre des amuse-gueules**.
   ☐ a. J'ai faim.
   ☐ b. J'ai pas faim.

2. **Il est rond comme une bille...**
   ☐ a. pasqu'il a rien bu.
   ☐ b. pasqu'il a trop bu.

3. **J'vais m'rincer l'sifflet.**
   ☐ a. J'ai soif.
   ☐ b. J'ai pas soif.

4. **J'ai la G.D.B.**
   ☐ a. J'ai trop bu hier soir.
   ☐ b. J'ai rien bu hier soir.

5. **On r'charge les accus!**
   ☐ a. Arrêtons de boire!
   ☐ b. Buvons encore!

6. **J'm'en suis payé une tranche chez Henriette.**
   ☐ a. Quelle soirée horrible!
   ☐ b. Quelle soirée fantastique!

7. **Quand je parlais au patron, j'étais en nage.**
   ☐ a. J'étais très nerveux.
   ☐ b. J'étais très calme.

8. **J'vais m'caler l'bide.**
   ☐ a. Il est temps d'prend' le déjeuner.
   ☐ b. J'ai déjà pris mon déjeuner.

9. **J'ai fait le tour du cadran.**
   ☐ a. Que j'étais fatigué!
   ☐ b. J'étais pas du tout fatigué!

10. **Tu t'frappes le biscuit?**
    ☐ a. T'as l'air inquiet.
    ☐ b. T'as l'air calme.

C. Match the columns.

☐ 1. That calls for a drink.

A. **On boit à son succès.**

☐ 2. Let's toast to his success.

B. **Il est rond comme une bille.**

☐ 3. That's what I call pretty.

C. **J'en ai vite dans l'casque.**

☐ 4. I had a blast.

D. **Ça vaut pas l'coup.**

☐ 5. Don't get yourself all worked up.

E. **Te frappe pas l'biscuit.**

F. **J'ai la tête en compote.**

☐ 6. It goes straight to my head.

G. **J'ai la G.D.B.**

☐ 7. I have a killer headache.

H. **Il est arrivé en un rien d'temps.**

☐ 8. I don't like to bar hop.

I. **J'm'en suis payé une tranche.**

☐ 9. He's dead drunk.

☐ 10. I have a hangover.

J. **Voilà c'qui s'appelle joli.**

☐ 11. He arrived in no time flat.

K. **J'aime pas écumer les bars.**

☐ 12. It's not worth it.

L. **Ça s'arrose.**

DICTATION
Test Your Aural Comprehension.

If you are following along with your cassette, you will now hear a paragraph containing many of the idioms from this section. The paragraph will be read at normal conversational speed (which may actually seem fast to you at first). In addition, the words will be pronounced as you would actually hear them in a conversation, including many common reductions.

The first time the paragraph is presented, simply listen in order to get accustomed to the speed and heavy use of reductions. The paragraph will then be read again with a pause after each group of words to give you time to write down what you heard. The third time the paragraph is read, follow along with what you have written.

A CLOSER LOOK:
Slang Suffixes

In spoken French, conventional words can be easily transformed into slang by attaching a slang suffix to the end of a word. These suffixes include: *-aille, -ard, -arès, -asse (ace), -oche, -os, -osse, -ouille, -ouse (ouze),* and *-uche.* By learning these slang suffixes, you will quickly be able to recognize them as well as create some interesting slang words of your own.

-aille(r)

boustifaille *f.* food, "grub.
NOTE: **boustifailler** *v.* to chow down.

crevaille *f.* huge meal.
ORIGIN: **crever** *v.* to die, to explode.

discutailler *v.* to discuss.
ORIGIN: **discuter** *v.*

duraille *adj.* hard.
ORIGIN: **dur(e)** *adj.*

Franchecaille *f.* France.

Franchouillard *adj.* very French.

gambergeailler *v.* to daydream.
ORIGIN: **gamberger** *v.*

godaille *f.* food.

godailler *v.*

joncaille *f.* money.
> **ORIGIN: jonc** *m.*

lichailler *v. to drink.*
> **ORIGIN: licher** *v.*

mangeaille *f.* grub.
> **ORIGIN: manger** *v. to eat*

pinailler *v. to quibble, nit-pick.*

poiscaille *m.* fish.
> **ORIGIN: poisson** *m.*

-ard

cottard(e) *adj.* difficult.

craspouillard(e) *adj.* dirty.

faiblard(e) *adj.* feeble.
> **ORIGIN: faible** *adj.*

pinard *m.* wine, "booze."

prétentiard(e) • **1.** *n.* pretentious • **2.** *adj.* pretentious person.
> **ORIGIN: prétentieux, -euse** *n. & adj.*

richard(e) *n. & adj.*
> **ORIGIN: riche** *adj.*

rigolard(e) *adj.* funny.
> **ORIGIN: rigoler** *v. to laugh.*

rêvard(e) *n.* dreamer.
> **ORIGIN: rêver** *v. to dream.*

tartouillard *adj.* ugly.
> **ORIGIN: tarte** *adj.*

-arès

bouclarès *adj.* closed.
> **ORIGIN: boucler** *v. to close.*

couparès *adj.* penniless.
> **ORIGIN: coupé(e)** *adj.* cut off (from funds).

emballarès *adj.* arrested.
> **ORIGIN: se faire emballer** *exp. to get arrested.*

-asse

blondasse *f.* blonde.

fadasse *adj.* dull.
> **ORIGIN: fade** *adj.*

follasse *adj. & n.* crazy woman.
> **ORIGIN: folle** *adj.*

pétasse *f.* vulgar woman.
> **ORIGIN: péter** *v.* • **1.** to fart • **2.** to explode.

paillasse *f.* straw mat.
> **ORIGIN: paille** *f.* straw.

-oche(r)

bidoche *f.* inferior meat.

cinetoche *m.* movie theater.
> **ORIGIN: cinéma** *m.*

cinoche *m.* movie theater.
ORIGIN: **cinéma** *m.*

espadoches *f.pl.* espadrilles.

fantoche *f.* fantasy.
ORIGIN: **fantaisie** *f.*

filocher *v.* to shadow
(someone).
ORIGIN: **filer** *v.*

glandocher *v.* to stroll and
hang out.
ORIGIN: **glander** *v.*

Invaloches *m.pl.* les Invalides.

lapinoche *m.* rabbit.
ORIGIN: **lapin(e)** *n.*

mardoche *m.* Tuesday.
ORIGIN: **mardi** *m.*

médoche *f.* medal.
ORIGIN: **médaille** *f.*

patoche *f.* hand.
ORIGIN: **patte** *f.*
• (lit.): paw.

peloche *f.* film.
ORIGIN: **pellicule** *f.*

pétoche *f.* fart; fear.
ORIGIN: **pet** *m.*

pistoche *f.* swimming pool.
ORIGIN: **piscine** *f.*

téloche *f.* television.
ORIGIN: **télévision** *f.*

-os

coolos *adj.* cool (attitude).

-ose

chouettose *exclam.* fantastic.
ORIGIN: **chouette** *exclam.*

matos *m.* equipment.

-ouille(r)

barbouiller *v.* to paint badly.

charmouille *adj.* charming.
ORIGIN: **charmant(e)** *adj.*

crachouiller *v.* to split.
ORIGIN: **cracher** *v.*

crassouille *f.* filth, dirt.
ORIGIN: **crasse** *f.* dirt.

gidouille *m.* **1.** stomach •
2. belly button.

glandouiller *v.* to stroll; hang
out.
ORIGIN: **glander** *v.*

gratouiller *v.* to itch.
ORIGIN: **gratter** *v.*

mâchouiller *v.* to eat without
appetite.
ORIGIN: **mâcher** *v.*

papouille f. • faire des papouilles à quelqu'un; to paw someone, to caress someone.

papouiller v. to paw and caress.

patouille f. • faire des patouilles à quelqu'un; to paw or caress someone.

péquenouille m. country hick.
ORIGIN: **péquenot** m.

pétouille f. fart, fear.
ORIGIN: **pet** m.

-ouse(r)

cartouse f. card.
ORIGIN: **carte** f.

cavouse f. wine cellar.
ORIGIN: **cave** f.

cravtouse f. tie.
ORIGIN: **cravate** f.

filetouse m. string bag.
ORIGIN: **filet** m.

languouse f. tongue.
ORIGIN: **langue** f.

limouse f. shirt.
ORIGIN: **lime** f.

palpouser v. to earn money.
ORIGIN: **palper** v.

paradouse m. paradise, heaven.
ORIGIN: **paradis** m.

perlouse f. pearl; fart.
ORIGIN: **perle** f.

pétouse f. fart, fear • (lit.): avoir la pétouse; to be scared to death.
ORIGIN: **pet** m.

piquouser v. to shoot up (with drugs).
ORIGIN: **piquer** v.

plaquouser v. to jilt, to drop (responsibilities).
ORIGIN: **plaquer** v.

sacouse m. purse.
ORIGIN: **sac** m.

tantouse f. gay man, "queen."
ORIGIN: **tante** f. • (lit.): aunt.

tartouse adj. ugly.
ORIGIN: **tarte** adj.

-uche

dabuche m. father.
ORIGIN: **dab** m.

dolluche m. dollar.
ORIGIN: **dollar** m.

méduche f. medal.
ORIGIN: **médaille** f.

paluche f. paw.
ORIGIN: **médaille** f.

PRACTICE SLANG SUFFIXES

A. Rewrite the following terms using slang suffixes.

1. télévision:

   _____

2. dur(e):

   _____

3. licher:

   _____

4. poisson:

   _____

5. fade:

   _____

6. folle:

   _____

7. cinéma:

   _____

8. prétentieux:

   _____

9. riche:

   _____

10. glander:

   _____

Elle est laide à pleurer!

(trans.): She's big-time ugly!
(lit.): She's ugly to cry over!

Dialogue in slang

Elle est laide à pleurer!

Christine: J'adore **faire du lèche-vitrines**. D'ailleurs, ce n'est pas comme si j'avais le choix. Je suis **dans la dèche la plus totale**, moi.

Pascale: Oh, **change de disque**! En fait tu es un peu **près de tes sous**. Tu m'as dit **maintes et maintes fois** que tu as un **bas de laine bien garni**, toi!

Christine: Mais ce n'est pas pour tout **fiche en l'air** sur **des fripes**!

Pascale: Tiens! Regarde cette robe. Elle **coûte un malheureux** trois cents **balles**. Et c'est **fait sur mesure**! C'**est donné**, ça! Ça doit être **au prix coûtant** et c'est **le dernier cri**.

Christine: Ce n'est pas logique ça. A mon avis, **la mariée est trop belle**. Je me méfierais de l'étoffe à ce prix-là.

Pascale: Qu'est-ce que tu racontes? C'est en promotion pour attirer la clientèle. On y **jette un coup d'œil**?

Christine: Tu vois? Cette robe n'est pas bien faite. Faut **appeler un chat un chat**, quand-même. Ça vaut cent balles **à tout casser**. Et même, trois cents balles...quel **coup de matraque**! Ce sont de vrais voleurs ici.

Pascale: Mais il me faut tout de même une **nouvelle dégaine**. Je veux être **bien mise** pour une fois dans ma vie. Regarde-moi. Je porte une robe horrible. Elle est affreuse! Elle me rend **laide à pleurer**!

Christine: **Chose curieuse**, quand je te l'ai offerte pour ton anniversaire, tu as **crié merveille** en me disant que c'était la plus belle robe que t'avais jamais vue de toute ta vie!

Translation in English

She's big-time ugly!

Christine: I love **going window-shopping**. Besides, it's not as if I had a choice. I'm **flat broke**.

Pascale: Oh, **get off it**! The fact is you're kind of **tight with your money**. You've told me **time and time again** that you have quite a **nest egg**!

Christine: But it's not **to blow** on **clothes**!

Pascale: Hey! Look at that dress. It **costs a measly** three hundred **francs**. And it's **tailor made**! That's **a real bargain**! It must be **at cost** and it's **the latest style**.

Christine: That doesn't make sense. If you ask me, **something is fishy**. I wouldn't trust the fabric at that price.

Pascale: What are you talking about? It's on sale to attract customers. What do you say we **take a look**?

Christine: You see? This dress isn't well made. Let's **call a spade a spade** for goodness sake. It's worth a hundred francs **at the outside**. Even three hundred francs...**what a rip-off**! They're real thieves here.

Pascale: But I need a new **look**. I want to be **well put together** for once in my life. Look at me. I'm wearing a horrible dress. It makes me look **big time ugly**!

Christine: **Interestingly enough**, when I gave it to you for your birthday, you **raved about it** telling me it was the prettiest dress you'd ever seen in your entire life!

Leçon Cinq

Elle est laide à pleurer!

Christine: J'adore **faire du lèche-vitrines**. D'ailleurs, c'est pas comme si j'avais l'choix. J'suis **dans la dèche la plus totale**, moi.

Pascale: Oh, **change de disque**! En fait t'es un peu **près d'tes sous**. Tu m'as dit **maintes et maintes fois** qu't'as un **bas d'laine bien garni**, toi!

Christine: Mais c'est pas pour tout **fiche en l'air** sur **des fripes**!

Pascale: Tiens! Regarde c'te robe. È **coûte un malheureux** trois cents **balles**. Et c'est **fait sur mesure**! C'**est donné**, ça! Ça doit être **au prix coûtant** et c'est **l'dernier cri**.

Christine: C'est pas logique ça. A mon avis, **la mariée, elle est trop belle**. J'me méfi'rais d'l'étoffe à c'prix-là.

Pascale: Qu'est-c'que tu racontes? C'est en promotion pour attirer la clientèle. On y **jette un coup d'œil**?

Christine: Tu vois? C'te robe, elle est pas bien faite. Faut **appeler un chat un chat**, quand-même. Ça vaut cent balles **à tout casser**. Et même, trois cents balles...quel **coup d'matraque**! Ce sont d'vrais voleurs ici.

Pascale: Mais y m'faut tout d'même une **nouvelle dégaine**. J'veux êt' **bien mise** pour une fois dans ma vie. Regarde-moi. J'porte une robe horrible. Elle est affreuse! È m'rend **laide à pleurer**!

Christine: **Chose curieuse**, quand j't'l'ai offerte pour ton anniversaire, t'as **crié merveille** en m'disant qu'c'était la plus belle robe que t'avais jamais vue d'toute ta vie!

Literal Translation

She's ugly to cry over!

Christine: I love **doing window-licking**. Besides, it's not as if I had the choice. I'm **in the most total poverty**.

Pascale: Oh, **change records**! In fact you're a little **close to your coins**. You've told me **time and time again** that you have quite a garnished **wollen sock**!

Christine: But it's not **to throw in the air** on **wrinkles**!

Pascale: Hey! Look at that dress. It **costs an unfortunate** three hundred **francs**. And it's **made on measurement**! That's **given**! It must be **at costing price** and it's **the latest cry**.

Christine: It's not logical. In my opinion, **the bride is too beautiful**. I wouldn't trust the fabric at that price.

Pascale: What are you talking about? It's on sale to attract customers. What do you say we **throw an eye-stroke**?

Christine: You see? This dress isn't well made. You have to **call a cat a cat**, anyway. It's worth a hundred francs **to break everything**. And even, three hundred francs…**what a hit by a bludgeon**! They're real thieves here.

Pascale: But I need a new look. I want to be **well put** for once in my life. Look at me. I'm wearing a horrible dress. It makes me **ugly enough to cry**.

Christine: **Interesting thing**, when I offered it to you for your birthday, you **screamed marvel** telling me that it was the prettiest dress you'd ever seen in your entire life!

Vocabulary

appeler un chat un chat *exp.* to call a spade a spade • (lit.): to call a cat a cat.

> example: C'est un escroc. J'*appelle un chat un chat.*

> as spoken: <u>C't</u>'un escroc. J'*appelle un chat un chat.*

> translation: He's a crook. I'm *calling a spade a spade.*

> **SNYONYM:** **dire le mot et la chose** *exp.* to call it like it is • (lit.): to say the word and the thing.

balle *f. (extremely popular)* franc.

> example: Est-ce que tu peux me prêter cent *balles*?

> as spoken: Tu peux <u>m'</u>prêter cent *balles*?

> translation: Can you lend me a hundred *francs*?

bas de laine *exp.* savings, money put aside for a rainy day • (lit.): woolen sock (into which money is hidden away).

> example: Elle a un *bas de laine* bien garni.

> as spoken: Elle a un *bas <u>d'</u>laine* bien garni.

> translation: She has a nice *nest egg.*

bien mis(e) (être) *exp.* to be well-dressed • (lit.): to be well put together.

> example: Tu as vu ses vêtements? Elle est toujours *bien mise.*

> as spoken: <u>T'</u>as vu ses vêtements? Elle est toujours *bien mise.*

> translation: Have you seen her clothes? She's always so *well-dressed.*

changer de disque *exp.* to change the subject • (lit.): to change the record.

> example: Oh, *change de disque!* Tu parles toujours du même sujet!
>
> as spoken: [no change]
>
> translation: Oh, *get off it!* You always talk about the same thing!

chose curieuse (étonnante, etc.) *exp.* strangely (surprisingly, etc.) enough • (lit.): strange (interesting, etc.) thing.

> example: *Chose curieuse*, il connaissait mon nom de famille!
>
> as spoken: *Chose curieuse*, y connaissait mon nom d'famille!
>
> translation: *Oddly enough*, he knew my last name!

coup de matraque *exp.* overcharging, rip-off, fleecing • (lit.): a blow or hit by a bludgeon.

> example: Ça coûte mille balles, ça? Quel *coup de matraque!*
>
> as spoken: Ça coûte mille balles, ça? Quel *coup d'matraque!*
>
> translation: That costs a thousand francs? What a *rip-off!*

coûter un malheureux *exp.* to cost a measly • (lit.): to cost an unfortunate.

> example: Ce tricot *coûte un malheureux* cinquante balles.
>
> as spoken: Ce tricot, y *coûte un malheureux* cinquante balles.
>
> translation: This sweater *costs a measly* fifty francs.

crier merveille *exp.* to rave about something • (lit.): to scream marvel.

> example: Quand Suzanne a acheté sa nouvelle bagnole, elle a *crié merveille*. Mais après avoir dépensé plus de quinze mille balles sur des réparations, elle est prête à la pousser dans le précipice.
>
> as spoken: Quand Suzanne a ach'té sa nouvelle bagnole, elle a *crié merveille*. Mais après avoir dépensé plus d'quinze mille balles sur des réparations, elle est prête à la pousser dans l'précipice.

translation: When Susan bought her new car, she *raved about it*. But after having spent more than fifteen thousand francs on repairs, she's ready to drive it off a cliff.

dèche (être dans la) *exp.* to be broke • (lit.): to be in poverty.

example: Ça fait deux mois qu'il est *dans la dèche*.

as spoken: [no change]

translation: It's been two months that he's been *on the skids*.

dégaine *f.* look • (lit.): outfit.

example: Mais je ne t'ai presque pas reconnu! Tu as une nouvelle *dégaine*!

as spoken: Mais <u>j'</u>t'ai presque pas <u>r'</u>connu! <u>T'</u>as une nouvelle *dégaine*!

translation: I almost didn't recognize you! You have a new *look*!

SYNONYM: **look** *m. (borrowed from English)*

dernier cri (être le) *exp.* to be the latest style • (lit.): to be the last cry.

example: Ce style est le *dernier cri* à Paris.

as spoken: Ce style, <u>c'</u>est <u>l'</u>*dernier cri* à Paris.

translation: This style is the *latest fashion* in Paris.

> **NOTE:** The expression "*dernier cri*" may also be used as an adjective:
>
> example: C'est une robe *dernier cri*.
>
> as spoken: <u>C't'</u>une robe *dernier cri*.
>
> translation: It's a dress of the *latest fashion*

donné(e) (être) *exp.* to be a bargain • (lit.): to be given away.

example: Cinquante balles pour ce déjeuner? C'est *donné*, ça!

as spoken: Cinquante balles pour <u>c'</u>déjeuner? C'est *donné*, ça!

translation: Fifty francs for this lunch? That's a *real bargain*!

fiche quelque chose en l'air *exp.* **1.** to throw something away frivolously • **2.** to kill • (lit.): to throw into the air.

　　　　　example (1):　Il a *fichu toute sa fortune en l'air*.

　　　　　as spoken:　[no change]

　　　　　translation:　He *blew* his entire fortune.

　　　　　example (2):　Le voleur a braqué son pistolet sur moi! J'ai failli me faire *fiche en l'air*.

　　　　　as spoken:　Le voleur, il a braqué son pistolet sur moi! J'ai failli m'faire *fiche en l'air*.

　　　　　translation:　The thief aimed his gun at me. I almost got myself *bumped off*.

fripe *f.* clothes, "threads" • (lit.): wrinkles (since fabic tends to wrinkle -- "*friper*" = to wrinkle).

　　　　　example:　Tu ne peux pas être vu avec des *fripes* comme ça à ce restaurant!

　　　　　as spoken:　Tu ~ peux pas ët' vu avec des *fripes* comme ça à c'resto!

　　　　　translation:　You can't be seen with *clothes* like that at this restaurant!

　SYNONYM:　**fringues** *f.pl.* clothing.

jeter un coup d'œil *exp.* to have a look • (lit.): to throw an eye-stroke.

　　　　　example:　Je vais *jeter un coup d'œil* au bébé.

　　　　　as spoken:　J'vais j'ter un coup d'œil au bébé.

　　　　　translation:　I'm going *to take a peek* at the baby.

la mariée est trop belle *exp.* there's a catch to it • (lit.): the bride is too beautiful.

　　　　　example:　Je ne me fie pas à ce qu'il me dit. *La mariée est trop belle*!

　　　　　as spoken:　J'me fie pas à c'qu'y m'dit. *La mariée, elle est trop belle*!

　　　　　translation:　I don't trust what he's telling me. *Something's fishy*.

　SYNONYM:　**ça ne tourne pas rond** *exp.* • (lit.): it doesn't turn round.

laid(e) à pleurer (être) *exp.* to be extremely ugly • to be ugly enough to cause crying.

>   example: Est-ce que tu as vu la chemise que Claude a porté ce
>   soir? Elle était *laide à pleurer.*
>
>   as spoken: T'as vu la ch'mise qu'il a porté c'soir, Claude? Elle était
>   *laide à pleurer.*
>
>   translation: Did you see the shirt that Claude wore tonight? It was
>   *hideously ugly.*

lèche-vitrines (faire du) *exp.* to go window-shopping • (lit.): to do window-licking.

>   example: Ma sœur peut passer des heures en ville à *faire du
>   lèche-vitrine.*
>
>   as spoken: Ma sœur, è peut passer des heures en ville à *faire du
>   lèche-vitrines.*
>
>   translation: My sister can spend hours in the city *window-shopping.*

maintes et maintes fois *exp.* time and time again • (lit.): many and many times.

>   example: Je t'ai demandé *maintes et maintes fois* de sortir les
>   poubelles!
>
>   as spoken: J't'ai d'mandé *maintes et maintes fois* d'sortir les
>   poubelles!
>
>   translation: I've asked you *time and time again* to take out the trash!

plus total(e) (le/la) *exp.* totally, "big time" • (lit.): the most total.

>   example: Après son divorce, Michelle est dans la dépression *la
>   plus totale.*
>
>   as spoken: Après son divorce, Michelle, elle est dans la dépression
>   *la plus totale.*
>
>   translation: After her divorce, Michelle has been in a *big time*
>   depression.
>
>   **SYNONYM:** **le plus complet/la plus complète** *exp.* • (lit.): the
>   most complete.

près de ses sous (être) *exp.* to be miserly • (lit.): to be close to one's coins.

> example: Chaque fois que je sors dîner avec Antoine, c'est moi qui paie. Il est très *près de ses sous,* lui!

> as spoken: Chaque fois qu'je sors dîner avec Antoine, c'est moi qui paie. Il est très *près d'ses sous,* lui!

> translation: Every time I go out to have dinner with Antoine, I'm the one who pays. He's such a *tightwad!*

prix coûtant (au) *exp.* at cost • (lit.): at costing price.

> example: Léon est un bon ami. Il m'a vendu sa voiture *au prix coûtant!*

> as spoken: Léon, c't'un bon ami. Y m'a vendu sa voiture *au prix coûtant!*

> translation: Leon's a great friend. He sold me his car *at cost.*

sur mesure (faire) *exp.* to be custom-made • (lit.): to make on measurement.

> example: Je suis tellement grand que tous mes complets doivent être *faits sur mesure.*

> as spoken: J'suis tellement grand qu'tous mes complets, y doivent êt' *faits sur mesure.*

> translation: I'm so tall that all of my suits have to be *custom-made.*

tout casser (à) *exp.* at the outside.

> example: Six cents balls pour une cravate?! Ça vaut vingt balles *à tout casser.*

> as spoken: [no change]

> translation: Six hundred francs for a tie?! It's worth twenty francs *at the outside.*

Practice the Vocabulary

[Answers to Lesson 5, p. 255]

A. Were the following idioms used correctly or incorrectly?

1. **Quelle jolie robe! T'es bien mise aujourd'hui.**
   ☐ correct usage   ☐ incorrect usage

2. **J'suis dans la dèche. J'ai beaucoup d'argent.**
   ☐ correct usage   ☐ incorrect usage

3. **Robert, il est près d'ses sous. Y m'prête jamais d'argent.**
   ☐ correct usage   ☐ incorrect usage

4. **Change de disque! Continue à m'parler d'lui.**
   ☐ correct usage   ☐ incorrect usage

5. **Quel coup d'matraque! Ça coûte pas cher, ça!**
   ☐ correct usage   ☐ incorrect usage

6. **On y jette un coup d'œil? J'veux y entrer.**
   ☐ correct usage   ☐ incorrect usage

7. **Ça coûte cher! C'est donné, ça!**
   ☐ correct usage   ☐ incorrect usage

8. **Il a un bas d'laine bien garni. Il est très pauvre.**
   ☐ correct usage   ☐ incorrect usage

9. **J'me méfie de c'qu'y m'dit. La mariée est trop belle.**
   ☐ correct usage   ☐ incorrect usage

10. **C'marchand-là, c't'un voleur. Faut appeler un chat un chat.**
    ☐ correct usage   ☐ incorrect usage

B. Choose the definition of the idiom shown in boldface.

1. J'vais aller en ville pour **faire du lèche-vitrines**.
   ☐ a. window-shop
   ☐ b. hang out

2. J'ai ach'té cette voiture **au prix coûtant**.
   ☐ a. second-hand
   ☐ b. at cost

3. Ça vaut cent francs **à tout casser**.
   ☐ a. at the outside
   ☐ b. maybe more

4. Thierry, il est dans la dépression **la plus totale**.
   ☐ a. a total
   ☐ b. at the outside

5. Quelle jolie coupe de ch'veux! J'adore ta nouvelle **dégaine**!
   ☐ a. look
   ☐ b. rip-off

6. J't'ai dit **maintes et maintes fois** d'enl'ver tes chaussures avant d'entrer!
   ☐ a. once
   ☐ b. time and time again

7. **La mariée est trop belle**.
   ☐ a. There's a catch to it
   ☐ b. She's a knock out

8. Ça **coûte un malheureux** cent francs.
   ☐ a. costs an enormous
   ☐ b. costs a measly

9. Mon complet, il était **fait sur mesure**.
   ☐ a. off the rack
   ☐ b. custom made

10. T'aimes ma robe? C'est **l'dernier cri**.
    ☐ a. very inexpensive
    ☐ b. the latest style

C. Underline the appropriate word that best completes the phrase.

1. J'peux pas l'acheter. J'suis dans la (**dèche**, **crèche**, **douche**).

2. Ça n'coûte que cent francs?! La mariée est trop (**grande**, **maigre**, **belle**).

3. Oh, change de (**chaussette**, **disque**, **chaussure**)! Tu parles toujours du même sujet!

4. Cette robe, c'est l'(**premier**, **deuxième**, **dernier**) cri d'Paris.

5. Ça vaut cent francs à tout (**casser**, **parler**, **appeler**).

6. J'adore faire du (**dèche**, **mèche**, **lèche**)-vitrines en ville.

7. Regarde la robe dans la vitrine. Elle est jolie! On y jette un coup d'(**œil**, **oreille**, **ongle**)?

8. Mon argent, il est pas pour fiche en l'(**océan**, **eau**, **air**) sur des vêtements.

9. Ça coûte mille francs? C'est (**pris**, **donné**, **emprunté**), ça!

10. J't'ai dit maintes et (**maintenant**, **maintes**, **main**) fois d'ranger ta chambre!

DICTATION
Test Your Aural Comprehension.

If you are following along with your cassette, you will now hear a paragraph containing many of the idioms from this section. The paragraph will be read at normal conversational speed (which may actually seem fast to you at first). In addition, the words will be pronounced as you would actually hear them in a conversation, including many common reductions.

The first time the paragraph is presented, simply listen in order to get accustomed to the speed and heavy use of reductions. The paragraph will then be read again with a pause after each group of words to give you time to write down what you heard. The third time the paragraph is read, follow along with what you have written.

A CLOSER LOOK:
Fish, Insects, and Animals that Have Infiltrated French Slang

We certainly owe a great deal of thanks to fish, insects, and animals that have graciously allowed themselves to be the subject of many American slang expressions such as: *to pig out, to be dog tired, to have a frog in one's throat, to worm something out of someone, to get one's goat, to smell fishy, to be a real fox, that's a lot of bull, "What are ya? ...Chicken?"*

Undeniably, the French hold their own in creating slang expressions out of anything that crawls, slithers, or flies. The following are several words and expressions that have been inspired by the animal kingdom and are now part of the imaginative world of French slang:

Bear *(Ours)*

ours *m.* manuscript that has been rejected repeatedly by publishers • (lit.): bear.

ours (avoir ses) *exp.* to have one's period • (lit.): to have one's bears.

Bird *(Oiseau)*

à bientôt, mon oiseau! *exp.* see ya later, alligator! • (lit.): see you later, my bird!
NOTE: The expression *mon oiseau,* literally meaning "my bird," is used to signify "my sweetheart" or "darling."

becquant *m.* slang term for "bird" • (lit.): "beaker."
NOTE: This comes from the masculine noun *bec* meaning "beak."

petit oiseau *exp.* child's terms for "penis" • (lit.): little bird.

piaf *m.* slang for "bird" • (lit.): sparrow.

pinçant *m.* slang for "bird" • (lit.): "pincher."

rossignols *m.pl.* old merchandise • (lit.): nightingales.

vilain oiseau (un) *m.* a shady customer • (lit.): a bad bird.

Camel *(Chameau)*

chameau *m.* a nasty person • (lit.): camel.

sobre comme un chameau (être) *exp.* to be stone-sober • (lit.): to be as sober as a camel.

Cat *(Chat)*

autres chats à fouetter (avoir d') *exp.* to have other fish to fry • (lit.): to have other cats to whip.

chat dans la gorge (avoir un) *exp.* to have a "frog" in one's throat • (lit.): to have a cat in the throat.

donner sa langue au chat *exp.* to give up (to a guess) • (lit.): to give one's tongue to the cat.

écriture de chat *exp.* illegible writing, chicken scratch • (lit.): cat's writing.

greffier *m.* slang for "cat" • (lit.): scratcher.
NOTE: This comes from the verb *griffer* meaning "to scratch."

griffard *m.* slang for "cat" • (lit.): scratcher.
NOTE: This comes from the verb *griffer* meaning "to scratch."

grippart *m.* slang for "cat" • (lit.): pouncer.

NOTE: This comes from the verb *gripper* meaning "to pounce."

lapin de gouttière *m.* slang for "cat" • (lit.): (roof-)gutter rabbit.

miron *m.* slang for "cat" • (lit.): looker.
NOTE: This comes from the slang verb *mirer* meaning "to look."

mistigri *m.* slang for "cat."

pas un chat *exp.* not a living soul • (lit.): not a cat.

Chicken/Rooster/Hen
(Poulet/Coq/Poule)

bouche en cul de poule (faire la) *exp.* to purse one's lips • (lit.): to make an expression with one's mouth like the ass of a hen.

coq à l'âne (sauter du) *exp.* to skip from one subject to another • (lit.): to go from chicken to donkey.
VARIATION: **faire des coq-à-l'ânes** *exp.*

mère-poule *f.* over protective mother • (lit.): mother hen.

mollets de coq (des) *m.pl.* thin legs, bird legs • (lit.): (leg-)calves of a rooster.

pique-en-terre *m.* slang for "chicken" • (lit.): earth peckers.

NOTE: This comes from the verb *piquer* meaning "to pick, to peck, to bite."

poule (la) *f.* the police, the cops • (lit.): the hen.

poulet (être du) *exp.* to be a cinch • (lit.): to be chicken.

poulet *m.* police officer, "pig" • (lit.): chicken.

poulette *f.* young girl, a "chick" • (lit.): young hen.

poussin *m.* child language for "darling," "sweetie" • (lit.): chick, spring chicken.

quand les poules auront des dents *exp.* never, when hell freezes over • (lit.): when hens have teeth.

Cow *(Vache)*

cornante *f.* slang for "cow" • (lit.): that which has horns.

plein(e) comme une vache (être) *exp.* to be roaring drunk • (lit.): to be as full as a cow.

pleurer comme une vache *exp.* to cry one's eyes out • (lit.): to cry like a cow.

pleuvoir comme vache qui pisse *exp.* to rain heavily • (lit.): to rain like a pissing cow.

tête de veau *m.* idiot, fool • (lit.): calf's head.

travailler comme un bœuf *exp.* to work like a "horse" • (lit.): to work like an ox.

vache *f. & adj.* **1.** mean, nasty, rotten. *Elle est vache avec lui;* She's really nasty with him. • **2.** despicable person. *Quelle bande de vaches!* What a bunch of rotten people! • **3.** police officer (derogatory) • **4.** *Oh, la vache!;* Wow! • (lit.): Oh, the cow!

vachement *adv.* extremely • (lit.): cow-like.

vacherie *f.* a rotten trick

Crane *(Grue)*

grue *f.* prostitute • (lit.): crane. **NOTE:** This comes from the image of a crane which, like a prostitute, spends much of its time standing in one position.

pied de grue (faire le) *exp.* to wait for a long time, to "cool one's heels" • (lit.): to do the crane foot (meaning "to stand in one place without moving").

Cricket *(Cricri)*

cricri *m.* cricket (due to the "cri-cri" sound it makes).

Dog *(Chien)*

cabot *m.* slang for "dog."

caractère de chien (avoir un) *exp.* to have a nasty disposition • (lit.): to have a dog's disposition.

chien (avoir du) *exp.* to have charm and sex appeal • (lit.): to have dog.

chien avec quelqu'un (être) *exp.* to be mean to someone • (lit.): to be dog(-like) to someone.

chien coiffé *m.* very ugly person, a "real dog." • (lit.): dog with a hairdo.

chien comme tout (être) *exp.* to be as mean as they come • (lit.): to be dog like anything.

chien pour quelqu'un (avoir un) *exp.* to have a crush on someone • (lit.): to have a dog for someone.

chien(ne) (être) *adj.* to be mean • (lit.): to be dog(-like).

chienchien *m.* affectionate term for dog, "doggy."

clébard *m.* slang for "dog."

clebs *m.* (pronounced: *kleps*) slang for "dog."

donner un mal de chien pour faire quelque chose (se) *exp.* to bend over backward to do something • (lit.): to cause oneself the pain of a dog (great pain) to do something.

humeur de chien *f.* very bad mood • (lit.): the mood of a dog.

mal de chien (avoir un) *exp.* to be in great pain • (lit.): to have pain like a dog.

mon chien *exp.* my darling • (lit.): my dog.

ouah-ouah *m.* (pronounced *wawa*) "doggy."

piquer un chien *exp.* to take a "cat" nap • (lit.): to take a dog (nap).

quel chien t'a mordu? *exp.* what's gotten into you? • (lit.): what dog bit you?

temps de chien *exp.* horrible weather • (lit.): dog's weather.

vie de chien *exp.* dog's life, hard life • (lit.): same.

Donkey (Ane)

coq-à-l'ânes (faire des) *exp.* to skip from one subject to another • (lit.): to go from chicken to donkey.

monté comme un âne (être) *exp.* to be hung as a horse • (lit.): to be equipped like a donkey.

oreillard *m.* slang for "donkey" • (lit.): that which has *oreilles* or "ears."

peau d'âne *f.* diploma • (lit.): donkey skin.

plein(e) comme une bourrique (être) *exp.* to be drunk as a "skunk" • (lit.): to be full (drunk) like a donkey.

Duck (Canard)

barbot *m.* slang for "duck" • (lit.): that which likes to paddle.

NOTE: This comes from the verb *barbotter* meaning "to paddle."

barboteux *m.* slang for "duck" • (lit.): that which likes to paddle.

NOTE: This comes from the verb *barbotter* meaning "to paddle."

canard *m.* newspaper.

sirop de canard *m.* water • (lit.): duck syrup.

Elephant (Eléphant)

comme un éléphant dans un magasin de porcelaine (être) *exp.* to be like a bull in a china shop • (lit.): to be like an elephant in a porcelain shop.

mémoire d'éléphant *f.* elephant's memory • (lit.): same.

Fish (Poisson)

finir en queue de poisson *exp.* to fizzle out • (lit.): to end up like a fish's tail.

gros poisson (un) *m.* a big shot • (lit.): a big fish.

pescal(e) *m.* slang for "fish."

poiscaille *m.* slang for "fish."

poisson d'avril *exp.* April fools • (lit.): fish of April.

yeux de merlan frit (faire des) *exp.* to make goo-goo eyes at someone • (lit.): to make fried marlin eyes at someone.

Flea (Puce)

chercher des puces à quelqu'un *exp.* to nitpick • (lit.): to look for fleas in someone.

puce à l'oreille (avoir la) *exp.* to be suspicious • (lit.): to have a flea in the ear.

saut de puce *m.* a quick flight in an airplane, a quick hop • (lit.): a flea jump.

secouer les puces à quelqu'un *exp.* to tell someone off • (lit.): to shake the fleas off someone.

Fly (Mouche)

fine mouche (une) *exp.* a crafty devil • (lit.): a fine fly.

quelle mouche te pique? *exp.* what's bugging you? • (lit.): what fly's biting you?

tuer les mouches à quinze pas *exp.* to have bad breath • (lit.): to kill flies fifteen steps away.

Fox (Renard)

renard (aller au) *exp.* to throw up • (lit.): to go to the fox.

renard *m.* a strike-breaker, a scab • (lit.): fox.

Frog (Grenouille)

grenouille de bénitier (une) *f.* an extremely devout churchwoman • (lit.): a frog of the holy-water basin.

homme-grenouille *m.* scuba diver, frog man • (lit.): man-frog.

sirop de grenouille *m.*
water • (lit.): frog syrup.

Goat (*Chèvre*)

bique *f.* slang for "nanny-goat."

chèvre coiffée *f.* very ugly
person • (lit.): goat with a
hairdo.

chèvre *f.* girl of easy morals •
(lit.): goat.

Goose (*Oie*)

oie (faire l') *exp.* to act silly.

oie blanche *exp.* a naive girl.

Horse (*Cheval*)

à cheval (être) *exp.* to be a
stickler about something •
(lit.): to be on a horse (riding
through the city with a
proclamation).

boudon *slang* for "horse, old
nag."

bourrin *m.* slang for "horse" •
(lit.): donkey.

canard *m.* slang for "horse,
old nag" • (lit.): duck.

canasson *m.* slang for "horse,
old nag."

carcan *m.* slang for "horse, old
nag."

carne *f.* slang for "old horse" •
(lit.): meat (Spanish).

**cela ne se trouve pas sous
le pas d'un cheval** *exp.* it
doesn't grow on trees •
(lit.): it's not found under the
step of a horse.

cocotte *f.* horse • used in *Hue,
cocotte!*; Giddy up!

dada *m.* "horsey" (child's
language).

fièvre de cheval *exp.* raging
fever • (lit.): fever of a horse.

gail *m.* slang for "horse."

**manger avec les chevaux
de bois** *exp.* to go without
food • (lit.): to eat with the
wooden horses.

mémoire de cheval *exp.*
excellent memory, memory
of an "elephant" • (lit.):
memory of a horse.

rosse *f.* **1.** old nag •
2. ill-natured, nasty person.

Kangaroo (*Kangourou*)

voler au kangourou *exp.* to
shoplift (and hide the stolen
goods under one's clothing
like a kangaroo would do in
its pouch) • (lit.): to steal
kangaroo style.

Louse/Lice *(Pou/Poux)*

chercher des poux à quelqu'un *exp.* to look for a fight with someone, to nitpick • (lit.): to look for lice in someone.

orgueilleux comme un pou *exp.* proud as a "peacock" • (lit.): to be proud as a louse.

sale comme un pou *exp.* filthy dirty • (lit.): dirty as a louse.

Monkey *(Singe)*

singe *m.* boss • (lit.): monkey.

singe (faire le) *exp.* to act up • (lit.): to act like a monkey.

Mouse *(Souris)*

c'est la montagne qui accouche d'une souris *exp.* it's a lot of fuss about nothing • (lit.): it's like the mountain giving birth to a mouse.

trottante *f.* slang for "mouse" • (lit.): that which trots around.
NOTE: This comes from the verb *trotter* meaning "to trot."

Oyster *(Huître)*

huître *f.* gob of snot, "loogie" • (lit.): oyster

plein(e) comme une huître (être) *exp.* to be drunk as a "skunk" • (lit.): to be full as an oyster.
NOTE: **plein(e)** *adj.* drunk • (lit.): full.

Pig *(Cochon)*

bacon *m.* slang for "pig" • (lit.): a (piece of) bacon.

bouant *m.* slang for "pig."
NOTE: This comes from the feminine noun *boue* meaning "mud."

cochonner *v.* to botch up • (lit.): to make something look "pig-like."

cochonnerie *f.* smut, dirty trick.

copains comme cochons (être) *exp.* to be great friends • (lit.): to be friends like pigs.

humeur de cochon *exp.* very bad mood • (lit.): the mood of a pig.

saoûl(e) comme un cochon *exp.* drunk as a "skunk" • (lit.): drunk as a pig.

tour de cochon à quelqu'un (jouer) *exp.* to play a dirty trick on someone • (lit.): to play a pig's trick on someone.

travail de cochon *exp.*
botched job, slap dash work;
dirty work • (lit.): the work of
a pig.

yeux porcins (avoir des)
exp. to have small, squinty
eyes • (lit.): to have the eyes
of a pig, to have porcine eyes.

Pigeon *(Pigeon)*

pigeon *m.* sucker •
(lit.): pigeon.

pigeonner *v.* to sucker
(someone) • (lit.): to take
someone for a pigeon.

Rabbit/Hare *(Lapin/Lièvre)*

chaud lapin *m.* a playboy, an
over-sexed man • (lit.): a hot
rabbit.

**courir deux lièvres à la
fois** *exp.* to try to do too
many things at once •
(lit.): to run after two hares
at the same time.

drôle de lapin (être un)
m. to be a strange person •
(lit.): to be a droll rabbit.

fameux lapin (un) *exp.* a
great guy • (lit.): a terrific
rabbit.

jeannot *m.* slang for "rabbit,
bunny."

lapinoche *m.* slang for
"rabbit."

SEE: *Lesson Two: A Closer
Look — Slang Suffixes, p. 86.*

lever un lièvre *exp.* to bring
up a touchy subject • (lit.): to
flush a hare (as in a hunt).

**mémoire de lièvre (avoir
une)** *exp.* to have a memory
like a sieve • (lit.): to have a
memory like a hare.

mère lapine (une) *f.* woman
with many children •
(lit.): mother rabbit.

mon petit lapin *exp.* my
darling • (lit.): my little rabbit.

**poser un lapin à
quelqu'un** *exp.* to stand
someone up • (lit.): to put a
rabbit to someone.

prendre le lièvre au gîte
exp. to catch someone
napping • (lit.): to take the
hare to the resting-place.

trottin *m.* slang for "rabbit."
NOTE: This comes from the
verb *trotter* meaning "to trot
(around)."

Rat *(Rat)*

**ennuyer comme un rat
mort (s')** *exp.* to be bored
to death • (lit.): to be bored
like a dead rat.

**fabriqué(e) comme un rat
(être)** *exp.* to be done for,
to have one's "goose"
cooked • (lit.): to be done
(for) like a rat.

gaspard *m.* slang for "rat."

mon petit rat *exp.* my darling • (lit.): my little rat.

mon petit raton *exp.* my darling • (lit.): my little baby rat.

rat d'église *m.* a devoted churchgoer • (lit.): a church rat.

rat de bibliothèque *exp.* a bookworm • (lit.): a library rat.

vivre comme un rat *exp.* to be miserly • (lit.): to live like a rat.

Sheep *(Mouton)*

bêlant *m.* slang for "sheep." **NOTE:** This comes from the verb *bêler* meaning "to bleat."

chercher le mouton à cinq pattes *exp.* to look for the impossible • (lit.): to look for the sheep with five paws.

revenons à nos moutons *exp.* let's get back to the subject • (lit.): let's get back to our sheep.

Squirrel *(Ecureuil)*

écureuil à roulettes *m.* cyclist • (lit.): squirrel on wheels.

Turkey *(Dindon/Dinde)*

dinde *f.* stupid woman • (lit.): turkey.

dindon de la farce (être le) *exp.* to play the fool, to be duped.

Whale *(Baleine)*

marrer comme une baleine (se) *exp.* to laugh like a "hyena" • (lit.): to laugh like a whale.

Wolf *(Loup)*

jeune loup (un) *m.* an ambitious young professional • (lit.): a young wolf.

mon petit loup/ma petite louve *exp.* my darling • (lit.): my little wolf.

vieux loup de mer (un) *exp.* an old sea-dog, an old salt • (lit.): an old wolf of the sea.

Worm *(Ver)*

nu(e) comme un ver (être) *exp.* to be naked as a "jaybird" • (lit.): to be naked as a worm.

tirer les vers du nez à quelqu'un *exp.* to worm something out of someone • (lit.): to pull worms from someone's nose.

PRACTICE USING FISH, INSECTS, AND ANIMALS IN IDIOMATIC EXPRESSIONS

A. Match the English with the French translations by writing the appropriate letter in the box.

☐ 1. It's raining cats and dogs.

☐ 2. She's always nasty.

☐ 3. I'm in such pain.

☐ 4. What a lousy disposition!

☐ 5. What horrible weather!

☐ 6. He's drunk as a skunk.

☐ 7. He's a crafty devil.

☐ 8. The project fizzled out.

☐ 9. He's cold sober.

☐ 10. I have a frog in my throat.

☐ 11. You keep jumping from one subject to the next!

☐ 12. Never!

☐ 13. He has terrible breath.

☐ 14. I've been waiting here for an hour!

A. **Il est plein comme une bourrique.**

B. **Le projet, il a fini en queue d'poisson.**

C. **Y pleut comme vache qui pisse.**

D. **Quel temps d'chien!**

E. **Elle est toujours vache.**

F. **C't'une fine mouche, lui.**

G. **J'ai un mal d'chien.**

H. **Quel caractère d'chien!**

I. **Il est sobre comme un chameau.**

J. **Tu continues à sauter du coq à l'âne!**

K. **J'ai un chat dans la gorge.**

L. **Quand les poules auront des dents!**

M. **Ça fait une heure que j'fais l'pied d'grue!**

N. **Y tue les mouches à quinze pas!**

B. Underline the appropriate word that best completes the sentence.

1. J'suis fatigué. J'vais piquer un (**éléphant**, **chien**, **poisson**).

2. Quelle mauvaise haleine! Y tue les (**mouches**, **cochons**, **lapins**) à quinze pas!

3. Quel travail d'(**souris**, **renard**, **cochon**)!

4. È l'a volé au (**cheval**, **kangourou**, **mouton**).

5. Elle a perdu du poids pasqu'è mange avec les (**pigeons**, **poux**, **chevaux**) d'bois.

6. J'suis malade, moi. J'ai une fièvre de (**cheval**, **cochon**, **lapin**).

7. Je m'suis marré comme une (**baleine**, **vache**, **mouche**).

8. Il a essayé d'me tirer les (**baleines**, **rats**, **vers**) du nez.

9. Rev'nons à nos (**moutons**, **rats**, **vers**).

10. Ça fait deux heures bien tassées qu'j'attends. J'crois qu'è m'a posé un (**oiseau**, **poisson**, **lapin**).

11. J'suis fabriqué comme un (**kangourou**, **mouton**, **rat**), moi.

12. Mais, pourquoi t'as d'mandé ça? Tu vois pas qu't'as levé un (**lièvre**, **cheval**, **lapin**)?

REVIEW EXAM FOR LESSONS 1-5

(Answers to Review, p. 256)

A. Underline the appropriate word(s).

1. Claire, elle est tombée au beau (**tabac**, **milieu**, **bide**) du supermarché.

2. Mais qu'est-c'que tu m'racontes?! Tu colportes des (**amuse-gueules**, **vieilles branches**, **cancans**), toi!

3. Demain, j'dois faire une présentation d'vant trois cent personnes! J'ai les (**boules**, **bides**, **ballons**), moi!

4. J'ai très faim. J'vais m'caler (**la sellette**, **l'œil au beurre noir**, **le bide**).

5. J'suis certain qu'tu vas recevoir ta promotion. (**C'est pas d'refus**, **C'est dans l'sac**, **C'est pas la mer à boire**).

6. Quelle soirée super! On s'en est payé une (**bêcheuse**, **vacherie**, **tranche**)!

7. Tu peux pas conduire! T'es (**rond comme une bille**, **dans la dèche**, **près d'tes sous**)!

8. Comment tu trouves ma nouvelle robe? C'est l'(**premier**, **second**, **dernier**) cri d'Paris.

9. Georges, y s'est (**frappé l'biscuit**, **pointé**, **rincé l'sifflet**) à 20h. Il est toujours en r'tard, c'ui-là!

10. Tu veux faire du lèche-(**fripes**, **vitrines**, **vacheries**) en ville?

B. Complete the following phrases by choosing the appropriate word(s) from the list below. Give the correct form of the verb.

biscuit	**disque**	**pleurer**
branche	**maintes**	**pommes**
bras	**matraque**	**rien**
casque	**œil**	**vingt**

1. Marcel, y veut dev'nir manequin? Mais il est laid à _____ !

2. Regarde la jolie ch'mise dans la vitrine! On y jette un coup d'_____?

3. J't'ai dit maintes et _____ fois d'fermer la porte derrière toi!

4. J'pourrai réparer ta voiture en un _____ de temps.

5. Mais pourquoi tu t'frappes le _____? Ton fiancé, il arriv'ra bientôt.

6. Salut ma vieille _____! Ça va?

7. Quand j'bois du vin, j'en ai vite dans l'_____.

8. Ça coûte trop cher! Quel coup d' _____!

9. Oh, change de _____. Tu t'plains toujours d'la même chose!

10. Nancy, elle est très grande, tandis que son frère, il est haut comme trois _____.

11. J'peux pas l'croire! Les _____ m'en tombent!

12. Tu sais pas c'qui s'est passé hier soir? Ça a fait les infos d'_____ heures!

C. CROSSWORD PUZZLE
Fill in the crossword puzzle on page 121 by choosing from the list below.

BAISSE	COTES	MATRAQUE	POIL
BEURRE	DECHE	MORCEAU	POT
BIDE	DENTELLE	MORDRE	ROSES
BISCUIT	DOIGTS	NAGE	SAC
BISE	EPONGE	NOISE	SALADES
BOIRE	FROID	PARTIE	TABAC
CAFARD	GUEULES	PEAU	TROMBE
CHEMISE	LAINE	PLEIN	VINGT

ACROSS

13. **battre _____ à** *exp.* to be cool toward.

21. **dans le _____ (être)** *exp.* to be a sure thing, to be in the bag.

25. **abandonner la _____** *exp.* to call it a day.

31. **caler le _____ (se)** *exp.* to eat.

35. **arriver en _____** *exp.* to storm in.

44. **passer quelqu'un à _____** *exp.* to beat someone up, to give someone a thrashing.

48. **envoyer sur les _____(se faire)** *exp.* • **1.** to get oneself fired • **2.** to get reprimanded.

53. **_____ (être en)** *exp.* to be going downhill.

57. **coup de _____** *exp.* overcharging, rip-off, fleecing.

64. **amuse-_____** *m.pl.* appetizers.

67. **bouger d'un _____(ne pas)** *exp.* not to budge an inch.

69. **passer l'_____ là-dessus** *exp.* to reconcile, to let bygones be bygones.

76. **battre son** _____ *exp.* to be in full swing.

80. **boire un** _____ *exp.* to have a drink.

85. **déballer ses** _____ *exp.* to reel off one's problems.

DOWN

4. **chercher** _____ **à quelqu'un** *exp.* to look for a fight.

11. **ce n'est pas la mer à** _____ *exp.* it's not such a big deal.

16. **assiette au** _____ *exp.* cush job.

19. _____ **les doigts (s'en)** *exp.* to regret something.

22. _____ **(avoir le)** *exp.* to be depressed.

30. **faire les infos de** _____ **heures** *exp.* everyone is talking about it.

33. **faire dans la** _____ *exp.* to put on kid gloves.

36. **frapper le** _____ **(se)** *exp.* to get oneself all worked up.

40. **cracher le** _____ *exp.* to fess up.

45. _____ **(faire la)** *f.* to kiss.

47. **entendre comme cul et** _____ **(s')** *exp.* to get along extremely well (with someone).

55. _____ **(être en)** *exp.* to be soaking wet from perspiraton.

60. _____ **(être dans la)** *exp.* to be broke.

65. **bas de** _____ *exp.* savings, money put aside for a rainy day.

66. **deux** _____ **(être à)** *exp.* on the brink.

67. _____ **neuve (faire)** *exp.* to turn over a new leaf.

75. **à-**_____ *exp.* perks.

CROSSWORD PUZZLE

D. Match the English with the French.

☐ 1. At the very beginning of our vacation, it started to rain.

☐ 2. She flew off the handle when she saw what happened to her new car.

☐ 3. I'll like you to meet my husband.

☐ 4. The party's is full swing.

☐ 5. Don't move a muscle.

☐ 6. Let's forget our quarrel and let bygones be bygones.

☐ 7. I'm crazy about him!

☐ 8. He pulled a dirty trick on me.

☐ 9. I can't stand her.

☐ 10. I'm in tip-top shape today.

☐ 11. You look depressed.

☐ 12. My new job has some great perks.

A. Elle est **sortie d'ses gonds** quand elle a vu c'qui est arrivé à sa nouvelle voiture.

B. J'te présente mon **tendre et cher**.

C. La soirée, è **bat son plein**.

D. **Bouge pas d'un poil**.

E. Oublions not'querelle et **passons l'éponge là-d'ssus**.

F. J'**en pince pour lui**!

G. Y m'a **fait une vach'rie**.

H. J'**peux pas la voir en peinture**.

I. J'**pète la forme** aujourd'hui.

J. On dirait que t'**as l'cafard**.

K. Mon nouveau boulot, il a de très bons **à-côtés**.

L. **Au tout début** de nos vacances, il a commencé à pleuvoir.

LECON SIX

On n'apprend pas à un vieux singe à faire la grimace

(trans.): You can't teach an old dog new tricks
(lit.): You can't teach an old monkey to smile

Leçon Six

On n'apprend pas à un vieux singe à faire la grimace

Cécile: Je te le dis mais **motus et bouche cousue**. Marc a été **laissé en carafe** pendant sa lune de miel à cause d'un autre gars!

Josette: Ah, l'angoisse, **dis**! Sophie a toujours aimé **fréquenter les lits**. Bon ben, ce n'est pas **demain la veille** qu'elle changera. **On n'apprend pas à un vieux singe à faire la grimace**!

Cécile: **Un de ces quatre**, elle va **se taper un réveil pénible**! C'est vraiment dommage...tout le monde pensait qu'elle **avait l'étoffe** d'une bonne épouse et d'une bonne mère.

Josette: C'est bizarre de penser que j'étais là au moment où Marc a **fait sa déclaration**. Alors dis-moi, quand **ça lui est tombé sur le nez**, il a dû être **pris au dépourvu**, non?

Cécile: **C'est le moins qu'on puisse dire!** Remarque, maintenant, je vais **t'en boucher un coin**. Après le **tissu de mensonges** qu'elle lui a **fait avaler**, elle a promis qu'elle **ferait peau neuve** s'il la laissait **rentrer au bercail**. Mais il lui a dit: «**Rien à faire! Comme on fait son lit, on se couche.**» Maintenant c'est lui qui **a le dessus** et elle se retrouve à la rue.

Josette: C'est **bien fait pour sa gueule**! Marc **n'est pas aussi bête qu'il en a l'air**. Elle pensait qu'elle pourrait lui **jeter de la poudre aux yeux** mais **rien ne lui échappe**.

Cécile: Ma devise en amour, ce n'est pas «**plus on est de fous, plus on rit**!»

Josette: Ben, non! C'est plutôt, « **à deux on se distrait, à trois on s'ennuie**!»

Leçon Six

Translation in English

You can't teach an old dog new tricks

Cécile: I have to tell you something but **it's just between you and me**. Marc was **dumped** during his honeymoon because of another guy!

Josette: How nerve-racking, **wow**! Sophie always did like **to sleep around**. Well, she's **not about to change any time soon. You can't teach an old dog new tricks**.

Cécile: **One of these days**, she's going to **have a rude awakening**! It's really a shame…everyone thought she **had the makings** of a good wife and a good mother.

Josette: It's strange to think that I was there at the moment Marc **popped the question**. So tell me, when he **found out**, he must have been **caught off guard**, huh?

Cécile: **That's putting it mildly**! **Listen**, now I'm really **gonna freak you out**. After the **pack of lies** she **made him buy**, she promised she'd **turn over a new leaf** if he let her **come back home**. But he told her, "**No way! You've made your bed, so now you can just lie in it**." Now he's the one **with the upper hand** and she's back on the street.

Josette: It **serves her right**! Marc **isn't as dumb as he looks**. She thought she could **pull one over on him** but **nothing gets by him**.

Cécile: When it comes to love, my motto is not, "**The more the merrier**!"

Josette: No way! It's more like, "**Two's company, three's a crowd**!"

Dialogue in slang as it would be spoken

On apprend pas à un vieux singe à faire la grimace

Cécile: J'te l'dis mais **motus et bouche cousue**. Marc, il a été **laissé en carafe** pendant sa lune de miel à cause d'un aut' gars!

Josette: Ah, l'angoisse, **dis**! Sophie, elle a toujours aimé **fréquenter les lits**. Bon ben, c'est pas **d'main la veille** qu'è chang'ra. **On apprend pas à un vieux singe à faire la grimace**!

Cécile: **Un d'ces quat'**, è va **s'taper un réveil pénible**! C'est vraiment dommage...tout l'monde pensait qu'elle **avait l'étoffe** d'une bonne épouse et d'une bonne mère.

Josette: C'est bizarre d'penser qu'j'étais là au moment où Marc, il a **fait sa déclaration**. Alors dis-moi, quand **ça lui est tombé sur le nez**, il a dû êt' **pris au dépourvu**, non?

Cécile: **C'est l'moins qu'on puisse dire!** Remarque, maintenant, j'vais **t'en boucher un coin**. Après l'**tissu d'mensonges** qu'è lui a **fait avaler**, elle a promis qu'è **f'rait peau neuve** s'y la laissait **rentrer au bercail**. Mais y lui a dit: «**Rien à faire! Comme on fait son lit, on se couche.**» Maintenant c'est lui qui **a l'dessus** et è s'retrouve à la rue.

Josette: C'est **bien fait pour sa gueule**! Marc, il **est pas aussi bête qu'il en a l'air**. È pensait qu'è pourrait lui **sh'ter d'la poudr'aux yeux** mais **rien lui échappe**.

Cécile: Ma devise en amour, c'est pas «**plus on est d'fous, plus on rit**!»

Josette: Ben, non! C'est plutôt, «**à deux on s'distrait, à trois on s'ennuie!**»

Literal Translation

On doesn't teach an old monkey to make faces

Cécile: I have to tell you something but **sewn up mouth**. Marc was **left (standing) in a carafe** during his honeymoon because of another guy!

Josette: Oh, the anguish, **say**! Sophie always did like **to visit beds**. Well, it's not **tomorrow the eve that she will change**. **You can't teach an old monkey to smile**.

Cécile: **One of these four (days)**, she's going **to hit back a painful awakening**! It's really a shame...everyone thought she **had the fabric** of a good wife and a good mother.

Josette: It's strange to think that I was there at the moment Marc **made his declaration (of love)**. So tell me, when **it fell on his nose**, he must have been **caught without resources**, no?

Cécile: **It's the least one can say**! **Notice**, now I'm really going **to plug up a corner of it for you**. After the **web of lies** she **made him swallow**, she promised she'd **make new skin** if he let her **come back to the crib**. But he told her, "**Nothing doing! As one makes one's bed, one lies down**." Now he's the one **with the top** and she's back on the street.

Josette: It's **well done for her mouth**! Marc **isn't as dumb as he looks it**. She thought she could **throw powder into his eyes** but **nothing escapes him**.

Cécile: When it comes to love, my motto is not, "**The more goofy people there are, the more we'll laugh**!"

Josette: No way! It's more like, "**With two it's fun, with three it's bothersome**!"

Vocabulary

à deux on se distrait, à trois on s'ennuie *exp.* two's company, three's a crowd • (lit.): with two it's fun, with three it's bothersome.

>   example: Comment veux-tu l'inviter à nous rejoindre? *A deux on se distrait, à trois on s'ennuie!*
>
>   as spoken: Comment tu veux l'inviter à nous r'joindre? *A deux on s'distrait, à trois on s'ennuie!*
>
>   translation: What do you mean you want to invite her? *Two's company, three's a crowd!*
>
>   **NOTE:**   In colloquial French, the inversion form (such as veux-tu) is not used. SEE: *Street French 1 — A Closer Look, Inversion and est-ce que forms, p. 37.*

aussi bête qu'on en a l'air (ne pas être) *exp.* not to be as dumb as one looks • (lit.): not to be as dumb as one looks it.

>   example: Je sais que tu crois qu'il n'a rien compris. Mais il *n'est pas aussi bête qu'il en a l'air.*
>
>   as spoken: Je sais qu'tu crois qu'il ~ a rien compris. Mais il *est pas aussi bête qu'il en a l'air.*
>
>   translation: I know you think he didn't understand anything. But he's *not as dumb as he looks.*

avaler quelque chose *v.* to accept something as truth • (lit.): to swallow something.

>   example: J'espère que tu n'as pas *avalé* toutes les excuses que Madeleine t'a donné!
>
>   as spoken: J'espère que t'as pas *avalé* toutes les excuses qu'è t'a donné, Madeleine!
>
>   translation: I hope you didn't *swallow* all the excuses Madeleine gave you!

bien fait pour sa gueule (être) *exp.* to serve someone right • (lit.): to be well done for one's face/mouth.

> example: Elle a échoué à l'examen? Bon. C'est *bien fait pour sa gueule.* Elle est toujours à tricher!

> as spoken: [no change]

> translation: She failed the test? Good. It *serves her right.* She's always cheating.

> **NOTE:** The feminine noun *"gueule,"* literally meaning the "mouth of animal," is commonly used in French slang to signify either "face" or "head" depending on the context.

boucher un coin (en) *exp.* to surprise, to flabbergast • (lit.): to stop up a corner of it (with a cork).

> example: Tu *m'en bouches un coin* avec tes notes extraordinaires! J'ai toujours pensé que tu étais un peu lent!

> as spoken: Tu *m'en bouches un coin* avec tes notes extr'ordinaires! J'ai toujours pensé qu't'étais un peu lent!

> translation: You *really surprise me* with your incredible grades! I always thought you were a little slow!

c'est le moins qu'on puisse dire *exp.* that's putting it mildly • (lit.): that's the least one can say.

> example: Tu crois qu'il est bizarre? *C'est le moins qu'on puisse dire!*

> as spoken: Tu crois qu'il est bizarre? *C'est l'moins qu'on puisse dire!*

> translation: You think he's strange? *That's putting it mildly!*

comme on fait son lit, on se couche *exp.* you've made your
bed, now lie in it • (lit.): since one makes one's bed, on lies down (in it).

> example: Tu es toujours à mentir et maintenant ton problème est
> que personne ne te croit. *Comme on fait son lit, on se
> couche.*

> as spoken: T'es toujours à mentir et maintenant ton problème, c'est
> que personne ~ te croit. *Comme on fait son lit, on se couche.*

> translation: You're always lying and now your problem is that no
> one believes you. *You made your bed, now lie in it.*

> **NOTE:** In the previous "as spoken" section, the phrase *"on se
> couche"* was not reduced to *"on s'couche"* since proverbs
> generally respect proper rules of pronunciation.

déclaration (faire sa) *exp.* to pop the question • (lit.): to make one's
declaration (of love).

> example: Maman! Jean vient de me *faire sa déclaration*! Admire
> la superbe bague!

> as spoken: Maman! Jean, y vient d'me *faire sa déclaration*! Admire
> la suberbe bagouse!

> translation: Mom! John just *popped the question*! Take a look at the
> incredible rock!

> **NOTE:** In French, an "engagement ring" is called *"une bague de
> fiançailles"* whereas a "wedding ring" is referred to as
> *"un anneau de marriage."*

demain la veille (ne pas être) *exp.* said of something that is not
likely to happen in the near future • (lit.): tomorrow is the eve (of something
happening).

> example: *Ce n'est pas demain la veille* qu'il changera son attitude.

> as spoken: *C'est pas d'main la veille* qu'y chang'ra son attitude.

> translation: *It's not likely to happen soon* that he's going to change
> his attitude.

dessus (avoir le) *exp.* to have the upper hand • (lit.): to have the top.

> example: Il a joué sa dernière carte. Maintenant, c'est moi qui *ai le dessus.*

> as spoken: Il a joué sa dernière carte. Maintenant, c'est moi qui *ai l'dessus.*

> translation: He played his last card. Now I'm the one with *the upper hand.*

dis *exclam.* (used at the end of a sentence) wow • (lit.): say.

> example: Je n'ai jamais rien vu de si beau, *dis!*

> as spoken: J'ai jamais rien vu d'si beau, *dis!*

> translation: I've never seen anything so beautiful, *wow!*

> **NOTE:** The exclamation *"dis"* is used when speaking in the informal, whereas *"dites"* would be applied in the formal.

étoffe (avoir l') *exp.* to have the makings (of something) • (lit.): to have the fabric.

> example: Elle *a l'étoffe* d'un bon médecin.

> as spoken: Elle *a l'étoffe* d'un bon méd'cin.

> translation: She *has the makings* of a fine doctor.

fréquenter les lits *exp.* to sleep around • (lit.): to frequent beds.

> example: Je n'aime pas les mecs qui *fréquentent les lits.*

> as spoken: J'aime pas les mecs qui *fréquentent les lits.*

> translation: I don't like guys who *sleep around.*

> **NOTE:** **mec** *m.* (extremely popular) guy, dude.

jeter de la poudre aux yeux à quelqu'un *exp.* to pull the wool over someone's eyes • (lit.): to throw powder in someone's eyes.

> example: C'est la dernière fois qu'il *me jète de la poudre aux yeux!*

> as spoken: C'est la dernière fois qu'y *m'jète d'la poudr'aux yeux!*

> translation: That's the last time he's gonna *pull the wool over on me!*

laissé(e) en carafe (être) *exp.* to jilt someone • (lit.): to leave someone like a carafe (after it's been all used up).

>   example: C'est vrai ce qu'on m'a raconté? Il l'a *laissée en carafe?*

>   as spoken: C'est vrai <u>c'</u>qu'on m'a raconté? <u>Y</u> l'a *laissée en carafe?*

>   translation: Is is true what I heard? He *dumped* her?

motus et bouche cousue *exp.* don't say a word to anyone • (lit.): ("*motus*" has no literal translation) and sewn up mouth.

>   example: C'est un secret. *Motus et bouche cousue!*

>   as spoken: <u>C't'</u>un secret. *Motus et bouche cousue!*

>   translation: It's a secret. *Mum's the word!*

on n'apprend pas à un vieux singe à faire la grimace
exp. you can't teach an old dog new tricks • (lit.): you can't teach an old male monkey to make faces.

>   example: A mon âge, tu veux m'apprendre à conduire? *On n'apprend pas à un vieux singe à faire la grimace.*

>   as spoken: A mon âge, tu veux m'apprendre à conduire? *On ~ apprend pas à un vieux singe à faire la grimace.*

>   translation: At my age, you want to teach me to drive? *You can't teach an old dog new tricks.*

peau neuve (faire) *exp.* to turn over a new leaf • (lit.): to have new skin.

>   example: Après le premier de l'an, je vais *faire peau neuve.*

>   as spoken: Après <u>l'</u>premier <u>d'</u>l'an, <u>j'</u>vais *faire peau neuve.*

>   translation: After the first of the year, I'm *turning over a new leaf.*

plus on est de fous, plus on rit *exp.* the more the merrier • (lit.): the more goofy people there are, the more we'll laugh.

>   example: Venez nous rejoindre! *Plus on est de fous, plus on rit!*

>   as spoken: <u>V'</u>nez nous rejoindre! *Plus on est <u>d'</u>fous, plus on rit!*

>   translation: Come join us! *The more the merrier!*

pris(e) au dépourvu (être) *exp.* to be taken off guard • (lit.): to be taken short (as in destitute).

    example: Quand il a donné sa démission, j'ai été *pris au dépourvu*.

    as spoken: [no change]

    translation: When he gave his resignation, I was *taken off guard*.

remarquer *v.* to take notice, to consider something.

    example: *Remarque.* Les gens dépassent la limite de vitesse tout le temps sans attraper de contraventions.

    as spoken: *Remarque.* Les gens, <u>y</u> dépassent la limite de vitesse tout <u>l'</u>temps sans attraper de contraventions.

    translation: *Think about it.* People break the speed limit all the time without getting a ticket for it.

rentrer au bercail *exp.* to return to the sanctity of one's own home • (lit.): to return to the crib.

    example: Après trois semaines de vacances, je suis prêt à *rentrer au bercail*.

    as spoken: Après trois <u>s'</u>maines de vacances, <u>j'</u>suis prêt à *rentrer au bercail*.

    translation: After three weeks of vacation, I'm ready to *get back home*.

réveil pénible *exp.* rude awakening • (lit.): painful awakening.

    example: Un de ces jours, il va avoir un *réveil pénible*.

    as spoken: Un <u>d'</u>ces jours, <u>y</u> va avoir un *réveil pénible*.

    translation: One of these days, he's going to have a *rude awakening*.

rien à faire *exp.* no way • (lit.): nothing doing.

    example: Tu veux que je te prête de l'argent? *Rien à faire!* Tu me dois toujours cent balles!

    as spoken: Tu veux que <u>j'</u>te prête <u>d'</u>l'argent? *Rien à faire!* Tu <u>m'</u>dois toujours cent balles!

    translation: You want me to lend you some money? *No way!* You still owe me one hundred francs!

rien ne lui échappe *exp.* • (lit.): nothing escapes him/her.

    example: Le professeur sait que tu as triché à l'examen. *Rien ne lui échappe.*

    as spoken: Le <u>prof</u>, <u>y</u> sait q<u>u't'</u>as triché à l'<u>exam</u>. *Rien ~ lui échappe.*

    translation: The teacher knows you cheated on the test. *Nothing gets by him.*

taper (se) *v.* to have • (lit.): to hit back.

    example: Je *me suis tapé* un bon dîner hier soir.

    as spoken: Je <u>m'</u>suis *tapé* un bon dîner hier soir.

    translation: I *had* a good dinner last night.

tissu de mensonges *exp.* pack of lies • (lit.): cloth of lies.

    example: Quand je lui ai demandé des détails sur sa famille, elle m'a raconté un *tissu de mensonges.*

    as spoken: Quand <u>j'</u>ui ai <u>d'</u>mandé des détails sur sa famille, <u>è</u> m'a raconté un *tissu <u>d'</u>mensonges.*

    translation: When I asked her details about her family, she handed me a *pack of lies.*

tomber sur le nez de quelqu'un *exp.* to come suddenly to someone (said of good/bad news) • (lit.): to fall on the nose of someone.

    example: Quand les nouvelles de sa banqueroute *me sont tombées sur le nez,* j'en étais stupéfait!

    as spoken: [no change]

    translation: When the news of his bankruptcy *came to me,* I was shocked!

un de ces quatre *exp.* one of these days • (lit.): one of these four.

    example: *Un de ces quatre,* je vais m'installer à Tahiti.

    as spoken: *Un <u>d'</u>ces quat',* <u>j'</u>vais m'installer à Tahiti.

    translation: *One of these days,* I'm going to move to Tahiti.

    NOTE: This is a shortened version of the expression *un de ces quatre matins* (pronounced: *un d'ces quat' matins*) meaning "one of these four mornings."

Practice The Vocabulary

(Answers to Lesson 6, p. 257)

A. Choose the correct definition of the idioms in boldface.

1. **Sous l'sceau du secret**, Antoine, y va d'mander à Marie d'l'épouser!
   ☐ a. This may sound unbelievable but...
   ☐ b. This may surprise you but...
   ☐ c. Just between you and me...

2. **Plus on est d'fous, plus on rit**.
   ☐ a. Two's company, three's a crowd
   ☐ b. The more the merrier
   ☐ c. Birds of a feather flock together

3. **Un d'ces quatre**, è va regretter c'qu'elle a fait.
   ☐ a. One of these days
   ☐ b. Once in a blue moon
   ☐ c. In four days

4. Il a toujours été prétentieux, mais il a dit qu'y va **faire peau neuve**.
   ☐ a. to continue his behavoir
   ☐ b. to get even worse
   ☐ c. to turn over a new leaf

5. **C'est bien fait pour sa gueule**!
   ☐ a. It serves him/her right
   ☐ b. He/she has a big mouth
   ☐ c. He/she is mouthing off again

6. È va avoir un **réveil pénible**.
   ☐ a. monster headache
   ☐ b. rude awakening
   ☐ c. nightmare

7. È pensait qu'è pourrait lui **j'ter d'la pourdr'aux yeux**.
   ☐ a. pull the wool over his eyes
   ☐ b. dump him
   ☐ c. turn over a new leaf.

8. **Comme on fait son lit, on se couche**.
   ☐ a. Early to bed, early to rise
   ☐ b. Don't let the bed bugs bite
   ☐ c. You've made your bed, now lie in it

9. Sophie, elle a toujours aimé **fréquenter les lits**.
   ☐ a. to make beds
   ☐ b. to bed hop
   ☐ c. collect beds

10. **On apprend pas à un vieux singe à faire la grimace**.
    ☐ a. You can't teach an old dog new tricks
    ☐ b. The more the merrier
    ☐ c. Two's company, three's a crowd

B. Underline the appropriate words that best complete the phrase.

1. Paule, elle a déménagé? C'est difficile à croire, (**lis**, **ris**, **dis**)!

2. Tu veux que j'te prête cent balles?! Rien à (**coucher**, **faire**, **rire**)!
   Tu m'dois toujours cent balles d'la s'maine dernière!

3. Après mes longues vacances, j'ai hâte de (**faire peau neuve**,
   rentrer au bercail, **faire ma déclaration**).

4. C't'un secret! Motus et (**bouche**, **tête**, **jambe**) cousue!

5. Plus on est d'fous, plus on (**pleure**, **parle**, **rit**).

6. Il est pas aussi bête qu'il en a l'(**air**, **eau**, **oxygène**).

7. Marc, il a été laissé en (**verre**, **cruche**, **carafe**) pendant sa lune
   de miel à cause d'un aut' gars!

8. J'ai soif. J'vais (**m'taper**, **m'frapper**, **m'cogner**) une boisson froide.

9. Tu crois vraiment qu'y pourrait faire (**main**, **peau**, **jambe**) neuve?

10. Jacques, il a (**l'étoffe**, **la langue**, **la bouche**) d'un bon père.

11. A deux on s'distrait, à (**trois**, **quatre**, **cinq**), on s'ennuie.

12. Quel (**papier**, **coton**, **tissu**) d'mensonges!

C. Match the columns.

☐ 1. Il est bizarre, lui! C'est l'moins qu'on puisse _____ !

A. **dépourvu**

☐ 2. Marc, il a fait sa _____ à Josette! Il vont s'marier dans un mois.

B. **déclaration**

☐ 3. Tu vas pas croire c'que j'vais te dire. J'vais t'en boucher un _____ .

C. **coin**

☐ 4. Elle est très intelligente. Rien lui _____ .

D. **échappe**

☐ 5. Quand il a appris la nouvelle, il a dû êt' pris au _____ .

E. **tissu**

☐ 6. C'est pas d'main la _____ qu'è chang'ra. Elle a toujours été méchante et è rest'ra méchante!

F. **étoffe**

☐ 7. On peut pas croire c'qu'y dit. Y raconte toujours un _____ d'mensonges.

G. **dire**

☐ 8. È veut rentrer, mais Marc, y va pas l'permettre. Maintenant c'est lui qui a l'_____ .

H. **veille**

☐ 9. Elle a l'_____ d'une bonne prof.

I. **motus**

☐ 10. J'ai quèque chose à te dire, mais _____ et bouche cousue!

J. **dessus**

DICTATION
Test Your Aural Comprehension.

If you are following along with your cassette, you will now hear a paragraph containing many of the idioms from this section. The paragraph will be read at normal conversational speed (which may actually seem fast to you at first). In addition, the words will be pronounced as you would actually hear them in a conversation, including many common reductions.

The first time the paragraph is presented, simply listen in order to get accustomed to the speed and heavy use of reductions. The paragraph will then be read again with a pause after each group of words to give you time to write down what you heard. The third time the paragraph is read, follow along with what you have written.

A CLOSER LOOK:
Expressions that Contain
Proper Names

In the previous chapter, we saw how animals have crept their way into French slang providing us with an unlimited supply of colorful expressions. But wait! People are animals, too! Have we humans been unfairly neglected? There is only one answer to that question, "No way, José!"

In American slang, we have certainly heard proper names crop up in expressions like: *for Pete's sake, good-time Charlie, plain Jane, Joe Blow, jack-of-all-trades, to go to the john, etc*. The French certainly keep pace when it comes to creating expressions of this sort. Proper names have given birth to many other imaginative expressions in French as demonstrated by the following list.

"Nom"

ça n'a pas de nom! *exp.* that's incredible! • (lit.): it has no name!

nom d'un chien! *exp.* holy cow! • (lit.): name of a dog!

nom d'un nom! *exp.* holy cow! • (lit.): name of a name!

nom de deux! *exp.* my gosh! • (lit.): name of two!
NOTE: This is a euphemism for *"nom de Dieu!"*

nom de Dieu! *exp.* my God! • (lit.): name of God!

nom de nom! *exp.* holy cow! • (lit.): name of name!

Adam

je ne le connais ni d'Eve ni d'Adam *exp.* I don't know him from Adam • (lit.): I don't know him from Eve nor Adam.

manger quelque chose avec la fourchette du père Adam *exp.* to eat with one's fingers • to eat something with the fork of father Adam.

pomme d'Adam *f.* • (lit.): Adam's apple.

tenue d'Adam (être dans sa) *exp.* to be naked, in one's birthday suit • (lit.): to be in Adam's clothing.

Alfred

le bonjour d'Alfred *exp.* tip, "pourboire" • (lit.): the hello from Alfred.

Anatole

ça colle, Anatole? *exp.* hey Joe, whadya know? • (lit.): does it stick, Anatole?

Arthur

appeler Arthur (se faire) *exp.* to get reprimanded • (lit.): to get oneself called Arthur.

Auguste

come de juste, Auguste! *exp.* you said it, Charlie! • (lit.): exactly, Auguste!
VARIATION: tout juste, Auguste!

Azor

appeler Azor (se faire)
exp. to get booed and
hissed at • (lit.): to get
oneself called Azor.

Azor *Prn.* Fido, Rover.

Ben Hur

**arrête ton char, Ben
Hur!** *exp.* stop
exaggerating! • (lit.): stop
your chariot, Ben Hur!

Bouffi

tu l'as dit, Bouffi! *exp.* you
said it, Charlie!

Charles

tu parles, Charles! *exp.*
you said it, Charlie!

Charlot

bascule à Charlot *f.*
guillotine.

Charlot *Prn. & m.*
1. good-time Charlie • **2.** a
silly person • **3.** a term of
affection for Charlie Chaplin.

Diane

prix de Diane (un) *exp.* a
very pretty girl •
(lit.): Diane's prize.

Etienne

à la tienne, Etienne! *exp.*
here's to you! • (lit.): to
yours, Steve!

Eve

**je ne le connais ni d'Eve
ni d'Adam** *exp.* I don't
know him from Adam •
(lit.): I don't know him from
Eve nor Adam.

**tenue d'Eve (être dans
sa)** *exp.* to be naked, in
one's birthday suit • (lit.): to
be in Eve's clothing.

François

**faire le coup du père
François à quelqu'un**
exp. to strangle someone •
(lit.): to do the Father
François hit to someone.

Georges

Georges *Prn. & m.* (aviation)
automatic pilot.

Jacques

Jacques *Prn. & m.* taxi meter.

Jacques (faire le) *exp.* to act dumb • (lit.): to act like Jacques.

Pierre, Paul et Jacques *exp.* Tom, Dick, and Harry.

Jean

comme un petit Saint Jean *exp.* naked • (lit.): like a little Saint John.

petit saint Jean (faire son) *exp.* (said of a child) to be on one's best behavior • (lit.): to do one's little Saint John.

Joseph

faire son Joseph *exp.* to act self-righteous and smug • (lit.): to do one's Joseph.

Joséphine

faire sa Joséphine *exp.* to play the prude, to be all good-goody • (lit.): to do one's Josephine.

Jules

Jules *Prn. & m.* • **1.** husband • **2.** boyfriend • **3.** pimp.

Julie *Prn. & f.* wife.

appeler Jules (se faire) *exp.* to get reprimanded • (lit.): to get oneself called Jules.

Jupiter

sorti(e) de la cuisse de Jupiter (se croire) *exp.* to think highly of oneself, to be conceited • (lit.): to believe oneself to have come from Jupiter's thigh.

Léon

vas-y, Léon! *exp.* • (lit.): go for it Leon!

Lisette

pas de ça, Lisette! *exp.* • (lit.): (let's have) none of that, Lisette!

Louis

**jambes Louis Quinze
(avoir des)** *exp.* to be
bowlegged • (lit.): to have
legs like Louis XV–style
chairs.

Louisette

Louisette (la) *Prn. & f.*
guillotine.

Madeleine

**pleurer comme une
Madeleine** *exp.* to cry
one's eyes out • (lit.): to cry
like a Madeleine.

Marcel

chauffe, Marcel! *exp.* go
for it! • (lit.): heat it up,
Marcel!

Marcel *Prn. & m.* tank top.

Marie

Marie-couche-toi-là *Prn.
& f.* woman of easy morals •
(lit.): Marie lay yourself
there.

Marie-Chantal

Marie-Chantal *Prn. & f.*
a pretentious woman •
C't'une Marie-Chantal; She's
a rich airhead.

Paul

Pierre, Paul et Jacques
exp. Tom, Dick and Harry.

Pierre

Pierre, Paul et Jacques
exp. Tom, Dick and Harry.

Robert

roberts *m.pl.* big breasts

Sophie

faire sa Sophie *exp.* to
behave prudishly • (lit.): to
do one's Sophie.

PRACTICE USING PROPER NAMES IN IDIOMATIC EXPRESSIONS

A. Choose the letter of the appropriate name that goes with the expression.

1. Ma mère, elle était furieuse. Je m'suis fait appeler _____ en rentrant.
   a. **Etienne**   b. **Auguste**   c. **Arthur**

2. Tu parles, _____ !
   a. **Georges**   b. **Charles**   c. **Gaston**

3. Y s'croit sorti d'la cuisse de _____ .
   a. **Jupiter**   b. **Paul**   c. **Pierre**

4. Ça colle, _____ ?
   a. **Henriette**   b. **Anatole**   c. **Marie**

5. En été, j'aime porter un _____ !
   a. **Georges**   b. **Marcel**   c. **Jules**

6. L'acteur, y s'est fait appeler _____ .
   a. **Auguste**   b. **François**   c. **Azor**

7. Allez! Chauffe _____ !
   a. **Léon**   b. **Joseph**   c. **Marcel**

8. Comme de juste, _____ !
   a. **Henriette**   b. **Madeleine**   c. **Auguste**

9. Elle a pleuré comme une _____ , la pauvre.
   a. **Louisette**   b. **Henriette**   c. **Madeleine**

10. Y s'est fait décapoter par la _____ .
    a. **Diane**   b. **Sophie**   c. **Louisette**

Elle file un mauvais coton!

(trans.): She's not doing well!
(lit.): She's spinning a bad cotton!

Leçon Sept

Elle file un mauvais coton!

Paul: Alors, tu as rencontré les nouveaux voisins? Comment sont-ils?

Irène: La femme **n'a pas la langue dans sa poche**. J'ai eu du mal à **en placer une**. Par contre, lui, il parlait **à peine** parce qu'il **relève d'une** grippe et **avait un coup de pompe**. Il **a filé un mauvais coton** pendant une semaine. C'est un couple intéressant. Ils sont **comme torchon et serviette**. Elle, elle **pète le feu** et lui, il est plutot réservé. Franchement, j'ai l'impression qu'elle **le mène à la baguette**.

Paul: **Arrête ton char**! Je **meurs d'envie** de savoir comment ils **gagnent leur vie**! Ils doivent **être cousus d'or**. Ils ont **pas mal d'**antiquités qui doivent **remonter au** dix-septième siècle ainsi qu'une Ferrari dans le garage! La première fois que j'ai vu la bagnole, j'**en suis resté comme deux ronds de flan**! Ça coûte **la peau des fesses**, ça!

Irène: **Pour autant que** je sache, ils ne travaillent même pas! Ils sont **frais émoulus** de l'université. Et quand je leur ai demandé comment ça se faisait qu'ils ont tous ces meubles, ils m'ont raconté une histoire **tirée par les cheveux**. Je **parie mon dernier sou** qu'ils ont **gagné gros** au lotto. Ils ne **jouent pas aux riches** comme ça mais ils le sont, **à l'évidence**! Peut-être qu'ils ont **fait fortune en partant de rien**, mais je n'en **mettrais pas ma main au feu**. Ils ne sont pas **sur la paille**, c'est sûr!

Paul: Ils ont peut être **touché un gros héritage**? Si c'est le cas, ils **ont leur pain cuit**.

Translation in English

She's not doing well!

Paul: So, did you meet the new neighbors? What are they like?

Irène: The wife **is a real blabbermouth**. I had trouble **getting a word in edgewise**. On the other hand, the guy, he **hardly** spoke because he is **getting over** the flu and **was totally exhausted**. He **hasn't been doing well** for a week. They're an interesting pair. They're **totally opposite**. She's **real hyper** and he's rather reserved. Frankly, I get the impression that she **has him wrapped around her little finger**.

Paul: **Stop exaggerating**! I'm **itching** to find out how they **make a living**! They must **be filthy rich**. They have **quite a few** antiques that must **date back to** the seventeenth century and a Ferrari in the garage! The first time I saw the car, I **was absolutely stunned**! That **costs an arm and a leg**!

Irène: **As far as** I know, they don't even work! They're **fresh out** of school. And when I asked them how it is that they have all these antiques, they gave me some **far-fetched** story. I **bet my bottom dollar** that they **hit it big** at the lottery. They **don't seem rich** but **obviously** they are! Maybe they **went from rags to riches** but **I wouldn't put money on it**. They're not **broke**, that's for sure!

Paul: Maybe they **came into a big inheritance**. If that's the case, they **have it made**.

Dialogue in slang as it would be spoken

È file un mauvais coton!

Paul: Alors, t'as rencontré les nouveaux voisins? Comment y sont?

Irène: La femme, elle **a pas la langue dans sa poche**. J'ai eu du mal à **en placer une**. Par contre, lui, y parlait **à peine** pasqu'y **r'lève d'une** grippe et **avait un coup d'pompe**. Il **a filé un mauvais coton** pendant une s'maine. C't'un couple intéressant. Y sont **comme torchon et serviette**. Elle, è **pète le feu** et lui, il est plutot réservé. Franchement, j'ai l'impression qu'è **l'mène à la baguette**.

Paul: **Arrète ton char**! J'**meurs d'envie** d'savoir comment y **gagnent leur vie**! Y doivent **êt' cousus d'or**. Y z'ont **pas mal d'**antiquités qui doivent **remonter au** dix-septième siècle ainsi qu'une Ferrari dans l'garage! La première fois qu'j'ai vu la bagnole, j'**en suis resté comme deux ronds d'flan**! Ça **coûte la peau des fesses**, ça!

Irène: **Pour autant que** j'sache, y travaillent même pas! Y sont **frais émoulus** d'l'université. Et quand j'leur ai d'mandé comment ça s'faisait qu'y z'ont tous ces meubles, y m'ont raconté une histoire **tirée par les ch'veux**. J'**parie mon dernier sou** qu'y z'ont **gagné gros** au lotto. Y **jouent pas aux riches** comme ça mais y l'sont, **à l'évidence**! P't-êt'qu'y z'ont **fait fortune en partant de rien**, mais j'en **mettrais pas ma main au feu**. Y sont pas **sur la paille**, c'est sûr!

Paul: Y z'ont p't'êt' **touché un gros héritage**? Si c'est l'cas, y z'**ont leur pain cuit**.

Literal Translation

She's spinning a bad cotton!

Paul: So, did you meet the new neighbors? What are they like?

Irène: The wife **doesn't have her tongue in her pocket**. I had trouble **placing a word**. On the other hand, the guy, he spoke **at difficulty** because he is **getting back up from** the flu and **was pumped of energy**. He **was spinning a bad cotton** for a week. They're an interesting pair. They're **like rag and napkin**. The wife **farts fire** and he's rather reserved. Frankly, I get the impression that she **leads him with a conductor's baton**.

Paul: **Stop your chariot**! I'm **dying with wanting to know** how they **win a life**! They must **be sewn with gold**. They have **not bad** antiques that must **go back in time to** the seventeenth century and a Ferrari in the garage! The first time I saw the car, I **was motionless like two rounds of custard**! That costs **the skin of the buttocks**!

Irène: **For as much that** I know, they don't even work! They're **freshly ground** from school. And when I asked them how it is that they have all these antiques, they gave me some **pulled by the hair** story. I **bet my last coin** that they **won big** at the lottery. They **don't act rich** but **by evidence** they are! Maybe they **made a fortune starting from nothing** but **I won't put my hand to the fire on it**. They're not **on the straw**, that's for sure!

Paul: Maybe they **touched a big inheritance**. If that's the case, they **have their bread cooked**.

Vocabulary

arrêter son char *exp.* to stop one's exaggerating • (lit.): stop your waggon.

>   example: "Aïe! Je crois que je me suis cassé le bras!"
>   "*Arrête ton char!* Tu te l'es foulé un peu. C'est tout!"

>   as spoken: "Aïe! J'crois qu'je m'suis cassé l'bras!"
>   "*Arrête ton char!* Tu t'l'es foulé un peu. C'est tout!"

> translation: "Ow! I think I broke my arm!"
>   "*Stop your exaggerating!* You just sprained it a little. That's all!

> **NOTE:** **charrier** *v.* to exaggerate.

comme deux ronds de flan (en rester) *exp.* to be dumbfounded • (lit.): to be motionless like two rounds of custard.

>   example: Martial n'a que vingt ans! Il fait pourtant beaucoup plus âgé! *J'en reste comme deux ronds de flan!*

>   as spoken: Martial, il ~ a qu'vingt ans! Y fait pourtant beaucoup plus âgé! *J'en reste comme deux ronds d'flan!*

> translation: Martial is only twenty years old! He looks a lot older! I'm *stunned!*

> **NOTE:** In the previous sentence, the verb *faire* was used to mean "to look." This is an extremely commonly usage for *faire*. (*Il fait beaucoup plus âgé!* = He looks a lot older!)

coup de pompe (avoir un) *exp.* to be exhausted • (lit.): to have the pump strike (meaning that one's energy has been pumped out).

>   example: J'ai fait du sport pendant trois heures aujourd'hui. *J'ai un coup de pompe*, moi!

>   as spoken: J'ai fait du sport pendant trois heures aujourd'hui. *J'ai un coup d'pompe*, moi!

> translation: I played sports for three hours today. I'm *pooped!*

cousu(e) d'or (être) *exp.* to be filthy rich • (lit.): to be sewn with gold.

> example: Tu lui as prêté de l'argent?! Mais il est *cousu d'or*, lui!

> as spoken: Tu lui as prêté <u>d</u>'l'argent?! Mais il est *cousu d'or*, lui!

> translation: You lent him money?! But he's *filthy rich*!

coûter la peau des fesses *exp.* to cost an arm and a leg • (lit.): to cost the skin of the buttocks.

> example: J'aimerais bien acheter cette robe mais elle *coûte la peau des fesses*.

> as spoken: J'aimerais bien ac<u>h</u>'ter cette robe mais <u>è</u> *coûte la peau des fesses*.

> translation: I'd really like to but this dress but it *costs an arm and a leg*.

> **VARIATION:** **coûter les yeux de la tête** *exp.* • (lit.): to cost the eyes from the head.

évidence (à l') *adv.* evidently • (lit.): at the evidence.

> example: Marcel a volé mon argent! J'ai toujours pensé que je pouvais me fier à lui, mais je ne peux pas, *à l'évidence*!

> as spoken: Marcel, <u>il</u> a volé mon argent! J'ai toujours pensé qu<u>'j</u>'pouvais <u>m</u>'fier à lui, mais <u>j</u>'peux pas, *à l'évidence*!

> translation: Marcel stole my money! I always thought I could trust him, but *evidently* I can't!

filer un mauvais coton *exp.* to be in a bad way (regarding health or business), not to be doing well • (lit.): to spin a bad cotton.

> example: Pauvre Jean. Il *file un mauvais coton* en ce moment. Il n'arrive pas à trouver d'emploi. Il ne sait même pas comment il va payer son loyer.

> as spoken: Pau<u>v</u>' Jean. <u>Y</u> *file un mauvais coton* en <u>c</u>'moment. Il ~ arrive pas à trouver d'emploi. <u>Y</u> ~ sait même pas comment <u>y</u> va payer son loyer.

> translation: Poor John. He's *not doing well* right now. He doesn't seem to be able to find a job. He doesn't even know how he's going to pay his rent.

fortune en partant de rien (faire) *exp.* to go from rags to
riches • (lit.): to make a fortune by starting from nothing.

> example: Elle a démarré sa companie avec un malheureux cent
>   dollars. En deux ans, elle a *fait fortune en partant de rien.*
>
> as spoken: [no change]
>
> translation: She started up her company with a measly one hundred
>   dollars. In two years, she *went from rags to riches.*

frais/fraîche émoulu de (être) *exp.* to be fresh out of • (lit.): to
be freshly ground (from the verb *"moudre"* meaning "to grind.").

> example: Marc est *frais émoulu de* l'université.
>
> as spoken: Marc, il est *frais émoulu d'*l'unif.
>
> translation: Mark is *fresh out of the univeristy.*

gagner gros *exp.* to make big bucks, to win big • (lit.): to win big.

> example: Bernard est un cadre dans une grande companie. Il
>   *gagne gros,* lui.
>
> as spoken: Bernard, *c't'*un cadre dans une grande companie. Y
>   *gagne gros,* lui.
>
> translation: Bernie is an executive in a large company. He *makes big
>   bucks.*

gagner sa vie *exp.* to make a living • (lit.): to earn life.

> example: Comment elle *gagne sa vie?*
>
> as spoken: Comment è *gagne sa vie?*
>
> translation: How does she *make a living?*

jouer à *exp.* to play or act a certain way • (lit.): to play at (something).

> example: François est très prétentieux. Il *joue à* l'important, mais
>   il ne l'est pas du tout.
>
> as spoken: François, il est très prétentieux. Y *joue à* l'important, mais
>   y ~ l'est pas du tout.
>
> translation: François is very pretentious. He *acts* important, but he's
>   not at all.

langue dans sa poche (ne pas avoir la) *exp.* to be a blabbermouth • (lit.): not to have one's tongue in one's pocket.

> example: Son mari est très gentil mais il faut dire qu'il *n'a pas la langue dans sa poche.* Il me parle sans arrêt!

> as spoken: Son mari, <u>il</u> est très gentil mais ~ faut dire qu'<u>il</u> ~ *a pas la langue dans sa poche.* <u>Y</u> m'parle sans arrêt!

> translation: Her husband is very nice but I've gotta tell you that *he's a real yacker.* He talks to me nonstop!

mener à la baguette *exp.* to boss around • (lit.): to lead with a conductor's baton.

> example: Son frère le *mène à la baguette.* Franchement, je pense qu'il a peur de lui!

> as spoken: Son frère, <u>y</u> l'*mène à la baguette.* Franchement, <u>i</u>'pense qu'il a peur de lui!

> translation: His brother *bosses him around.* Frankly, I think he's afraid of him!

mettre sa main au feu (en) *exp.* to be absolutely sure of something • (lit.): to put one's hand in fire over it.

> example: Je te dis qu'elle ment. J'*en mettrais ma main au feu.*

> as spoken: <u>J</u>'te dis qu'<u>è</u> ment. J'*en mettrais ma main au feu.*

> translation: I'm telling you she's lying. I *would swear to it.*

mourir d'envie de faire quelque chose *exp.* to be dying to do something • (lit.): to die with desire to do something.

> example: Je *meurs d'envie* d'aller à Paris un de ces jours!

> as spoken: <u>J</u>'*meurs d'envie* d'aller à Paris un <u>d</u>'ces jours!

> translation: I'm *dying* to go to Paris one of these days!

parier son dernier sou *exp.* to bet one's bottom dollar • (lit.): to bet one's last cent.

> example: Je *parie mon dernier sou* qu'il vont finir par divorcer.
>
> as spoken: J'*parie mon dernier sou* qu'y̲ vont finir par divorcer.
>
> translation: I'll *bet my bottom dollar* that they end up getting divorced.

pas mal *exp.* quite a bit • (lit.): not [a] bad [number of].

> example: Je n'aime pas ce parc. Il y a *pas mal* de moustiques ici!
>
> as spoken: J'̲aime pas c̲'parc. Y̲ ~ a *pas mal* d̲'moustiques ici!
>
> translation: I don't like this park. There are *quite a few* mosquitos here!

peine (à) *exp.* hardly • (lit.): to difficulty.

> example: Je le connais *à peine*.
>
> as spoken: J'̲le connais *à peine*.
>
> translation: I *hardly* know him.

pèter le feu *exp.* to be hyperactive, to have tons of energy • (lit.): to fart fire.

> example: Il *pète le feu*, cet enfant. C'est épuisant!
>
> as spoken: Y̲ *pète le feu*, c̲'t̲'enfant. C̲'t̲'épuisant!
>
> translation: This child *is so hyper*. It's exhausting!

placer une (en) *exp.* to get a word in edgewise • (lit.): to place one.

> example: Il parle tellement que je ne peux même pas *en placer une*.
>
> as spoken: Y̲ parle tellement qu'i̲'peux même pas *en placer une*.
>
> translation: He talks so much that I can't even *get a word in edgewise*.
>
> **NOTE:** In this expression, *une* represents *une parole* meaning "speech" or a "word."
>
> **VARIATION:** **placer un mot** *exp.* • (lit.): to place a word.

pour autant que *exp.* as far as • (lit.): for as much as that.

> example: *Pour autant que* je sache, il va arriver à midi.

> as spoken: *Pour autant que* j'sache, y va arriver à midi.

> translation: *As far as* I know, he is going to arrive at noon.

> **SYNONYM:** **jusqu'à** *exp.* • (lit.): up to.

> **NOTE:** As seen above, the expression *autant que* (as well as "*jusqu'à*") are followed by the subjunctive tense).

relever de *exp.* to be getter over (a sickness) • (lit.): to get back up (from something).

> example: Mon père est très fatigué parce qu'il *relève d'*une grippe.

> as spoken: Mon père, il est très fatigué pasqu'y *relève d'*une grippe.

> translation: My father is very tired because he's *getting over* the flu.

remonter à *exp.* to date back to • (lit.): to go back (in time) to.

> example: Cette peinture *remonte au* dix-septième siècle!

> as spoken: Cette peinture, è r'monte au dix-septième siècle!

> translation: This painting *dates back to* the seventeenth century!

son pain cuit (avoir) *exp.* to have it made, to be on easy street • (lit.): to have one's bread cooked.

> example: David a hérité d'un million de dollars! Il *a son pain cuit*, lui.

> as spoken: David, il a hérité d'un million d'dollars! Il *a son pain cuit*, lui.

> translation: David inherited a million dollars! He *has it made*.

sur la paille (être) *exp.* to be down and out, broke • (lit.): to be on the straw.

> example: C'est difficile à croire que l'année dernière Silvie était riche et maintenant elle *est sur la paille*. Elle a perdu tout son argent aux courses.

> as spoken: C'est difficile à croire que l'année dernière Silvie, <u>elle</u> était riche et maint'nant <u>elle</u> *est sur la paille*. Elle a perdu tout son argent aux courses.

> translation: It's hard to believe that last year Silvia was rich and now she's *totally broke*. She lost all her money at the horse races.

tiré(e) par les cheveux (être) *exp.* to be farfetched • (lit.): to be pulled by the hair.

> example: Son excuse était *tirée par les cheveux*.

> as spoken: Son excuse, <u>elle</u> était *tirée par les ch'veux*.

> translation: His excuse was *farfetched*.

torchon et serviette (être comme) *exp.* said of two people who are completely opposite in personality • (lit.): to be like rag and napkin.

> example: Guillaume et Charlotte se sont mariés? Mais pourtant ils sont *comme torchon et serviette*!

> as spoken: Guillaume et Charlotte, <u>y</u> <u>s'</u>sont mariés? Mais pourtant <u>y</u> sont *comme torchon et serviette*!

> translation: Guillaume and Charlotte got married? But they're *about as opposite as two people could be*!

toucher un gros héritage *exp.* to get a large inheritance • (lit.): to touch a big inheritance.

> example: Comme j'ai *touché un gros héritage*, je pourrai passer tout mon temps à voyager.

> as spoken: Comme j'ai *touché un gros héritage*, <u>j'</u>pourrai passer tout mon temps à voyager.

> translation: Since I *got a big inheritance*, I'll be able to spend all my time traveling.

Practice The Vocabulary

(Answers to Lesson 7, p. 257)

A. Choosing from the list below, complete the idiom by writing the correct word in the crossword puzzle on the following page.

AUTANT
BAGUETTE
CHEVEUX
COTON
EMOULU
FESSES
FEU

FLAN
FORTUNE
GROS
MAL
OR
PAILLE
PAIN

PEINE
POCHE
POMPE
RELEVE
SOU
VIE

ACROSS

12. J'ai un coup de _____ .
    J'vais aller m'coucher.

18. Pour _____ qu'je sache,
    y travaillent même pas!

20. Ça fait une s'maine que
    j'file un mauvais _____ .

28. Son histoire, elle est tirée
    par les _____ .

34. Y z'ont fait _____ en
    partant de rien.

36. Carole, è _____ d'une
    grippe.

44. J'ai gagné _____ au
    lotto!

48. J'parie mon dernier
    _____ qu'elle a menti!

DOWN

5. J'pouvais pas l'croire. En
   apprenant la nouvelle, j'en
   suis resté comme deux ronds
   de _____ .

12. J'la connais à _____ . J'l'ai
    rencontrée hier.

13. Elle a pas la langue dans sa
    _____ . È parle sans arrêt!

15. J'ai l'impression qu'è l'mène
    à la _____ .

21. T'as vu sa maison?! Y doit
    être cousu d'_____ !

23. Il a beaucoup d'énergie. Y
    pète le _____ , c't'enfant!

34. Ça coûte la peau des _____ !

35. Il est frais _____ d'l'unif.

50. Y z'ont pas d'argent. Ils sont sur la _____ .

52. J'ai r'çu pas _____ d'cadeaux pour mon anniversaire!

47. J'ai l'impression qu'y sont riches. J'me d'mande comment y gagnent leur _____ .

50. Avec l'héritage qu'il a r'çu, il a son _____ cuit.

CROSSWORD PUZZLE

B. Choose the correct idiom that goes with the phrase.

1. **Y parle sans arrêt!**
   ☐ a. Il a pas la langue dans sa poche!
   ☐ b. Y fait fortune en partant de rien!

2. **J'ai travaillé toute la journée.**
   ☐ a. J'suis sur la paille.
   ☐ b. J'ai un coup d'pompe.

3. **J'peux pas l'croire!**
   ☐ a. J'en reste comme deux ronds d'flan!
   ☐ b. J'fais fortune en partant de rien!

4. **Il a été très malade.**
   ☐ a. Il est cousu d'or.
   ☐ b. Y file un mauvais coton depuis longtemps.

5. **Il a r'çu un gros héritage.**
   ☐ a. Il a son pain cuit.
   ☐ b. Y r'monte au dixième siècle.

6. **Elle a pas d'argent du tout.**
   ☐ a. È pète le feu.
   ☐ b. Elle est dans la dèche.

7. **Il a beaucoup d'énergie.**
   ☐ a. Y pète le feu.
   ☐ b. Il est sur la paille.

8. **Quelle jolie voiture!**
   ☐ a. Tu dois êt' cousu d'or!
   ☐ b. Tu doit êt' frais émoulu d'l'école!

9. **J'crois pas son histoire.**
   ☐ a. Elle est tirée par les ch'veux.
   ☐ b. È gagne gros.

10. **C'est la première fois que j'le rencontre.**
    ☐ a. J'le connais à peine.
    ☐ b. J'en suis resté comme deux ronds d'flan.

C. Complete the dialogue using the list below. Note that one of the words is used twice.

autant	feu	or	pompe
baguette	flan	paille	relève
char	fortune	pas mal	remonter
cheveux	frais	peau	serviette
coton	gros	peine	sou
cuit	jouent	placer	touché
évidence	meurs	poche	vie

Paul: Alors, tu as rencontré les nouveaux voisins? Comment sont-ils?

Irène: La femme n'a pas la langue dans sa **(1)**_____. J'ai eu

du mal à en **(2)**_____une. Par contre, lui, il parlait

à **(3)**_____parce qu'il **(4)**_____d'une

grippe et avait un coup de **(5)**_____. Il a filé un

mauvais **(6)**_____pendant une semaine. C'est un couple

intéressant. Ils sont comme torchon et **(7)**_____.

Elle, elle pète le **(8)**_____et lui, il est plutôt

réservé. Franchement, j'ai l'impression qu'elle le mène à la

(9)_____.

Paul: Arrête ton **(10)**_____! Je **(11)**_____d'envie de

savoir comment ils gagnent leur **(12)**_____! Ils doivent être

cousus d'**(13)**____. Ils ont **(14)**_____d'antiquités qui doivent **(15)**_____au dix-septième

siècle ainsi qu'une Ferrari dans le garage! La première fois que

j'ai vu la bagnole, j'en suis resté comme deux ronds de

(16)_____! Ça coûte la **(17)**_____

des fesses, ça!

Irène: Pour **(18)**_____que je sache, ils ne travaillent même

pas! Ils sont **(19)**_____émoulus de l'université.

Et quand je leur ai demandé comment ça se faisait qu'ils aient

tous ces meubles, ils m'ont raconté une histoire tirée par les

(20)_____. Je parie mon dernier **(21)**_____

qu'ils ont gagné **(22)**_____au lotto. Ils ne

(23)_____pas aux riches comme ça mais ils le sont, à

l'**(24)**_____! Peut-être qu'ils ont fait

(25)_____en partant de rien, mais je n'en mettrais

pas ma main au **(26)**_____. Ils ne sont pas sur la

(27)_____, c'est sûr!

Paul: Ils ont peut être **(28)**_____un gros héritage? Si c'est le

cas, ils ont leur pain **(29)**_____!

DICTATION

Test Your Aural Comprehension.

If you are following along with your cassette, you will now hear a paragraph containing many of the idioms from this section. The paragraph will be read at normal conversational speed (which may actually seem fast to you at first). In addition, the words will be pronounced as you would actually hear them in a conversation, including many common reductions.

The first time the paragraph is presented, simply listen in order to get accustomed to the speed and heavy use of reductions. The paragraph will then be read again with a pause after each group of words to give you time to write down what you heard. The third time the paragraph is read, follow along with what you have written.

A CLOSER LOOK:
The Use of Numbers in Slang Expressions

From time to time, numbers creep into our own slang in expressions such as: *to be dressed to the 9's, to be in 7th heaven, catch 22, cloud 9, to 86 someone, to put 2 and 2 together, etc.*

The French seem to have beaten us hands down in the "numbers game" with an assortment of colorful phrases:

"Numéro"

connaître le numéro *exp.* to know one's number, to have someone all sized up • (lit.): to know the number.

numéro (faire son) *exp.* to pull a scene • (lit.): to do one's number.

numéro cent *m.* the restroom • (lit.): number one hundred.

NOTE: This is actually a play on words since *"cent"* is pronounced the same as *"sent"* from the verb *"sentir,"* meaning "to smell."

tirer un bon numéro *exp.* to pick a winner • (lit.): to pull a good number.

un drôle de numéro *m.* a weird person • (lit.): a strange number.

vieux numéro (un) *m.* an old fogey • (lit.): and old number.

O (zéro)

à zéro *adv.* completely • (lit.): to zero.

avoir le moral à zéro *exp.* to be very depressed • (lit.): to have the morale down to zero.

double zéro *m.* a real loser • (lit.): a double zero.

les avoir à zéro *exp.* to be frightened • (lit.): to have them (one's testicles) down to zero.

partir à zéro *exp.* to start from the beginning • (lit.): to start from zero.

vrai zéro (un) *m.* a real loser, a big zero • (lit.): a real zero.
   VARIATION (1): **zéro à gauche (un)** *m.* • (lit.): a zero to the left.

VARIATION (2): **zéro en chiffre (un)** *m.* • (lit.): a zero in letters.
VARIATION (3): **zéro fini (un)** *m.* • (lit.): a finished zero (meaning, "a complete zero").

zéro pointé (un) *m.* a complete zero (used to denote an extremely low grade in school, etc.) • (lit.): a pointed zero.

1/3 (tiers)

devoir au tiers et au quart *exp.* to owe money right and left • (lit.): to owe a third (party) and a quarter (party).

moquer du tiers comme du quart (s'en) *exp.* not to give a damn • (lit.): not to care a third or a fourth about it.

1/4 (quart)

devoir au tiers et au quart *exp.* to owe money right and left • (lit.): to owe a third (party) and a quarter (party).

faire passer un mauvais quart d'heure *exp.* to worry (someone) greatly • (lit.): to make (someone) go through a bad quarter of an hour.

les trois quarts du temps
exp. most of the time •
(lit.): three-quarters of the
time.

**moquer du tiers comme
du quart (s'en)** *exp.* not
to give a damn • (lit.): not
to care a third or even a
fourth about it.

pour le quart d'heure
exp. for the time being •
(lit.): for the quarter-hour.

quart (faire le) *exp.* to
walk one's beat (said of a
prostitute) • (lit.): to do a
quarter of an hour (said of a
watchman or sailor who is
on watch duty).

quart *m.* police station, the
station where watchmen or
sailors go on watch duty.
SEE: quart (faire le)
exp.

1 (un/une)

il était moins une *exp.* it
was a close shave, it was a
narrow escape • (lit.): it was
one minute to the hour.

la une *f.* front page of a
newspaper • (lit.): the
number one (page) • *C't'un
événement qui fait la une*; It's
an event that made the
front page.

**pouvoir en placer une
(ne pas)** *exp.* not to be
able to get a word in edgewise • (lit.): not to be able
to place one ("*une parole*").

sans faire ni une ni deux
exp. without further
hesitation, urgently •
(lit.): without saying one
or two (counts).

sans un (être) *exp.* to be
broke • (lit.): to be without
one (a franc).

tirer à moins une (s'en)
exp. to have a narrow
escape • (lit.): to pull
oneself out of it with less
than one (minute left).

un(e) de ces *exp.* a real... •
(lit.): one of these • *C't'un
d'ces menteurs!*; He's a real
liar!

2 (deux)

casser en deux (se) *exp.* to
double up with laughter •
(lit.): to break oneself in two.

**deux temps, trois
mouvements (en)** *adv.*
quickly, lickety-split •
(lit.): in two beats, three
movements.

il était moins deux *exp.* it
was a close shave • (lit.): it
was two minutes to the
hour.

moins de deux (en) *adv.* quickly • (lit.): in less than two (seconds).

plier en deux (se) *exp.* to bend over backwards in order to do something • (lit.): to fold oneself in two.

six-quat'-deux (à la) *adv.* quickly, lickety-split • (lit.): in six-four-two.

3 *(trois)*

deux temps, trois mouvements (en) *adv.* quickly, lickety-split • (lit.): in two beats, three movements.

trois quarts du temps (les) *exp.* most of the time • (lit.): three-quarters of the time.

4 *(quatre)*

entre quat'z'yeux *exp.* just between you and me • (lit.): between four eyes.

fichu(e) comme quat'sous *exp.* to be dressed any old way • (lit.): to be made like four small coins.

malle à quat'nœuds *f.* handkerchief containing one's savings • (lit.): trunk with four knots.

quatre à quatre *adv.* very quickly • (lit.): four by four • *Il a descendu l'escalier quatre à quatre;* He took the stairs four at a time.

quatrième vitesse (en) *adv.* quickly • (lit.): in fourth gear.

semaine des quat'jeudis (la) *exp.* never • (lit.): the week of the four Thursdays.

six-quat'-deux (à la) *exp.* quickly, lickety-split • (lit.): in six-four-two.

tiré(e) à quatre épingles (être) *exp.* to be dressed to the "nines" • (lit.): pulled with four pins.

un de ces quatre matins *exp.* one of these days • (lit.): one of these four mornings.
NOTE: This is commonly pronounced *un d'ces quat'matins.*
VARIATION: **un de ces quat'** *exp.*

5 *(cinq)*

cinq secs (en) *adv.* very quickly • (lit.): in five seconds.

il était moins cinq *exp.* it was a narrow escape, a close shave • (lit.): it was five minutes to the hour.

je t'en écrase cinq *exp.*
gimme five • (lit.): I'll crash
five of them (fingers) down
on you.

**je vous reçois cinq sur
cinq** *exp.* I read you loud
and clear • (lit.): I receive
you five on five.

tape cinq *exp.* gimme five •
(lit.): hit five (fingers).

y aller de cinq *exp.* to
shake hands • (lit.): to go at
it with five (fingers).

6 (six)

six-quat'-deux (à la) *adv.*
quickly, lickety-spit • (lit.): in
six-four-two.

7 (sept)

septième ciel (être au)
exp. to be in 7th heaven •
(lit.): to be in the seventh
sky.

11 (onze)

**prendre le train d'onze
heures** *exp.* to go by foot •
(lit.): to take the 11:00 train.

12 (douze)

douze (faire un) *exp.* to
make a mistake • (lit.): to
make a twelve.

13 (treize)

treizième mois *m.*
Christmas bonus • (lit.): the
thirteenth month.

14 (quatorze)

**chercher midi à
quatorze heures** *exp.* to
look for problems where
there are none • (lit.): to
look for noon at 2:00 (p.m.)

15 (quinze)

**tuer les mouches à
quinze pas** *exp.* to have
bad breath • (lit.): to kill
flies fifteen paces away.

22 (vingt-deux)

vingt-deux! *interj.* let's
scram!

31 (trente et un)

**mettre sur son trente et
un (se)** *exp.* to get all
dressed up, to dress to the
"nines" • (lit) to get on
one's thirty-one.

33 (trente-trois)

trente-trois *interj.* (doctor
to patient) *Dites trente-trois!;*
Say "ah!"

36 (trente-six)

tous les trente-six du mois *exp.* once in a blue moon • (lit.): each thirty-sixth of the month.

trente-six volontés de quelqu'un (faire les) *exp.* to be at someone's beck and call • (lit.): to do the thirty-six wills of someone.

voir trente-six chandelles (en) *exp.* to see stars after getting hit in the head • (lit.): to see thirty-six candles.

40 (quarante)

mettre en quarantaine *exp.* to put in quarantine • (lit.): to put in the fortieth.

mettre en quarante (se) *exp.* to get angry • (lit.): to put oneself in forty.

quarante-quatre *interj.* (doctor to patient) *Dites quarante-quatre!;* Say "ah!"

quarante-quatre *interj.* (doctor to patient) *Dites quarante-quatre!;* Say "ah!"

"50" (cinquante)

fifti (faire) *exp.* (Americanism) to go halves, "fifty-fifty."

100 (cent)

cent coups (être aux) *exp.* to be worried sick • (lit.): to be at one hundred blows, to feel as though you've been hit in the head one hundred times due to so much worrying.

numéro cent *m.* restroom • (lit.): the number one hundred.
NOTE: This is actually a play on words since *"cent"* is pronounced the same as *"sent"* from the verb *"sentir,"* meaning "to smell."

1000 (mille)

c'est du mille feuilles *exp.* It's a piece of cake • (lit.): it's a Napoléon pastry (referred to as a *mille feuilles* since its layers look like thousands of thin leaves).

je te le donne en mille *exp.* you will never guess in a thousand years. • (lit.): I'll give it to you in a thousand.

millimètre (faire du) *exp.* to economize • (lit.): to make millimeters.

taper dans le mille *exp.* to be successful • (lit.): to hit the thousand (when playing darts).

PRACTICE EXPRESSIONS THAT CONTAIN NUMBERS

A. Choose the correct French translation of the words in italics by check the box.

1. I was **totally** bombed.
   - ☐ a. à la six-quat'-deux
   - ☐ b. à zéro
   - ☐ c. la une

2. I'll do it **right** away.
   - ☐ a. double zéro
   - ☐ b. vingt-deux
   - ☐ c. à la six-quat'-deux

3. He **made a mistake** on his test.
   - ☐ a. a fait un douze
   - ☐ b. était sans un
   - ☐ c. s'est plié en deux

4. She's **such a big** liar.
   - ☐ a. un drôle de numéro
   - ☐ b. une de ces
   - ☐ c. treizième mois

5. **Let's beat it!**
   - ☐ a. vingt-trois
   - ☐ b. vingt-cinq
   - ☐ c. vingt-deux

6. She couldn't sleep because she was **terribly worried**.
   - ☐ a. aux cents coups
   - ☐ b. un d'ces quat'
   - ☐ c. j't'en écrase cinq

7. After he got hit in the head, he **saw stars**.
   - ☐ a. en a vu trente-six chandelles
   - ☐ b. y est allé d'cinq
   - ☐ c. était aux cent coups

8. He **got so angry** about it.
   - ☐ a. s'est mis en quarante
   - ☐ b. y est allé d'cinq
   - ☐ c. a fait fifti

9. I have to go to the **bathroom**.
   - ☐ a. quarante-quatre
   - ☐ b. vingt-deux
   - ☐ c. numéro cent

10. He sure is **a strange guy**.
    - ☐ a. un drôle de numéro
    - ☐ b. un d'ces
    - ☐ c. à zéro

11. Boy, what a **loser**!
    - ☐ a. drôle de numéro
    - ☐ b. double zéro
    - ☐ c. trente-trois

12. Could you hand me **the front page**, please?
    - ☐ a. deux de jeu
    - ☐ b. treizième mois
    - ☐ c. la une

Je pète les plombs!

(trans.): *I'm freaking out!*
(lit.): *I'm blowing fuses!*

Leçon Huit

Je pète les plombs!

Paul: Alors, ça **marche** bien avec ton invité?

Anne: Ah, celui-là, il **se la coule douce** ici. Il **n'en fiche pas une rame** toute la journée. Qu'est-ce qu'il **les a palmées**, lui! Tous les jours, c'est la même chose. Il fait **la grasse matinée** jusqu'à midi, puis il **se rempli la bedaine** au déjeuner jusqu'à ce qu'il ait **les dents du fond qui baignent**. Après ça, il **pique une ronflette**. Ce qu'il **est porté sur la bouffe**, lui! Je **n'en peux plus**! Il va me faire **perdre les pédales** et je vais **péter les plombs** un de ces quatre! Je te jure que tu n'as jamais rien vu de pareil! **A lui le pompon**!

Paul: Tu **as interêt** à **ronger ton frein** en attendant qu'il **plie bagages**. C'est pour ce weekend, n'est-ce pas?

Anne: Ouais, mais pour le moment, j'ai l'impression qu'il va **mourir de sa belle mort** chez moi. J'**en ai soupé**, tu sais?

Paul: Dis, il passe toujours des **coups de fil** à l'étranger?

Anne: Ah, que non! Là, j'**y ai mis mon véto**. J'ai voulu **étouffer ça dans l'œuf** avant que ça dégénère. Je ne veux pas **toujours cirer le même bouton**, mais il est quand même **bête comme ses pieds**. Hier, il a insisté pour faire la cuisine et sans le **faire exprès**, il a failli **faire sauter** la maison!

Paul: C'est vrai qu'**il a du culot**. Heu, Anne, heu, essaie de **la garder froide**, mais je crois bien qu'il parle au téléphone **de nouveau**.

Anne: Quoi?! **C'est le bouquet**, ça! **Son compte est bon**! **A nous deux**, vieille **fripouille**!

Leçon Huit

I'm freaking out!

Paul: So, are **things going well** with your houseguest?

Anne: Man, that guy **has it easy** here. He **doesn't lift a finger** all day. Is he ever **lazy**! Every day, it's the same thing. He **sleeps in** until noon, then then he **stuffs his face** until **he's about to explode from overeating**. After that, he **takes a nap**. Is this guy ever **driven by food**! I **can't take it any more**! He's going to make me **lose control** and **freak out** one of these days! I swear you've never seen anything like it! **He takes the cake**!

Paul: It would really be **in your best interest** to **chill out** until he **takes off**. It's this weekend, isn't it?

Anne: Yeah, but for the moment, I feel like he's going **to die of old age** at my house. I've really **had it**, you know?

Paul: Say, is he still making **phone calls** abroad?

Anne: Absolutely not! I **drew the line** on that one. I wanted **to nip that in the bud** before things get worse. I don't want **to keep harping**, but he's really **dumber than dumb**. Yesterday, he insisted on cooking and without **doing it on purpose**, he almost **blew up** the house!

Paul: He really **has some nerve**! **Um**, Anne, um, try **to stay cool** but I think he's talking on the phone **again**.

Anne: What?! **That did it**! **He's dead meat**! **Put 'em up**, you old **snake**!

Dialogue in slang as it would be spoken

J'pète les plombs!

Paul: Alors, ça **marche** bien avec ton invité?

Anne: Ah, s'ui-là, y **s'la coule douce** ici. **Il en fiche pas une rame** toute la journée. Qu'est-c'qu'y **les a palmées**, lui! Tous les jours, c'est la même chose. Y fait **la grasse matinée** jusqu'à midi, puis y **s'rempli la bedaine** au déjeuner jusqu'à c'qu'il ait **les dents du fond qui baignent**. Après ça, y **pique une ronflette**. C'qu'il **est porté sur la bouffe**, lui! J'**en peux plus**! Y va m'faire **perd' les pédales** et **j'vais péter les plombs** un d'ces quatre! J'te jure que t'as jamais rien vu d'pareil! **A lui l'pompon**!

Paul: T'**as interêt** à **ronger ton frein** en attendant qu'y **plie bagages**. C'est pour c'weekend, n'est-ce pas?

Anne: Ouais, mais pour le moment, j'ai l'impression qu'y va **mourir de sa belle mort** chez moi. J'**en ai soupé**, tu sais?

Paul: Dis, il passe toujours des **coups d'fil** à l'étranger?

Anne: Ah, que non! Là, j'**y ai mis mon véto**. J'voulais **étouffer ça dans l'œuf** avant qu'ça dégénère. J'veux pas **toujours cirer le même bouton**, mais il est quand même **bête comme ses pieds**. Hier, il a insisté pour faire la cuisine et sans l'**faire exprès**, il a failli **faire sauter** la maison!

Paul: C'est vrai qu'**y a du culot**. Heu, Anne, heu, essaie d'**la garder froide**, mais j'crois bien qu'y parle au téléphone **de nouveau**.

Anne: Quoi?! **C'est l'bouquet**, ça! **Son compte est bon**! **A nous deux**, vieille **fripouille**!

Literal Translation

I'm blowing fuses!

Paul: So, is everything **working** well with your houseguest?

Anne: He sure **flows it sweetly** here. He **doesn't do an oar** all day. Does he ever **have them webbed**! Every day, it's the same thing. He **makes the fat morning** until noon, then he **fills up his gut** at lunch until his **back teeth are floating**. After that, he **takes a little snore**. Is this guy ever **carried on food**! I **can't do of it any more**! He's going to make me **lose the pedals** and **blow my fuses**! I swear you've never seen anything like it! **To him the pom-pom**!

Paul: **You have interest** to chew at the bit waiting for him **to fold suitcases**. It's for this weekend, isn't it?

Anne: Yeah, but for the moment, I feel like he's going **to die of his pretty death** at my house. I've really **souped of it**, you know?

Paul: Say, is he still making **wire calls** abroad?

Anne: Absolutely not! I **put my veto** on that one. I wanted **to smother that in the egg** before it degenerates. I don't want **to wax the same button**, but he's **as stupid as his shoes**. Yesterday, he insisted on cooking and without **doing it on purpose**, he almost **made** the house **jump**!

Paul: He really **has nerve**. **Um**, Anne, um, try **to keep it cold**, but I think he's on the phone **of new**.

Anne: **That's the bouquet! His account is good! To us both**, old **unscrupulous man**!

Vocabulary

à lui le pompon *exp.* he takes the cake • (lit.): to him the pom-pom.

    example: Il a mangé tout notre dessert! *A lui le pompom!*

    as spoken: Il a mangé tout not' dessert! *A lui l'pompom!*

    translation: He ate all of our dessert! *He takes the cake!*

à nous deux *exp.* an expression used to signify one's intention to start a fight, "Let's take it outside," "Just you and me" • (lit.): to both of us.

    example: Tu oses m'insulter?! *A nous deux!*

    as spoken: T'oses m'insulter?! *A nous deux!*

    translation: How dare you insult me?! *C'm'on! You and me right now!*

c'est le bouquet! *exp.* that's the last straw! • (lit.): that's the bouquet!

    example: Il a pris ma voiture sans permission?! *C'est le bouquet,* ça!

    as spoken: Il a pris ma voiture sans permission?! *C'est l'bouquet,* ça!

    translation: He took my car without permission?! *That's the last straw!*

    SYNONYM: **c'est la fin des haricots!** *exp.* • (lit.): that's the end of the beans!

cirer toujours le même bouton *exp.* to harp on a subject • (lit.): always to wax the same button.

    example: Je ne veux pas *cirer toujours le même bouton,* mais tu ne m'écoutes jamais!

    as spoken: J'veux pas *cirer toujours le même bouton,* mais tu m'écoutes jamais!

    translation: I don't want *to keep harping all the time,* but you never listen to me!

couler douce (se la) *exp.* to have it easy • (lit.): to flow it sweetly.

    example: Il veut devenir riche pour *se la couler douce* un de ces jours.

    as spoken: Y̲ veut dev̲'nir riche pour s̲'la couler douce un d̲'ces jours.

    translation: He wants to become rich and *have it easy* one of these days.

coup de fil *exp.* telephone call • (lit.): wire call.

    example: Grégoire! Tu as un *coup de fil!*

    as spoken: Grégoire! T̲'as un *coup d̲'fil!*

    translation: Gregory! You have a *phone call!*

    NOTE: The previous expression, *"fil"* may be replaced with any number of slang synonyms for the word "telephone" such as: *bigophone, bigorneau, cornichon, escargot, phonard, ronfleur, télémuche, etc.*

culot (avoir du) *exp.* to have nerve.

    example: J'ai invité Rémy à manger chez moi et il n'a pas arrêté de critiquer le dîner. Qu'est-ce qu'il a *du culot,* lui!

    as spoken: J'ai invité Rémy à manger chez moi et il ~ a pas arrêté de critiquer l̲'dîner. Qu'est-c̲'qu'il a *du culot,* lui!

    translation: I invited Rémy to eat at my house and he didn't stop criticizing the dinner. Does he ever *have nerve!*

étouffer quelque chose dans l'œuf *exp.* to nip something in the bud • (lit.): to smother something in the egg (so that it can never become full grown).

    example: Elle pense qu'elle peut se servir de mes affaires comme ça? Je vais *étouffer ça dans l'œuf* tout de suite!

    as spoken: È̲ pense qu'è̲ peut s̲'servir d̲'mes affaires comme ça? J̲'vais *étouffer ça dans l'œuf* tout d̲'suite!

    translation: She thinks she can use my things just like that? I'm gonna *nip that in the bud* right now!

exprès (faire quelque chose) *exp.* to do something on purpose.

> example: Georgette a cassé mon poste de télévision et l'a *fait exprès!*
>
> as spoken: Georgette, <u>elle</u> a cassé mon poste <u>télé</u> et l'a *fait exprès!*
>
> translation: Georgette broke my television and did it *on purpose!*

fiche une rame (ne pas) *exp.* to be terribly lazy • (lit.): not to do an oar (that is, "an oar's worth of work," referring to someone who does not do his/her share of the work).

> example: Il est paresseux. Il *ne fiche pas une rame* toute le journeé.
>
> as spoken: Il est paresseux. <u>Y</u> ~ *fiche pas une rame* toute la journée.
>
> translation: He's lazy. He *doesn't lift a finger* all day.
>
> **NOTE:**   Oddly enough, "*fiche*" <u>is</u> a verb, although it does not have a traditional ending. "*Fiche*" has replaced the verb "*ficher*" which is a slang version of "*faire,*" meaning "to do/make."

fripouille *f.* a man without scruples, a shady character, a *snake.*

> example: Tu vas sortir avec Antoine? Je ne me fierais pas à cette *fripouille* si j'étais à ta place!
>
> as spoken: Tu vas sortir avec Antoine? Je <u>m'fi'</u>rais pas à <u>c</u>'te *fripouille* si j'étais à ta place!
>
> translation: You going out with Antoine? I wouldn't trust that *snake* if I were in your shoes!
>
> **NOTE:**   This term is slightly outdated yet is commonly heard used in jest or ironically.

garder froide (la) *exp.* to keep one's cool • (lit.): to keep it cool.

> example: Je sais que tu es fâché avec lui, mais essaie de *la garder froide* quand tu lui parleras.
>
> as spoken: Je sais <u>qu't</u>'es fâché avec lui, mais essaie <u>d'</u>*la garder froide* quand tu lui parleras.
>
> translation: I know you're angry at him, but try and *keep your cool* when you speak to him.

heu *interj. (pronounced "ø")* um.

> example: Au supermarché, je dois acheter du lait, des œufs, et *heu*... du pain.

> as spoken: Au supermarché, j̲'dois ac̲h̲'ter du lait, des œufs, et *heu*... du pain.

> translation: At the market, I have to buy some mike, some eggs, and *um*... some bread.

interêt à faire quelque chose (avoir) *exp.* to be better off doing something • (lit.): to have interest to do something.

> example: Tu *as interêt à* partir tout de suite. Sinon, tu risques d'être en retard.

> as spoken: T'*as interêt à* partir tout d̲'suite. Sinon, tu risques d'êt̲r̲'en r̲'tard.

> translation: You'd *better* leave right away. Otherwise, you run the risk of being late.

mettre son véto (y) *exp.* to draw the line, to put one's foot down • (lit.): to put one's veto there.

> example: Vous ne pouvez pas jouer au ballon dans la maison. Là, j'*y met mon véto*.

> as spoken: Vous ~ pouvez pas jouer au ballon dans la maison. Là, j'*y met mon véto*.

> translation: You can't play ball in the house. I'm *drawing the line* there.

mourir de sa belle mort *exp.* to die of old age • (lit.): to die of one's pretty death.

> example: Elle n'a jamais été malade. Elle est *morte de sa belle mort*.

> as spoken: Elle ~ a jamais été malade. Elle est *morte de sa belle mort*.

> translation: She's never been sick. She *died of old age*.

nouveau (de) *exp.* again • (lit.): of new.

> example: Demain, je vais faire du ski *de nouveau*.
>
> as spoken: Demain, j'vais faire du ski *d'nouveau*.
>
> translation: Tomorrow, I'm going skiing *again*.
>
> **NOTE:**   *de nouveau* = again • *à nouveau* = in a new and different way (*Je vais le faire à nouveau*; I'm going to go about it differently).

palmées (les avoir) *exp.* to be extremely lazy • (lit.): to have them (hands) webbed (and therefore unable to do any work).

> example: Elle ne m'aide jamais. Ce qu'elle *les a palmées*!
>
> as spoken: È m'aide jamais. C'qu'è *les a palmées*!
>
> translation: She never helps me. Is she ever *lazy*!
>
> **NOTE:**   **l'envers (les avoir à)** *exp.* • (lit.): to have them (hands) inside out.

perdre les pédales *exp.* to lose it (one's sanity and patience) • (lit.): to lose the pedals.

> example: S'il n'arrête pas de jouer cette musique de hardrock, je vais *perdre les pédales*!
>
> as spoken: S'y ~ arrête pas d'jouer c'te musique de hardrock, j'vais *perd' les pédales*!
>
> translation: If he doesn't stop playing that hardrock music, I'm gonna *lose it*!

piquer une ronflette *exp.* to take a nap • (lit.): to take a little snore.

> example: Je suis fatigué. Je crois que je vais *piquer une ronflette* pendant une heure.
>
> as spoken: J'suis fatigué. J'crois que j'vais *piquer une ronflette* pendant une heure.
>
> translation: I'm tired. I think I'll *take a little snooze* for an hour.
>
> **NOTE (1):**   The verb *"piquer"* has a slang meaning of "to take" or "to swipe." For example: *Qui a piqué mon stylo?*; Who took my pen?
>
> **NOTE (2):**   The feminin noun *ronflette* comes from the verb *ronfler*, meaning "to snore."

plier bagages *exp.* to leave, to scram • (lit.): to fold (up) suitcases.

      example:　On a finit de déjeuner, là. On *plie bagages*?

      as spoken:　On a finit d'déjeuner, là. On *plie bagages*?

      translation:　There! We're done with lunch. Let's *beat it*!

porté(e) sur quelque chose (être) *exp.* to be driven by something • (lit.): to be carried by something.

      example:　Il est *porté sur* la bouffe.

      as spoken:　[no change]

      translation:　He's *driven by* food.

      NOTE:　**bouffe** *f.* (very popular) food, grub • **bouffer** *v.* (very popular) to eat.

      SYNONYM:　**raffoler de quelque chose** *exp.* to be wild for something.

          example:　Je *raffole du* chocolat!

          as spoken:　J'*raffole du* chocolat!

          translation:　I'm *crazy for* chocolate!

pouvoir (ne plus en) *exp.* to be unable to stand it any longer • (lit.): to be no longer capable of it.

      example:　Il m'énerve sans arrêt. Je *n'en peux plus*!

      as spoken:　Y m'énerve sans arrêt. J'*en peux plus*!

      translation:　He bothers me nonstop. I *can't take it any more*!

remplir la bedaine (se) *exp.* to eat • (lit.): to fill one's gut.

      example:　Le dîner était excellent. Je *me suis bien rempli la bedaine* ce soir!

      as spoken:　Le dîner, il était excellent. Je *m'suis bien rempli la bedaine* c'soir!

      translation:　The dinner was excellent. I *really ate well* tonight.

ronger son frein *exp.* to keep one's self-control, to chomp at the bit •
(lit.): to chew one's bit.

>   example: Je *ronge mon frein* en attendant que mon argent arrive!

>   as spoken: J'*ronge mon frein* en attendant qu'<u>'</u>mon argent arrive!

>   translation: I'm *chomping at the bit* en waiting for my money to
>   arrive!

sauter (faire) *exp.* to blow up • (lit.): to make jump.

>   example: Pendant la manifestation, les étudiants ont *fait sauter* la
>   voiture du directeur.

>   as spoken: Pendant la <u>manif</u>, les étudiants, <u>y z'</u>ont *fait sauter* la
>   voiture du <u>dirlo</u>.

>   translation: During the demonstration, the students *blew up* the
>   principal's car.

serrer les fesses *exp.* to hang in there • (lit.): to squeeze the cheeks of
one's buttocks.

>   example: Tu vas demander au patron de t'augmenter? Bravo
>   pour toi! *Serre les fesses*!

>   as spoken: Tu vas <u>d'</u>mander au patron <u>d'</u>t'augmenter? Bravo pour
>   toi! *Serre les fesses*!

>   translation: You're going to ask the boss to give you a raise? Good
>   for you! *Be strong*!

>   **SYNONYM:**   **tenir bon** *exp.* to hold tight, to stick to your guns • (lit.):
>   to hold good.

son compte est bon! *exp.* he's/she's a dead duck! • (lit.): his/her
account is good!

>   example: Elle m'a trompé! *Son compte est bon*!

>   as spoken: <u>È</u> m'a trompé! *Son compte est bon*!

>   translation: She tricked me! *She's dead meat*!

soupé (en avoir) *exp.* to have had it, to be fed up • (lit.): to have souped from it.

example: Le professeur nous a donné encore des devoirs pour le weekend. J'*en ai soupé*, moi!

as spoken: Le <u>prof</u>, <u>y</u> nous a donné encore des <u>d</u>'voirs pour le weekend. J'*en ai soupé*, moi!

translation: The teacher gave us homework over the weekend again. I'm *fed up*!

NOTE: The noun *"professeur"* is always masculine even when referring to a woman. However, in its popular abbreviated form *"prof,"* it can be either masculine or feminine: *"le prof,"* *"la prof."*

SYNONYM: **ras le bol (en avoir)** *exp.* • (lit.): to have had it to the brim of the bowl.

Practice The Vocabulary

(Answers to Lesson 8, p. 258)

A. Underline the word that best completes the phrase.

1. Y fait rien toute la journée. Y s'la coule (**sucrée**, **douce**, **forte**) ici.

2. J'peux pas croire c'qu'il a fait! Son compte est (**médiocre**, **mauvais**, **bon**)!

3. J'(**ronge**, **mange**, **bois**) mon frein en attendant qu'il arrive.

4. Elle est bête comme ses (**chaussures**, **pieds**, **chaussettes**).

5. Il est tard. J'dois (**plier**, **couper**, **casser**) bagages.

6. Les enfants, y voulaient peindre sur les murs mais là, j'y ai mis mon (**œuf**, **véto**, **bouquet**)!

7. En faisant la cuisine, il a fait (**sauter**, **courir**, **marcher**) la maison!

8. J'peux plus l'supporter! J'perds les (**roues**, **pneus**, **pédales**)!

9. Il est paresseux. Y fiche pas la (**pédale**, **rame**, **lame**) toute la journée.

10. Il est (**transporté**, **porté**, **apporté**) sur la bouffe, lui!

11. J'ai fait la (**grasse**, **grosse**, **grande**) matinée. Maintenant, je m'sens en pleine forme!

12. Tu m'as insulté pour la dernière fois! A nous (**un**, **deux**, **trois**)!

13. Gisèle, elle a emprunté mon tricot sans m'demander. Elle a du (**compte**, **bouton**, **culot**), celle-là!

14. J'ai trop mangé. J'ai les (**bagages**, **bouquets**, **dents**) du fond qui baignent.

15. Regarde tous ces desserts! J'vais m'remplir la (**balle**, **boule**, **bedaine**)!

16. Y l'a pas fait (**express**, **expressions**, **exprès**). C'était un accident.

17. C't'une bonne question, mais (**hein**, **heu**, **aïe**), j'connais pas la réponse!

18. Ton bus, y va arriver à la gare dans dix minutes! T'as (**intéressé**, **intérêt**, **interférence**) à partir tout d'suite!

B. Complete the idioms by choosing the appropriate word from the list below.

bagages	**nouveau**
bouquet	**œuf**
bouton	**palmées**
compte	**pieds**
fil	**porté**
frein	**ronflette**
mort	**soupé**

1. Y mange constamment! Il est _____ sur la bouffe, lui!

2. Elle est bête comme ses _____ !

3. È fait rien toute la journée. È les a _____ .

4. Elle a fait quoi?! C'est le _____ !

5. J'suis fatigué, moi. J'vais piquer une _____ .

6. Y m'a fait une vach'rie! Son _____ est bon!

7. Hier, j'ai r'çu un coup d' _____ de mon frère. Y m'a téléphoné des Etas-Unis!

8. J'crois qu'y vont s'battre! Bon. J'vais l'étouffer dans l'_____ tout d'suite!

9. J'plie _____ . A d'main.

10. Si tu réussis pas la première fois, essaie de _____ .

11. Arrête de cirer toujours le même _____ !

12. J'ronge mon _____ an attendant d'ses nouvelles.

13. Elle avait quatre-vingt-dix ans. Elle est morte de sa belle _____ .

14. J'peux plus l'supporter! J'en ai _____ , moi!

C. CONTEXT EXERCISE
Choose the idiom from the right column that best defines the word(s) in italics from the left column.

☐ 1. Y *fait rien* toute la journée.

A. **A lui le pompon**

☐ 2. T'as l'air fatigué. Pourquoi pas *dormir un peu?*

B. **bête comme ses pieds**

☐ 3. J'ai faim. J'vais *manger.*

C. **de nouveau**

☐ 4. Je *ne peux plus le supporter!*

D. **me remplir la bedaine**

☐ 5. J'vais lui en parler *encore une fois.*

E. **n'en peux plus**

F. **ne fiche pas la rame**

☐ 6. J'dois *partir* tout d'suite.

G. **piquer une ronflette**

☐ 7. Il est *motivé par* la bouffe!

☐ 8. *Il est incroyable!*

H. **plier bagages**

☐ 9. Il est *très stupide.*

I. **porté sur**

☐ 10. Je *vais pas l'permettre.*

J. **vais y mettre mon véto**

DICTATION

Test Your Aural Comprehension.

If you are following along with your cassette, you will now hear a paragraph containing many of the idioms from this section. The paragraph will be read at normal conversational speed (which may actually seem fast to you at first). In addition, the words will be pronounced as you would actually hear them in a conversation, including many common reductions.

The first time the paragraph is presented, simply listen in order to get accustomed to the speed and heavy use of reductions. The paragraph will then be read again with a pause after each group of words to give you time to write down what you heard. The third time the paragraph is read, follow along with what you have written.

A CLOSER LOOK 1:

Slang and Idioms Used in the World of Movies and Theater

Slang has infiltrated just about every profession from the distinguished medical community to the flamboyant world of the performing arts. Depending upon whether you're in a pastry shop, a bookstore, at the races or in a casino at Monte Carlo, you will inevitably hear a different type of slang being spoken, since each group has created a "lingo" all its own.

The same certainly holds true in the English language. For instance, when speaking with a friend about a television show or movie, we might use expressions such as: *that show was a turkey, she brought the house down, he really bombed, what a flop, that actor's a real ham, he got panned by the critics, she can act circles around the others, she flubbed her lines,* etc.

In French slang, the movie and theater industries have inspired the creation of numerous words and expressions bound to be heard at any theatrical presentation. Once you've studied the following list, you'll know that if someone says that a movie is a real "turnip" or *navet,* you'd be better off not going!

acteuse *f.* actress devoid of talent.
SEE: *cabotin • panne • ringard • théâtreux, euse.*

balayer les planches *exp.* to act as the show opener • (lit.): to sweep the boards (of the stage).

bide (faire un) *exp.* to flop (on stage) • (lit.): to do a belly (flop) • *J'ai fait un bide hier soir;* I really flopped last night.

bouler *v.* to fluff (one's lines) • (lit.): to make a *boulette* meaning "blunder, mistake."

brûler les planches *exp.* to act with fire • (lit.): to burn the boards (of the stage).

cabotin *m.* bad or ham actor.
VARIATION: **cabot** *m.*
SEE: *acteuse • panne • ringard • théâtreux, euse.*

casser la baraque *exp.* to bring the house down • (lit.): to break the house.
NOTE: **baraque** *f.* (*extremely popular*) house.

casserole *f.* projector, spotlight • (lit.): casserole.

chahuter *v.* **1.** to boo. *L'acteur s'est fait chahuter par le public;* The actor got himself booed (off the stage) by the audience. • **2.** to make a lot of noise (used often in school). *Arrêtez de chahuter!;* Stop making such a racket!
SEE: *cueillir (se faire).*

chauffer une salle/auditoire *exp.* to warm up an audience • (lit.): to warm up a room.

couteau *m.* lead role • (lit.): knife.
NOTE: **couteau** *m.* head surgeon.

cueillir (se faire) *v.* **1.** to get booed, hissed • **2.** to get arrested • (lit.): to get oneself picked (over).
SEE: *chahuter.*

emboîter quelqu'un *v.* to boo, hiss someone • (lit.): to box up (in a coffin) • *L'acteur s'est fait emboîter;* The actor got himself booed at (or "put into a coffin" since he died a miserable death on stage).

éreinter *v.* to pan (an author, actor, book, etc) • (lit.): to exhaust • *L'actrice s'est fait éreinter par les critiques;* The actress got herself raked over the coals by the critics.

flop m. (Americanism) flop • La pièce a fait flop; The play was a total flop.
SEE: four.

four m. flop • J'ai fait four; I totally flopped.
SEE: flop.

frimant(e) f. bit player • (lit.): show-off.
SEE: frime (faire de la) • jouer les utilités • marcheur, euse • servir la soupe.

frime (faire de la) exp. to have walk-on parts • (lit.): to make pretense • Il fait de la frime; He's a bit player.
SEE: frimant(e) • jouer les utilités • marcheur, euse • servir la soupe.

guignol m. prompt box • (lit.): theater of puppets.

jouer avec ses tripes exp. to act with guts and feeling • (lit.): to act with one's guts.

jouer devant les banquettes vides exp. to play to an empty house • (lit.): to play before empty seats.

jouer les utilités exp. to play bit parts • (lit.): to play the utilities.
SEE: frime (faire de la) • frimant(e) • marcheur, euse • servir la soupe.

kilos (en faire des) exp. to overact, to be going at it too strongly • (lit.): to make a lot of kilos out of something (that should be "lighter") • Elle en fait des kilos, cette acteuse; That lousy actress is really overdoing it.

louper v. to flub a line or entrance • (lit.): to miss, fail.
NOTE: loup m. flubbed line or entrance.

malheur (faire un) exp. to be a big hit • (lit.): to do a misfortune • Félicitations! J'ai entendu dire que tu as fait un malheur!; Congratulations! I heard you were a hit!
SEE: tabac (faire un).

marcheur, euse n. walk-on, extra, bit player • (lit.): walker.
SEE: frime (faire de la) • frimant(e) • jouer les utilités • servir la soupe.

navet m. lousy film • (lit.): turnip • Quel navet!; What a turkey!

panne *f.* **1.** small part • *Je refuse de faire les pannes*; I refuse to do small parts • **2.** bad actor or actress.
SEE: *cabotin* • *acteuse* • *ringard* • *théâtreux, euse.*

paradis (le) *m.* the top balcony section of the theatre, the cheap seats • (lit.): heaven.

pastille *f.* microphone • (lit.): lozenge.

poulaille *f.* audience.
NOTE: This refers to the people who sit in the *poulailler*.
SEE: *poulailler.*

poulailler *m.* cheap balcony seats, "nose bleed section" • (lit.): hen house • *J'ai pris des places au poulailler*; I got some seats in the nose bleed section.

projo *m.* projector in a movie theater.

recevoir des pommes cuites *exp.* to get "tomatoes" thrown at oneself (due to a bad performance) • (lit.): to receive cooked apples (thrown by the audience).

recevoir son morceau de sucre *exp.* to be applauded the moment one first appears on stage, to have one's moment of glory • (lit.): to receive one's piece of sugar.

ringard *m.* bad actor.
NOTE: *ringard* *m.* hopeless individual, a real zero.
SEE: *cabotin* • *panne* • *acteuse* • *théâtreux, euse.*

sécher ses lignes *exp.* to forget one's lines • (lit.): to dry up one's lines.

servir la soupe *exp.* to take bit parts, to play small roles • (lit.): to serve soup.
SEE: *frime (faire de la)* • *frimant(e)* • *jouer les utilités* • *marcheur, euse.*

tabac (faire un) *exp.* to be a big hit • (lit.): to do a tobacco • *Elle a fait un tabac hier soir*; She was a big hit last night.
SEE: *malheur (faire un).*

télé *f.* abbreviation of *télévision.*

théâtreux, euse *n.* bad performer • (lit.): one who does theatrics.
SEE: *cabotin* • *panne* • *ringard* • *acteuse.*

trac (avoir le) *m.* to have stage fright • *Il refuse de monter sur la scène. Il a le trac!*; He refuses to go on stage. He has stage fright!

PRACTICE USING MOVIE AND THEATER SLANG

A. Match the columns.

☐ 1. bad or ham actor

A. **poulaille**

☐ 2. to get booed

B. **navet**

☐ 3. to be a complete flop

C. **cabotin**

☐ 4. lead role

D. **avoir le trac**

☐ 5. to be a big hit

E. **se faire chahuter**

☐ 6. to play bit parts

F. **recevoir des pommes cuites**

☐ 7. to bring the house down

G. **couteau**

☐ 8. audience

H. **faire un bide**

☐ 9. microphone

I. **jouer les utilités**

☐ 10. turkey of a film

J. **casser la baraque**

☐ 11. to get "tomatoes" thrown at oneself

K. **pastille**

☐ 12. to have stage fright

L. **faire un tabac**

A CLOSER LOOK 2:
The Language of "Verlan"

Slang was originally thought up as a way for crooks to make themselves unintelligible to the police. However, it didn't take long for this "secret" language to become unmasked. Something else had to be done. Thus emerged verlan. By the way, this is how pig-latin got its start! However, it must be stressed that, unlike pig-latin, *verlan* (as well as *largonji*, to be discussed later) is an actively spoken slang "language."

It merely consists of turning around the most important word (Usually a slang word) in the sentence. For instance, the slang word **falzar** meaning "pants" would become **zarfal**. In the heading itself, *verlan* is actually the reverse of *l'envers* meaning "the reverse." It became even more popular when the French slang singer Renaud released his popular song, **"Laisse béton"** which is *verlan* for *"Laisse tomber"* or "Let it drop." The existence of *verlan* takes slang one step further and makes it that much more interesting and fun. After having learned slang, you will find it easier and easier to recognize *verlan*. The following are a few well-known *verlan* transformations:

balpeau *adv.* nothing, "zip" • (lit.): skin of the ball.
> **ORIGIN:** *peau de balle.*

barjot *adj.* crazy, insane.
> **ORIGIN:** *jobard.*

beur *m.* Arab.
> **NOTE:** This term is considered very politically correct.
> **ORIGIN:** *Arabe* (pronounced: *Ara-beuh*) becomes *beuh-ara* in verlan. As it so often the case in colloquial speech, a shortcut (or reduction) in pronunciation was made, creating *beur*.

bléca (être) *adj.* to be trendy, "with it" • (lit.): to be plugged in or "cabled."
> **ORIGIN:** *être cablé(e).*

brelica *m.* revolver.
> **ORIGIN:** *calibre.*

cecla *f.* class.
> **ORIGIN:** *classe.*

chébran (être) *adj.* to be trendy, "with it" • (lit.): to be plugged in.
> **ORIGIN:** *être branché(e).*

cinepi *f.* swimming pool.
> **ORIGIN:** *piscine.*

deban f. group (of friends, for example).
ORIGIN: *bande.*

féca m. café.
ORIGIN: *café.*

fumpar (être au) exp. to be up-to-date • (lit.): to be in the perfume.
ORIGIN: *être au parfum.*

jourbon interj. hello.
ORIGIN: *bonjour.*

keuf m. police officer.
NOTE: This is a *verlan* transformation of *flic*, an extremely popular term meaning "police officer." Although backwards, *flic* should be pronounced *kiffe*, the French tend to attach an "euh" sound (pronounced: ø as in sœur) to many words which then becomes part of the verlan transformation as seen in the case of *Arabe = beur* on the previous page. For this reason *flic* (commonly pronounced: "flic-euh") is pronounced "k<u>euf</u>."

laisse béton exp. just forget about it, drop it.
ORIGIN: *laisse tomber.*

lépou m. (derogatory) police officer, "pig" • (lit.): chicken.
ORIGIN: *poulet.*

looc adj. great, "cool."
ORIGIN: *cool* (borrowed from English).

meuf f. woman, wife.
NOTE: This is a *verlan* transformation of *femme*. Since *femme* is commonly pronounced "fam-euh," it has become part of the verlan transformation, creating *meuf*.

ouf adj. crazy.
ORIGIN: *fou.*

péclot f. cigarette.
ORIGIN: *clope* (extremely popular).

pera (le) m. rap music.
ORIGIN: *le rap* (borrowed from English).

quèm m. guy, "dude."
ORIGIN: *mec* (extremely popular).
NOTE: An accent grave (è) is used in order to retain the sound of the "e" in the word "mec."

raquebar f. house • (lit.): barracks.
ORIGIN: *baraque* (extremely popular).

rempa m.pl. parents.
ORIGIN: *parents.*

reuf m. brother.
> **ORIGIN:** *frère*. Since *frère* is commonly pronounced "*frèr-euh*," it has become part of the verlan transformation, creating *reuf*.

reup m. father.
> **ORIGIN:** *père*.

reus f. sister.
> **ORIGIN:** *sœur*.

ripou adj. rotten, corrupt.
> **ORIGIN:** *pourri*.

siquemu f. music.
> **ORIGIN:** *musique*.

sub m. bus.
> **ORIGIN:** *bus*.

tarcol (être dans le) exp. to be exhausted.
> **ORIGIN:** *être dans le coltar*.

tirape v. to leave (*Le train est tirapé;* The train left).
> **ORIGIN:** *partir*.

tisor v. to leave.
> **ORIGIN:** *sortir*.

tromé m. subway.
> **ORIGIN:** *métro*.

zesgon f. girl, "chick."
> **ORIGIN:** *gonzesse* (extremely popular).

PRACTICE "VERLAN"

A. Below is a list of words transformed into verlan.

(1) Write down the original word;

(2) Write down its English translation.

Example:

balpeau:

(1) *peau de balle*

(2) *nothing*

1. **brelica**:

    (1)_____   (2)_____

2. **être au fumpar**:

    (1)_____   (2)_____

3. **lépou**:

    (1)_____   (2)_____

4. **péclot**:

    (1)_____   (2)_____

5. **quèm**:

    (1)_____   (2)_____

6. **zesgon**:

    (1)_____   (2)_____

7. **raquebar**:

    (1)_____   (2)_____

8. **être dans le tarcol**:

    (1)_____   (2)_____

9. **zarfal**:

    (1)_____   (2)_____

10. **meuf**:

    (1)_____   (2)_____

11. **barjot**:

    (1)_____   (2)_____

12. **ripou**:

    (1)_____   (2)_____

B. Fill in the blank with the appropriate word from the list below.

balpeau	lépou	raquebar
barjot	meuf	tarcol
brelica	péclot	zarfal
fumpar	quèm	zesgon

1. J'habite dans une grande _____ .

2. Pour mon anniversaire, on m'a donné _____ !

3. Tu savais pas qu'il est mort? T'es pas au _____ ?

4. Il a pris son _____ et l'a tué!

5. Voleur! Appelle un _____ !

6, Ce _____-là, c'est mon prof d'anglais.

7. J'te présente ma _____ et nos enfants.

8. J'vais m'coucher. J'suis dans le _____ .

9. Tu m'passes une _____ , s'te plaît? J'ai envie d'fumer.

10. Elle est bien roulée, c'te _____ .

11. Il est _____ . Y s'parle tout l'temps!

12. Aujourd'hui, j'vais porter mon nouveau _____ .

J'en ai gros sur la patate.

(trans.): I have a lot on my mind.
(lit.): I have a lot of it on my potato.

Leçon Neuf

J'en ai gros sur la patate

Martine: **On dirait que** tu **n'es pas dans ton assiette** aujourd'hui. Tu **en as gros sur la patate**?

Lise: Non, ce n'est pas ça. La semaine dernière, j'étais pratiquemment **à l'article de la mort**. Je me suis tapé **une fièvre de cheval** pendant quatre jours. J'étais presque à penser que j'allais **passer l'arme à gauche**! Petit à petit, je commence à **retrouver mes forces**. Je suis sûre que je serai **d'attaque** dans quelques jours. C'est la première fois depuis deux semaines que je m'entraîne.

Martine: Dans ce cas, vas-y **mollo** aujourd'hui. Après tout, tu ne veux pas **te claquer un muscle**.

Lise: **Sans rigoler**! **Il ne me manquerait plus que ça**. Tiens! Regarde le costume qu'elle porte, Jeannette. Elle est presque **à poil**. Un petit coup de vent lui décrocherait le maillot.

Martine: Je dois t'avouer qu'elle me **tape sur le système**, celle-là. Elle **ne se prend pas pour de la petite bière**, c'est sûr.

Lise: Mais avec **les jambes en parenthèses** qu'elle a, c'est un miracle qu'elle se tienne encore debout!

Martine: Oh, tu es **vache** et c'est si bon! Hé! Regarde ces deux là qui **roulent des biscottos**. Je crois qu'ils **font de l'œil à** Jeanette!

Lise: Mais non! Tu es **à côté de la plaque**! Ils **la mettent en boîte** comme le reste de la **gym**!

Leçon Neuf

Translation in English

I've got a lot on my mind

Martine: **It looks like** you're **out of it** today. You **have a lot on your mind**?

Lize: No, it's not that. Last week, I was practically **at death's door**. I had **a fever that was sky high** for four days. I was beginning to think that I was gonna **croak**! Little by little, I'm starting **to get back to my old self**. I'm sure I'll be **up and at 'em** in a few days. This is the first time in two weeks that I've worked out.

Martine: In that case, go at it **easy** today. After all, you don't want **to pull a muscle**.

Lize: **You're not kidding**! **I'd need that like a hole in the head**. Hey! Look at the costume Jeannette's wearing. She's practically **in the raw**. A little breeze would rip off her t-shirt.

Martine: I have to admit she **gets on my nerves**, that one. She's **stuck up**, that's for sure.

Lize: But with **those bowed legs** of hers, it's a miracle she's still standing.

Martine: Oh, you're **mean** but it sure fits! Hey! Look at those guys **flexing their biceps**. I think they're **giving Jeannette the eye**!

Lize: No way! You're **out of your mind**! They're **making fun of her** like the rest of the **gym**!

Dialogue in slang as it would be spoken

J'en ai gros sur la patate

Martine: **On dirait qu'** t'**es pas dans ton assiette** aujourd'hui. T'**en as gros sur la patate**?

Lise: Non, c'est pas ça. La s'maine dernière, j'étais pratiquemment **à l'article d'la mort**. Je m'suis tapé **une fièv' de ch'val** pendant quat' jours. J'étais presque à penser qu'j'allais **passer l'arme à gauche**! P'tit à p'tit, j'commence à **retrouver mes forces**. J'suis sûre que je s'rai **d'attaque** dans quèques jours. C'est la première fois depuis deux s'maines que j'm'entraîne.

Martine: Dans ce cas, vas-y **mollo** aujourd'hui. Après tout, tu veux pas **t'claquer un muscle**.

Lise: **Sans rigoler**! **Y m'manqu'rait pu qu'ça**. Tiens! Regarde le costume qu'è porte, Jeannette. Elle est presque **à poil**. Un p'tit coup d'vent lui décroch'rait l'maillot.

Martine: J'dois t'avouer qu'è m'**tape sur le système**, celle-là. **È s'prend pas pour d'la p'tite bière**, c'est sûr.

Lise: Mais avec **les jambes en parenthèses** qu'elle a, c't'un miracle qu'è s'tienne encore debout!

Martine: Oh, t'es **vache** et c'est si bon! Hé! Regarde ces deux là qui **roulent des biscottos**. J'crois qu'y **font d'l'œil à** Jeannette!

Lise: Mais non! T'es **à côté d'la plaque**! Y **la mettent en boîte** comme le reste de la **gym**!

Leçon Neuf

Literal Translation

I have a lot of it on my potato

Martine: **One would say that** you're **not in your plate** today. You **have a lot of it on the potato**?

Lize: No, it's not that. Last week, I was practically **at the end of the roller**. I had **a horse's fever** for four days. I thought I was going to **pass my firearm to the left**! Little by little, I'm starting **to find my forces again**. I'm sure I'll be **of attack** in a few days. This is the first time I've worked out in two weeks.

Martine: In that case, go at it **mellow** today. After all, you don't want **to burst a muscle**.

Lize: **Without laughing**! **The last thing I need is that**. Hey! Look at the costume Jeannette's wearing. She's practically **to hair**. A little wind would rip off her t-shirt.

Martine: I have to admit that she **hits on my system**. She **doesn't take herself for a little beer**, that's for sure.

Lize: But with **the legs like parentheses** that she has, it's a miracle she's still standing!

Martine: Oh, you're **cow(-like)** and it's so good! Hey! Look at those guys **rolling their biceps**. I think they're **making some eye** at Jeannette!

Lize: But no! You're **next to the plaque**! They're **putting her in a box** like the rest of the gym!

Vocabulary

article de la mort (être à l') *exp.* to be at death's door • (lit.): to be at the article of death.

> example: Tu devrais lui rendre visite dès aujourd'hui. Je crois qu'il est *à l'article de la mort.*
>
> as spoken: Tu d'vrais lui rend' visite dès aujourd'hui. J'crois qu'il est *à l'artic' d'la mort.*
>
> translation: You should go pay him a visit today. I think he's *at death's door.*
>
> **SYNONYM:** **bout du rouleau (être au)** *exp.* • (lit.): to be at the end of the roller.

attaque (être d') *exp.* to be going strong • (lit.): to be of attack.

> example: Ma grand-mère a quatre-vingt ans mais elle est toujours *d'attaque.*
>
> as spoken: Ma grand-mère, elle a quatre-vingt ans mais elle est toujours *d'attaque.*
>
> translation: My grandmother is eighty years old but she's still *going strong.*

claquer un muscle (se) *exp.* to pull a muscle • (lit.): to burst a muscle.

> example: Quand j'ai essayé de bouger mon réfrigérateur, je *me suis claqué un muscle.*
>
> as spoken: Quand j'ai essayé d'bouger mon frigo, je *m'suis claqué un muscle.*
>
> translation: When I tried to move my refrigerator, I *pulled a muscle.*

côté de la plaque (être à) *exp.* to be out of one's mind (lit.): to be next to the plaque.

>   example: Si tu penses que je vais prêter du fric à Augustin, tu es *à côté de la plaque*! Il ne m'a jamais remboursé la dernière fois.

>   as spoken: Si tu penses que j'vais prêter du fric à Augustin, t'es *à côté d'la plaque*! Y ~ m'a jamais remboursé la dernière fois.

>   translation: If you think I'm going to lend money to Augustin, you're *out of your mind*. He never reimbursed me the last time.

>   **NOTE:** **fric** *m.* *(extremely popular)* money.

dans son assiette (ne pas être) *exp.* to be out of it, not to be with it • (lit.): not to be in one's plate.

>   example: Je ne suis pas *dans mon assiette* aujourd'hui. J'ai trop d'ennuis.

>   as spoken: J'suis pas *dans mon assiette* aujourd'hui. J'ai trop d'ennuis.

>   translation: I'm *out of it* today. I have too many worries.

>   **SYNONYM:** **sentir tout chose (se)** *exp.* • (lit.): to feel all thing.

fièvre de cheval (avoir une) *exp.* to have a high fever • (lit.): to have a horse's fever.

>   example: Je ne peux pas t'accompagner au cinéma ce soir. J'ai une *fièvre de cheval*.

>   as spoken: J'peux pas t'accompagner au ciné c'soir. J'ai une *fièu' de ch'val*.

>   translation: I can't go with you to the movies tonight. I have a *raging fever*.

gros sur la patate (en avoir) *exp.* to have a lot on one's mind •
(lit.): to have a lot of it on the head.

        example: Je ne peux pas me concentrer sur mon travail. J'*en ai*
                            gros sur la patate.

        as spoken: J'peux pas m'concentrer sur mon travail. J'*en ai gros sur*
                            la patate.

        translation: I can't concentrate on my work. I *have a lot on my mind.*

        NOTE: **patate** *f.* head • (lit.): potato.

gym *f.* a common abbreviation of "*gymnase*" meaning "gym" or
"gymnasium."

        example: Je vais à la *gym* cinq fois par semaine pour m'entraîner.

        as spoken: J'vais à la *gym* cinq fois par s'maine pour m'entraîner.

        translation: I go to the *gym* five days a week to work out.

jambes en parenthèses (avoir les) *exp.* to be bow-legged •
(lit.): to have legs like parentheses.

        example: Regarde comment il a *les jambes en parenthèses.* Il doit
                            monter à cheval. C'est un vrai cowboy!

        as spoken: Regarde comment il a *les jambes en parenthèses.* Y doit
                            monter à ch'val. C't'un vrai cowboy!

        translation: Look at those *bowed legs.* He must ride horses. He's a
                            real cowboy!

manquer plus que ça *exp.* to be the one thing one needs • (lit.): not
to miss any more than that.

        example: Mes invités arrivent dans une heure et mon four vient
                            de cesser de fonctionner. *Il ne me manquait plus que ça!*

        as spoken: Mes invités, y z'arrivent dans une heure et mon four, y
                            vient d'cesser d'fonctionner. *Y ~ m'manquait pu qu'ça!*

        translation: My guests are arriving in an hour and my oven just
                            stopped working. *I need this like a hole in the head.*

mettre quelqu'un en boîte *exp.* to make fun of someone • (lit.): to put someone in a box.

> example: Je ne peux pas sortir avec cette nouvelle coupe de cheveux. C'est affreux! Tout le monde va *me mettre en boîte*!

> as spoken: J'peux pas sortir avec c'te nouvelle coupe de ch'veux. C't'affreux! Tout l'monde va *m'mettr'en boîte*!

> translation: I can't go out with this new haircut. It's horrible! Everyone's going to *make fun of me*!

mollo *exp.* carefully and slowly • (lit.): [no literal translation].

> example: Tu vas jouer au football? Vas-y *mollo*, hein? Tu as été malade pendant une semaine.

> as spoken: Tu vas jouer au foot? Vas-y *mollo*, hein? T'as été malade pendant une s'maine.

> translation: You're going to play soccer? Take it *easy*, huh? You've been sick for a week.

œil à quelqu'un (faire de l') *exp.* to give someone the eye • (lit.): to make the eye to someone.

> example: Il te *fait de l'œil*! Va lui parler!

> as spoken: Y t'*fait d'l'œil*! Va lui parler!

> translation: He's *giving you the eye*! Go talk to him!

On dirait que... *exp.* "It looks like..." • (lit.): "One would say that..."

> example: *On dirait qu'*il va pleuvoir.

> as spoken: *On dirait qu'*y va pleuvoir.

> translation: *It looks like* it's going to rain.

passer l'arme à gauche *exp.* to die, to kick the bucket • (lit.): to pass the firearm to the left.

> example: Que j'étais malade hier soir. Je pensais que j'allais *passer l'arme à gauche*.

as spoken: Que j'étais malade hier soir. J'pensais qu'j'allais *passer l'arme à gauche.*

translation: Was I ever sick last night. I thought I was gonna *kick the bucket.*

SYNONYM: **avaler son extrait de naissance** *exp.* • (lit.): to swallow one's birth certificate.

poil (être à) *exp.* to be butt naked • (lit.): to be to [the] hair.

example: Dans les colonies de nudistes, tout le monde est complètement *à poil.*

as spoken: Dans les colonies d'nudistes, tout l'monde est complètement *à poil.*

translation: In nudist camps, everyone is completely *naked.*

prendre pour de la petite bière (ne pas se) *exp.* said of someone who is conceited • (lit.): not to take oneself for a small beer.

example: Cette vedette-là *ne se prend pas pour de la petite bière.*

as spoken: Cette vedette-là, è ~ *s'prend pas pour d'la p'tite bière.*

translation: That movie star *is so conceited.*

ANTONYM: **terre à terre (être)** *exp.* to be down to earth • (lit.): to be earth to earth.

retrouver ses forces *exp.* to get back to one's old self again (after an illness) • (lit.): to find one's forces again.

example: Petit à petit, je *retrouve mes forces* après l'opération.

as spoken: P'tit à p'tit, je r'trouve mes forces après l'opération.

translation: Little by little, I'm *getting back to my old self* after the operation.

rouler des biscottos *exp.* to flex one's biceps • (lit.): to roll one's biceps.

example: Regarde cet athlète-là. Il *roule des biscottos.*

as spoken: Regarde c't'athlète-là. Y *roule des biscottos.*

translation: Look at that athlete. He's *flexing his biceps.*

NOTE: **biscotto** *m.* bicep.

sans rigoler *exp.* no kidding • (lit.): without laughing.

> example: Tu as trouvé mille francs? *Sans rigoler?*

> as spoken: T'as trouvé mille francs? *Sans rigoler?*

> translation: You found a thousand francs? *No kidding?*

> **SYNONYM:** **sans blague** *exp.* • (lit.): without joke.

taper sur le système à quelqu'un *exp.* to bug someone, to get on someone's nerves • (lit.): to hit on someone's system.

> example: Je ne veux pas l'inviter à ma soirée. Elle me *tape sur le système.* Elle parle sans arrêt!

> as spoken: J'veux pas l'inviter à ma soirée. È m'*tape sur l'système.* È parle sans arrêt!

> translation: I don't want to invite her to my party. She *gets on my nerves.* She talks nonstop!

> **SYNONYM (1):** **taper sur les nerfs à quelqu'un** *exp.* • (lit.): to hit on someone's nerves.

> **SYNONYM (2):** **casser les pieds à quelqu'un** *exp.* • (lit.): to break someone's feet.

vache *adj. (extremely popular)* mean, nasty • (lit.): cow.

> example: Daniel était de mauvaise humeur aujourd'hui. Il a été *vache* envers moi pour aucune raison!

> as spoken: Daniel, il était d'mauvaise humeur aujourd'hui. Il a été *vache* envers moi pour aucune raison!

> translation: Daniel was in a bad mood today. He was *nasty* to me for no reason!

> **NOTE:** **Oh, la vache!** *exclam.* Wow!

> example: *Oh, la vache!* Tu as vu les prix dans ce restaurant? Ils sont astronomiques!

> as spoken: *Oh, la vache!* T'as vu les prix dans c'resto? Y sont astronomiques!

> translation: *Wow!* Did you see the prices at this restaurant? They're sky-high!

Practice The Vocabulary

(Answers to Lesson 9, p. 260)

A. CROSSWORD
Fill in the crossword puzzle on the opposite page by choosing the correct word(s) from the list below.

ARTICLE	**CLAQUER**	**PLAQUE**
ASSIETTE	**FORCES**	**POIL**
ATTAQUE	**GAUCHE**	**RIGOLER**
BIERE	**MOLLO**	**SYSTEME**
CHEVAL	**PARENTHESES**	**VACHE**

ACROSS

20. Tu vas soul'ver ça? Attention d'ne pas t' _____ un muscle!

21. Normalement, j'suis très énergique. Mais aujourd'hui, j'suis pas dans mon _____ .

40. Regarde c'ui-là! Y descend la montagne sans skis! Il est à côté d'la _____ , non?

45. Oh, c'te musique, elle est trop forte! È m'tape sur l' _____ !

50. Antoine, y va s'marier?! Sans _____ ?

56. C't'un verre en cristal que tu laves? Vas-y _____ , hein? Tu veux pas l'casser!

DOWN

5. Je m'sens beaucoup mieux après l'opération. J'commence à retrouver mes _____ .

12. Mon oncle, il est à l'hôpital. Il est à l'_____ d'la mort.

18. J'étais tellement malade que j'pensais qu'j'allais passer l'arme à _____ .

19. Regarde comment è marche. Elle a les jambes en _____ .

27. J'aime pas c'te prof. Elle est toujours _____ envers nous!

30. Hier j'étais fatigué toute la journée. Aujourd'hui, j'suis d'_____ !

38. J'peux pas sortir c'soir. J'ai une fièvre de _____ .

39. Elle est très prétentieuse. È s'prend pas pour d'la p'tite _____ .

47. Tu peux pas sortir comme ça! T'es presque à _____ !

CROSSWORD PUZZLE

B. Choose the correct phrase that best fits the idiom.

1. **Y roule les biscottos.**
   - ☐ a. Quels muscles!
   - ☐ b. Quelle intelligence!

2. **È s'prend pas pour d'la p'tite bière!**
   - ☐ a. Elle est très gentille.
   - ☐ b. Elle est très prétentieuse.

3. **Vas-y mollo!**
   - ☐ a. Tu veux pas l'casser!
   - ☐ b. T'as l'air triste.

4. **J'commence à retrouver mes forces.**
   - ☐ a. Je m'sens beaucoup mieux.
   - ☐ b. J'aime pas voyager.

5. **J'ai failli passé l'arme à gauche.**
   - ☐ a. Que j'étais content!
   - ☐ b. Que j'étais malade!

6. **È préfère êtr' à poil.**
   - ☐ a. Elle adore porter les vêtements.
   - ☐ b. Elle aime pas porter les vêtements.

7. **J'suis en froid avec elle.**
   - ☐ a. On s'parle tout l'temps.
   - ☐ b. On s'parle plus.

8. **Y m'tape sur le système!**
   - ☐ a. J'peux pas l'supporter!
   - ☐ b. C'est mon meilleur ami!

9. **J'crois qu'elle est à côté d'la plaque.**
   - ☐ a. Elle a toujours été charmante.
   - ☐ b. Elle a toujours été bizarre.

10. **J'ai une fièvre de ch'val.**
    - ☐ a. J'suis très malade.
    - ☐ b. J'suis en bonne santé.

C. Complete the dialogue using the appropriate idioms from the list below.

arme	claquer	patate
article	dirait	plaque
assiette	forces	poil
attaque	gym	rigoler
bière	manquerait	système
biscottos	mollo	vache
boîte	œil	
cheval	parenthèses	

Martine: On **(1)**_____que tu n'es pas dans ton **(2)**_____

aujourd'hui. Tu en as gros sur la **(3)**_____?

Lise: Non, ce n'est pas ça. La semaine dernière, j'étais pratiquemment

à l'**(4)**_____de la mort. Je me suis tapé une fièvre de

(5)_____pendant quatre jours. J'étais presque à

penser que j'allais passer l'**(6)**_____à gauche! Petit à petit,

je commence à retrouver mes **(7)**_____. Je suis

sûre que je serai d'**(8)**_____dans quelques jours.

C'est la première fois depuis deux semaines que je m'entraîne.

Martine: Dans ce cas, vas-y **(9)**_____aujourd'hui. Après tout, tu

ne veux pas te **(10)**_____un muscle.

Lise: Sans **(11)**_____! Il ne me **(12)**_____

plus que ça. Tiens! Regarde le costume qu'elle porte, Jeannette.

Elle est presque à **(13)**_____. Un petit coup de vent

lui décrocherait le maillot.

Martine: Je dois t'avouer qu'elle me tape sur le **(14)** _____,

         celle-là. Elle ne se prend pas pour de la petite **(15)** _____,

         c'est sûr.

Lise: Mais avec les jambes en **(16)** _____ qu'elle a,

         c'est un miracle qu'elle se tienne encore debout!

Martine: Oh, tu es **(17)** _____ et c'est si bon! Hé! Regarde ces

         deux là qui roulent des **(18)** _____. Je crois qu'ils

         font de l'**(19)** _____ à Jeanette!

Lise: Mais non! Tu es à côté de la **(20)** _____! Ils la mettent

         en **(21)** _____ comme le reste de la **(22)** _____!

DICTATION
Test Your Aural Comprehension.

If you are following along with your cassette, you will now hear a paragraph containing many of the idioms from this section. The paragraph will be read at normal conversational speed (which may actually seem fast to you at first). In addition, the words will be pronounced as you would actually hear them in a conversation, including many common reductions.

The first time the paragraph is presented, simply listen in order to get accustomed to the speed and heavy use of reductions. The paragraph will then be read again with a pause after each group of words to give you time to write down what you heard. The third time the paragraph is read, follow along with what you have written.

A CLOSER LOOK 1:

Slang Terms of Affection

Throughout the world, the French are well known for being hopeless romantics. In fact, I don't know of any other language that has such a variety of slang terms of endearment. All of the words in the main list below are used to mean "my sweetheart." However, for added passion, you may insert *petit(e)* before any one of these nouns:

ma poule ⇒ ***ma petite poule***

my hen ⇒ my little hen

If you want to get even "mushier," you may rearticulate the first syllable of the noun (the more common ones are given in the main list below):

ma petite poule ⇒ ***ma petite poupoule***

my little hen ⇒ my little "henny-wenny"

You can even take this sweetness one step further by adding *en sucre* (of sugar) to any of these:

ma petite poupoule ⇒ ***ma petite poupoule en sucre***

my little "henny-wenny" ⇒ my little sugar "henny-wenny"

Now, if you want to get positively saccharine, you can use the "mushier" form of *sucre* which becomes *susucre:*

ma petite poupoule en sucre ⇒ ***ma petite poupoule en susucre***

my little sugar "henny-wenny" ⇒ my little "sugary-wugary henny-wenny"

If your teeth managed to survive all that sweetness, you're ready to delve right in. Remember, any one of the following terms can be custom tailored:

mon bellot *m.* • (lit.): my pretty one.

> **NOTE:** This comes from the feminine adjective *belle* meaning "pretty."

ma bellotte *f.* the feminine form of *mon bellot.*

ma biche *f.* my sweetheart • (lit.): my doe.

ma bibiche *f.* my sweetie pie.
NOTE: *bibiche* is an affectionate variation of the feminine noun *biche* meaning "doe."

mon biquet *m.* • (lit.): my young (male) goat, kid.

ma biquette *f.* • (lit.): my young (female) goat, kid.

ma bobonne *f.* my "wifey" • (lit.): my goody-good.
NOTE: This comes from the feminine adjective *bonne* meaning "good."

mon canard *m.* • (lit.): my duck.

mon chien *m.* • (lit.): my dog.

ma chocotte *f.* my sweety pie.

mon chou *m.* • (lit.): my cream puff (from *choux à la crème*).

mon chou en sucre *m.* • (lit.): my sugar cream puff.

mon chou en susucre *m.* • (lit.): my sugar cream puff.
NOTE: *susucre* is an affectionate variation of the masculine noun *sucre* meaning "sugar."

mon chouchou *m.* my sweetheart; my favorite • (lit.): my cream puff.
NOTE: *chouchou* is an affectionate variation of the masculine noun *chou* meaning "cream puff."

ma chouchoute *f.* the feminine form of : *mon chouchou.*

ma choute *f.* the feminine form of: *mon chou.*

mon coco *m.* my sweetheart.

ma cocotte *f.* the feminine form of: *mon chou.*

mon lapin *m.* • (lit.): my rabbit.

mon loulou *m.* my sweetheart.

ma louloute *f.* the feminine form of: *mon loulou.*

mon mimi *m.* my sweetheart.

ma mimine *f.* the feminine form of: *mon mimi.*

mon minet *m.* • (lit.): my pussycat.

ma minette *f.* the feminine form of: *mon minet.*

ma minoche *f.* • (lit.): my pussycat.
NOTE: This is a slang variation of *minet* since *minoche* was created by using the slang suffix *-oche.*

ma poule *f.* • (lit.): my hen.

mon poulet *m.* • (lit.): my chicken.

ma poulette *f.* • (lit.): my little hen.

ma poupoule *f.* • (lit.): my little hen.
NOTE: *poupoule* is an affectionate variation of the feminine noun *poule* meaning "hen."

mon poussin *m.* • (lit.): my chick.

ma puce *f.* • (lit.): my flea.

mon rat *m.*• (lit.): my rat.
VARIATION: **mon petit rat** *m.*

mon raton *m.* • (lit.): my little rat.
VARIATION: **mon petit raton** *m.*

ma totoche *f.* my sweetie pie.

mon trésor *m.* • (lit.): my treasure.

PRACTICE SLANG TERMS OF AFFECTION.

A. Give the feminine form of each.

1. mon bellot:

   _____

2. mon biquet:

   _____

3. mon chou:

   _____

4. mon chouchou:

_____

5. mon coco:

_____

6. mon loulou:

_____

7. mon mimi:

_____

8. mon poulet:

_____

A CLOSER LOOK 2:
The Language of Largonji

Longonji is another interesting "language" that has produced many slang words in French. It consists of replacing the first letter of the word with the letter "l" and putting that first letter at the end of the word. Then the suffix **i**, **ic**, **é**, **èm**, **gue**, **ot**, **que**, or **uche** is generally attached. Therefore, you can start to see that the word *largonji* is merely the word *"jargon"* transformed by this formula.

Largonji takes slang one step further in that it not only rearranges the words as does *verlan*, but it also adds an extra suffix to make the recognition of the word that much more difficult...which is just what crooks wanted!

The following are some common results of *largonji*:

à loilpé, **à loilpuche** *adv.*
    naked • (lit.): to the hair.
    ORIGIN: *à poil.*

lacsé *m.* ten francs • (lit.): sack.
    ORIGIN: *sac.*

lamefé *f.* woman/wife.
    ORIGIN: *femme.*
    NOTE: The letter *"a"* in *lamefé* was added to retain the first *"e"* sound in femme (pronounced "fahme").

larteaumic *m.* crazy •
(lit.): hammer.
ORIGIN: *marteau.*

lateaubèm *m.* boat.
ORIGIN: *bateau.*

latrompèm *m.* boss.
ORIGIN: *patron.*

laubé, laubiche *adj.*
handsome.
ORIGIN: *beau.*

lerche, lerchot, lerchèm *adj.*
expensive.
ORIGIN: *cher.*

leurrebèm *m.* money •
(lit.): butter.
ORIGIN: *beurre.*

linvé *m.* a 20-franc piece •
(lit.): twenty.
ORIGIN: *vingt.*

listrobèm *m.* café.
ORIGIN: *bistrot.*

loinqué *m.* corner.
ORIGIN: *coin.*

loubé *m.* end.
ORIGIN: *bout.*

loucedoc (en) *adv.* quietly.
ORIGIN: *en douce.*

loucherbèm *m.* butcher.
ORIGIN: *boucher.*

louf, loufoque, louftingue
adj. crazy.
ORIGIN: *fou.*

PRACTICE "LARGONJI"

A. Below is a list of words transformed into largonji.

(1) Write down the original word;

(2) Write down its English translation.

Example:

à loilpé
(1) à poil
(2) naked

1. larteaumic

   _____

   _____

2. lamefé

   _____

   _____

3. lacsé

   _____

   _____

4. loubé

   _____

   _____

5. lateaubèm

   _____

   _____

6. laubiche

   _____

   _____

7. lerche

   _____

   _____

8. leurrebèm

   _____

   _____

9. linvé

   _____

   _____

10. listrobèm

    _____

    _____

B. Fill in the blank with the appropriate word from the list below:

lacsé   **lerche**   **loucedoc**
lamefé   **listrobèm**   **loucherbèm**
laubiche   **loinqué**   **loufoque**

1. Regarde c'te nana...è s'parle! Mais elle est _____ !

2. Not' prof de français, il est tellement _____ ! Y d'vrait êt'
   mannequin!

3. J'habite au _____ d'la rue.

4. Mais si, il est marié! Jeanette, c'est sa _____ .

5. J'veux pas qu'y nous entende. Parlons en _____ .

6. Son père, c't'un _____ . C'est pour ça on mange si
   bien chez lui!

7. J'ai soif, moi. Tu veux m'accompagner au _____ ?

8. Tu peux m'prêter un _____ ?

9. Mais, ça coûte _____ , c'truc!

Elle est enceinte jusqu'aux dents!

(trans.): *She's pregnant out to here!*
(lit.): *She's pregant up to her teeth!*

Dialogue in slang

Elle est enceinte jusqu'aux dents!

Michèle:	Dis-moi. Tu n'es que **l'ombre de toi-meme**! **Quoi de neuf**?
Suzanne:	Mais, ça **crève les yeux**!
Michèle:	Que je suis bête! Je **n'ai pas les yeux en face des trous** aujourd'hui. Qu'il est adorable ton nouveau bébé! Tu sais, c'est le **portrait tout craché de son père**. Et bien sûr, il n'a pas encore de **pavé dans la cour**! Je pourrais **le manger tout cru**. Alors, racontes-moi. Tout s'est passé **sans histoire**?
Suzanne:	Pas exactement. **Au plus profond de la nuit** je me suis réveillé en sachant que c'était **l'heure H**. Mais je suis restée **maîtresse de la situation**. J'ai **pris mes cliques et mes claques** et on a **mis les bouts** pour arriver **dans les délais**. Pas de **veine**. Il y avait un accident sur l'autoroute! Donc, **pour éponger le retard**, Robert **a donné plein gaz**. Il **prenait les virages sur les chapeaux de roues**! J'étais **blanche comme un cachet d'aspirine**. Tu penses comme **je n'en menais pas large**! J'ai finalement insisté pour qu'il ralentisse parce que je n'avais pas envie de **mordre la poussière** en route! Juste à ce moment-là, on s'est fait arrêter. Le **flic** pouvait bien voir que j'étais **enceinte jusqu'aux dents** mais c'était **clair comme de l'eau de roche** qu'il voulait **appliquer le règlement** et comptait nous **coller une prune**. Mais quand j'ai **crié à tue-tête** au cours d'une contraction, je crois qu'il a pris peur et nous a **laissé déguerpir**.
Michèle:	Mais, c'est malin, ça! Quelle **combine** pour **s'en tirer à bon compte**! Qu'est-ce qui s'est passé ensuite?
Suzanne:	On est arrivé à l'hôpital avec juste cinq minutes **de rab**! Quelle aventure! Mais je **m'en suis tirée haut la main**. Et admire le résultat!

Translation in English

She's pregnant out to here!

Michèle: You're **a shadow of your former self! What's new**?

Suzanne: It's **staring you in the face**!

Michèle: Am I ever a moron! I'm **not with it** today. Your new baby is so cute! You know, he's the **spitting image of** his father. And of course, he doesn't have **a single tooth**! I couldn't just **eat him up**! So, tell me. Everything went **without a hitch**.

Suzanne: Not exactly. **In the middle of the night** I woke up knowing that it was **the big moment**! But I remained **in control of the situation**. I **grabbed all my things**, and we **took off immediately** in order to arrive **in time**. No **luck**. There was an accident on the freeway! So, **to make up for lost time**, Robert **gave it the gas**. He **was going around curves at lightening speed**! I was **as white as a ghost**. I thought I thought **I was going to lose it**! Finally, I insisted that he slow down because I didn't feel like **biting the dust** on the way there! At that very moment, we got stopped. The **cop** could easily see that I was **pregnant out to here** but it was clear he wanted **to go by the book** and planned on **sticking us with a ticket**. But when I **screamed at the top of my lungs** during a contraction, I think he got scared and let us **take off fast**.

Michèle: That's really clever! What a **good trick** to **get off the hook**! What happened next?

Suzanne: We arrived at the hospital with just five minutes **to spare**! What an adventure! But I **came through with flying colors**. And just look at the result!

Leçon Dix 🔲

Dialogue in slang as it would be spoken

Elle est enceinte jusqu'aux dents!

Michèle: T'es que **l'ombre de toi-meme! Quoi d'neuf**?

Suzanne: Mais, ça **crève les yeux**!

Michèle: Que j'suis bête! **J'ai pas les yeux en face des trous** aujourd'hui. Qu'il est adorable ton nouveau bébé! Tu sais, c'est l'**portrait tout craché d'son père**. Et bien sûr, il a pas encore de **pavé dans la cour**! J'pourrais l'**manger tout cru**. Alors, racontes-moi. Tout s'est passé **sans histoire**?

Suzanne: Pas exactement. **Au plus profond d'la nuit** je m'suis réveillé en sachant qu'c'était **l'heure H**. Mais j'suis restée **maîtresse de la situation**. J'ai **pris mes cliques et mes claques** et on a **mis les bouts** pour arriver **dans les délais**. Pas d'**veine**. Il avait un accident sur l'autoroute! Donc, **pour éponger le r'tard**, Robert, il **a donné plein gaz**. Y **prenait les virages sur les chapeaux d'roues**! J'étais **blanche comme un cachet d'aspirine**. Tu penses comme **j'en m'nais pas large**. J'ai finalement insisté pour qu'y ralentisse pasque j'avais pas envie d'**mord' la poussière** en route! Juste à c'moment-là, on s'est fait arrêter. Le **flic**, y pouvait bien voir que j'étais **enceinte jusqu'aux dents** mais c'était **clair comme de l'eau d'roche** qu'y voulait **appliquer l'règlement** et comptait nous **coller une prune**. Mais quand j'ai **crié à tue-tête** au cours d'une contraction, j'crois qu'il a pris peur et nous a **laissé déguerpir**.

Michèle: Mais, c'est malin, ça! Quelle **combine** pour **s'en tirer à bon compte**! Qu'est-c'qui s'est passé ensuite?

Suzanne: On est arrivé à l'hôpital avec juste cinq minutes **de rab**! Quelle aventure! Mais j'**en suis tirée haut la main**. Et admire le résultat!

Leçon Dix

Literal Translation

She's pregnant up to her teeth!

Michèle: You're **nothing but a shadow of yourself**. **What of new**?

Suzanne: **It's puncturing your eyes**!

Michèle: Oh, I'm stupid! I **don't have eyes in front of their holes** today. Your new baby's so cute! You know, he's the **portrait all spit of** his father. And of course, he doesn't have **any flagstones in the courtyard**! So, tell me. Everything went **without a story**?

Suzanne: Not exactly. **In the deepest of the night** I woke up knowing that it was the **H hour**. But I remained **mistress of the situation**. I **took my odds and ends**, and we **put the ends together** in order to arrive **in the delays**. No **luck**. There was an accident on the freeway! So, **to sponge up the tardiness**, Robert **gave full gas**. He **took the curves on the hats of the tires**! I was **white as an aspirin tablet**. Imagine how **I wasn't leading large**. I finally insisted that he slow down because I didn't feel like **biting the dust** on the road! Just at that moment, we got stopped. The **cop** could easily see that I was **pregnant up to my teeth** but it was **clear as rock water** that he wanted **to apply the rule** and counted on **sticking us with a plum**. But when I **screamed to kill one's head** during a contraction, I think he got scared and **let us go**.

Michèle: That's really clever! What a **trick** to **pull oneself out to a good accounting**! What happened next?

Suzanne: We arrived at the hospital with just five minutes **more**! What an adventure! But I **pulled myself out with the hand high**. And admire the result!

Vocabulary

appliquer le règlement *exp.* to go by the book • (lit.): to apply the rule.

> example: J'ai expliqué au professeur que je n'ai pas pu faire mes devoirs parce que j'avais attrapé la grippe, mais il ne fait pas d'exceptions. Il est connu pour *appliquer le règlement*.

> as spoken: J'ai <u>es</u>piqué au <u>prof</u> que <u>j'</u>ai pas pu faire mes <u>d'</u>voirs <u>pasque</u> j'avais attrapé la grippe, mais <u>y</u> ~ fait pas d'exceptions. Il est connu pour *appliquer le règlement*.

> translation: I explained to the teacher that I couldn't do my homework because I had caught the flu, but he doesn't make any exceptions. He's known for *going by the book*.

arriver dans les délais *exp.* to arrive on time • (lit.): to arrive in the delays.

> example: La circulation sur l'autoroute était horrible ce matin. Heureusement, je suis *arrivé à l'aéroport dans les délais!*

> as spoken: La circulation sur l'autoroute, <u>elle</u> était horrible <u>c'</u>matin. Heureusement, <u>j'</u>suis *arrivé à l'aéroport dans les délais!*

> translation: The traffic on the freeway was horrible today. Luckily, I *made it to the airport on time!*

blanc(he) comme un cachet d'aspirine (être) *exp.* to be as white as a ghost (from shock) • (lit) to be as white as an aspirin tablet.

> example: Quand j'ai appris la nouvelle, j'étais *blanc comme un cachet d'aspirine!*

> as spoken: [no change]

> translation: When I heard the news, I turned *white as a ghost!*

coller une prune à quelqu'un *exp.* to give someone a traffic citation • (lit.): to stick a plum to someone.

example: Je *me suis fait coller une prune* aujourd'hui pour avoir dépassé la limite de vitesse.

as spoken: Je *m'suis fait coller une prune* aujourd'hui pour avoir dépassé la limite de vitesse.

translation: I *got a ticket* today for going over the speed limit.

NOTE (1): **prune** *f.* traffic citation • (lit.): plum.

NOTE (2): The term *prune* falls into the category of *faux amis* ("false friends") referring to the many words which resemble English words but have different definitions. For example: *prune* = plum; *pruneau* = prune.

combine *f.* said of a clever ploy or scheme.

example: Je connais la *combine* pour entrer au cinéma sans payer. Suis-moi!

as spoken: J'connais la *combine* pour entrer au *ciné* sans payer. Suis-moi!

translation: I know a *ploy* to get us into the movie theater without paying. Follow me!

crever les yeux *exp.* to be obvious • (lit.): to puncture the eyes.

example: "Pourquoi es-tu si heureuse ce matin?"
"Ça *crève les yeux!* Tu n'as pas remarqué la bague de fiançailles que Xavier m'a donné?!"

as spoken: "Pourquoi *t'*es si heureuse *c'*matin?"
"Ça *crève les yeux!* *T'*as pas *r'*marqué la bague de fiançailles que Xavier m'a donné?!"

translation: "Why are you so happy this morning?"
"*It's staring you in the face!* Didn't you notice the engagement ring Xavier gave me?"

NOTE: **crever** *v.* to die.

example: Je *crève* de faim!
as spoken: J'*crève* de faim!
translation: I'm *dying* of hungar!

crier à tue-tête *exp.* to scream at the top of one's lungs • (lit.): to scream to the point of killing one's head.

> example: J'ai du mal à dormir parce que j'ai des voisins qui *crient à tue-tête* à toute heure de la nuit.

> as spoken: J'ai du mal à dormir <u>pasque</u> j'ai des voisins qui *crient à tue-tête* à toute heure <u>d'</u>la nuit.

> translation: I have trouble sleeping because my neighbors *scream at the top of their lungs* at all hours of the night.

déguerpir *v.* to leave quickly.

> example: Nous devons *déguerpir* tout de suite pour arriver chez eux à l'heure.

> as spoken: Nous <u>d'</u>vons *déguerpir* tout <u>d'</u>suite pour arriver chez eux à l'heure.

> translation: We have *to leave* right away in order to get to their house on time.

> **NOTE:**   **à l'heure** *exp.* on time • (lit.): at the hour.

enceinte jusqu'aux dents (être) *exp.* to be pregnant out to here • (lit.): to be pregnant up to one's teeth.

> example: Ma mère était *enceinte jusqu'aux dents* mais même le docteur ne savait pas qu'elle allait accoucher de jumeaux!

> as spoken: Ma mère, <u>elle</u> était *enceinte jusqu'aux dents* mais même le docteur, <u>y</u> ~ savait pas qu'<u>elle</u> allait accoucher de jumeaux!

> translation: My mother was *pregnant out to here* but even the doctor didn't know she was going to have twins.

éponger un retard *exp.* to make up for lost time • (lit.): to sponge up a tardiness.

> example: Vite! Il faut *éponger le retard*!

> as spoken: Vite! ~ Faut *éponger le r'tard*!

> translation: Hurry! We have *to make up for lost time*!

flic *f.* *(extremely popular)* police officer, "cop."

> example: Mais qu'est-ce qui se passe ici? Il y a des *flics* partout!

> as spoken: Mais qu'est-c'qui s'passe ici? Y a des *flics* partout!

> translation: What's going on here? There are *cops* everywhere!

> **SYNONYM:** **flicard** *m.* • (lit.): [no literal translation].

heure H (l') *exp.* said of an important moment, "the big moment" • "H" hour.

> example: Les acteurs! Vous êtes tous à vos places? La pièce va commencer. C'est *l'heure H*!

> as spoken: Les acteurs! Vous êtes tous à vos places? La pièce, è va commencer. C'est *l'heure H*!

> translation: Actors! Are you all in your places? The play is about to begin. It's *the big moment*!

> **NOTE:** **jour J** *exp.* D-day

maître/maîtresse de la situation (être) *exp.* to be in control of the situation • (lit.): to be master/mistress of the situation.

> example: Après le désastre, je suis resté *maître de la situation*. Je n'ai jamais paniqué.

> as spoken: Après l'désastre, j'suis resté *maître d'la situation*. J'ai jamais paniqué.

> translation: Afer the disaster, I remained *in complete control*. I never panicked.

manger quelqu'un tout cru (pouvoir) *exp.* to devour someone with the eyes, to eat someone up • (lit.): to eat someone totally raw.

> example: Il est adorable, votre bébé! Je pourrais le *manger tout cru*!

> as spoken: Il est adorable, votre bébé! J'pourrais l'*manger tout cru*!

> translation: Your children are adorable! I could just *eat him up*!

mener large (ne pas en) *exp.* to be very upset, not to know which way to turn • (lit.): not to lead some wide.

>   example: Je n'ai pas assez de fric pour payer mon loyer ce mois. Je *n'en mène pas large!*

>   as spoken: J'ai pas assez d'fric pour payer mon loyer ce mois. J'en *mène pas large!*

>   translation: I don't have enough money to pay the rent this month. I'm *freaking out!*

>   **NOTE:** Notice the construction of the phrase above, "*payer mon loyer*," not "*payer pour mon loyer*," a common mistake made by many Americans.

mettre les bouts *exp.* to leave • (lit.): to put the ends (together).

>   example: Pascale a *mis les bouts* sans me dire au revoir!

>   as spoken: Pascale, il a *mis les bouts* sans m'dire au revoir!

>   translation: Pascale *took off* without saying good-bye to me!

>   **SYNONYM:** **prendre la tangeante** *exp.* • (lit.): to take the tangent.

mordre la poussière *exp.* to bite the dust • (lit.): [no change].

>   example: En redescendant de la montagne, j'ai *mordu la poussière* quand j'ai glissé sur un caillou.

>   as spoken: En r'descendant d'la montagne, j'ai *mordu la poussière* quand j'ai glissé sur un caillou.

>   translation: Coming back down the mountain, I *bit the dust* when I slipped on a stone.

ombre de soi-meme (n'être que l') *exp.* to be but a shadow of one's (former) self • (lit); [no change].

>   example: Est-ce que tu as été malade? Tu *n'es que l'ombre de toi-même!*

>   as spoken: T'as été malade? T'es *que l'ombre de toi-même!*

>   translation: Have you been sick? You're nothing but *a shadow of your former self!*

pavé dans la cour (avoir du) *exp.* to have teeth • (lit.): to have flagstones in the courtyard.

> example: Mon grand-père *n'a pas de pavé dans la cour.*
>
> as spoken: Mon grand-père, <u>il</u> ~ a pas <u>d'</u>pavé dans la cour.
>
> translation: My grandfather *doesn't have a tooth in his head.*

plus profond de la nuit (au) *exp.* in the dead of night • (lit.): at the deepest of the night.

> example: *Au plus profond de la nuit,* j'ai entendu un bruit sourd au salon! C'était le chien qui avait renversé un fauteuil.
>
> as spoken: *Au plus profond <u>d'</u>la nuit,* j'ai entendu un bruit sourd au salon! C'était <u>l'</u>chien qui avait renversé un fauteuil.
>
> translation: *In the dead of night,* I heard a thud in the living room! It was the dog who had turned over an armchair.

portrait tout craché de quelqu'un (être le) *exp.* to be the spitting image of someone • (lit.): to be the portrait all spit of someone.

> example: Tu es le *portrait tout craché* de ton père.
>
> as spoken: <u>T'</u>es <u>l'</u>portrait tout craché <u>d'</u>ton père.
>
> translation: He's the *spit and image* of his father.

prendre ses cliques et ses claques *exp.* to take one's personal belongings • (lit.): to take one's "this and that."

> example: *Prends tes cliques et tes claques* et déguérpis!
>
> as spoken: [no change]
>
> translation: *Take your things* and get out of here!

quoi de neuf? *exp.* what's new? • (lit.): what of new?

> example: Salut Etienne! *Quoi de neuf?*
>
> as spoken: Salut Etienne! *Quoi <u>d'</u>neuf?*
>
> translation: Hi Steve! *What's new?*
>
> **SYNONYM:** **qu'est-ce qu'il y a de nouveau?** *exp.* • (lit.): what is there of new?

rab (de) *exp. (borrowed from Arabic)* to spare • (lit.): more.

> example: On est arrivé au théâtre avec deux minutes *de rab*.
>
> as spoken: [no change]
>
> translation: We arrived at the theater with two minutes *to spare*.
>
> > **NOTE:** This expression is also commonly used to mean "more." For example:
> >
> > > example: Je veux des pommes de terre *de rab*.
> > >
> > > as spoken: J'veux des pommes de terre *de rab*.
> > >
> > > translation: I want some *more* potatoes.
> > >
> > > **SUB-NOTE:** This expression may also be used in front of the object, but note the resulting changes to the articles! For example:
> > >
> > > > example: Je veux **du** rab **de** pommes de terre.

sans histoire(s) *exp.* without a problem • (lit.): without a story.

> example: La construction de la maison s'est passée *sans histoires*.
>
> as spoken: La construction d'la maison, è s'est passée *sans histoires*.
>
> translation: The construction of the house went without *a hitch*.

tirer à bon compte (s'en) *exp.* to get off easy (cheap) • (lit) to pull oneself out of it at good accounting.

> example: Il a démoli la bagnole, mais lui *s'en est tiré à bon compte*!
>
> as spoken: Il a démoli la bagnole, mais lui, y *s'en est tiré à bon compte*!
>
> translation: He totaled the car, but he *got out unscathed*.
>
> **SYNONYM:** **être quitte à bon compte (en)** *exp.* • (lit.): to be even at good accounting.

tirer haut la main (s'en) *exp.* to come through with flying colors • (lit.): to pull oneself out of it with the hand high.

> example: L'examen était difficile, mais je *m'en suis tiré haut la main*.
>
> as spoken: L'exam, il était difficile, mais j'm'en suis tiré *haut la main*.
>
> translation: The exam was difficult, but I *came through with flying colors*.

veine (avoir de la) *exp.* to be lucky.

> example: Tu as gagné au loto? Mais tu as de la *veine*, toi!

> as spoken: T'as gagné au loto? Mais t'as d'la *veine*, toi!

> translation: You won the lottery? Do you ever have *luck*!

> **ANTONYM:** **déveine (avoir la)** *exp.* to be unlucky.

>> **SUB-NOTE:** Note that in the expression "*avoir la déveine*" that the article "*de*" is dropped, whereas "*avoir **de** la veine*" keeps the article "*de.*"

virages sur les chapeaux de roues (prendre les) *exp.* to take curves at a high speed • to take curves on the wheel covers.

> example: Il conduit trop vite. Il *prend toujours les virages sur les chapeaux de roues.*

> as spoken: Y conduit trop vite. Y *prend toujours les virages sur les chapeaux d'roues.*

> translation: He drive too fast. He *always takes curves at high speed.*

yeux en face des trous (ne pas avoir les) *exp.* to be unaware, out of it • (lit.): not to have eyes in front of their holes (or sockets).

> example: Tu n'as pas vu Georges à la soirée? Mais il était droit devant toi pendant une demi-heure! Tu *n'avais pas les yeux en face des trous* hier soir!

> as spoken: T'as pas vu Georges à la soirée? Mais il était droite devant toi pendant une demi-heure! T'*avais pas les yeux en face des trous* hier soir!

> translation: You didn't see George at the party? He was right in front of you for a half hour! You were *really out of it* last night!

Practice The Vocabulary

(Answers to Lesson 10, p. 259)

A. Were the following idioms used correctly or incorrectly?

1. C'est l'**portrait tout craché** d'son père. Y s'ressemblent beaucoup!
   ☐ correct usage   ☐ incorrect usage

2. Elle est **enceinte jusqu'aux dents**. È d'vrait s'mettre au régime.
   ☐ correct usage   ☐ incorrect usage

3. En conduisant à l'hôpital, Robert, il a **donné plein gaz**. Evidemment, il était pas pressé!
   ☐ correct usage   ☐ incorrect usage

4. **J'm'en suis tiré haut la main**. J'ai complètement échoué.
   ☐ correct usage   ☐ incorrect usage

5. Antoine, il était **maître d'la situation**. Y savait exactement quoi faire.
   ☐ correct usage   ☐ incorrect usage

6. Il est tard. J'dois **mett' les bouts**.
   ☐ correct usage   ☐ incorrect usage

7. Elle a **crié à tue-tête**. J'avais du mal à l'entendre!
   ☐ correct usage   ☐ incorrect usage

8. J'dois partir. **Quoi d'neuf**?
   ☐ correct usage   ☐ incorrect usage

9. **Au plus profond d'la nuit**, j'suis allé à la plage pour me bronzer.
   ☐ correct usage   ☐ incorrect usage

10. Ton bébé, il a pas d'**pavé dans la cour**! J'me d'mande comment il arrive à manger!
    ☐ correct usage   ☐ incorrect usage

B. Underline the appropriate word that best completes the phrase.

1. T'as été malade ou quoi? T'es que l'(**ombrelle**, **ombre**, **omelette**) de toi-même.

2. J'suis arrivé à l'hôpital avec juste trois minutes de (**rabbin**, **rab**, **rage**).

3. Salut Madeleine! T'es ici depuis longtemps? J'ai pas les (**jambes**, **yeux**, **mains**) en face des trous aujourd'hui!

4. Les invités, y viennent d'arriver. C'est l'heure (**J**, **D**, **H**)!

5. Ce p'tit chien, il est adorable! J'pourrais l'manger tout (**nu**, **lu**, **cru**)!

6. Si tu conduis comme ça, tu vas t'faire coller une (**prune**, **pomme**, **poire**).

7. En faisant du ski, j'ai failli (**mordre**, **manger**, **boire**) la poussière.

8. Vite! Faut éponger le (**gaz**, **retard**, **règlement**)!

9. J'dois partir! Laisse-moi (**déguiser**, **déguster**, **déguerpir**).

10. Tu comprends pas?! Mais c'est clair comme de l'eau de (**rocher**, **caillou**, **roche**)!

11. Mais regarde le ventre de cette dame-là! Elle est enceinte jusqu'aux (**yeux**, **dents**, **bras**)!

12. La réponse, elle est évidente. Ça crève les (**yeux**, **oreilles**, **bras**)!

C. Choose the most appropriate definition of the words in boldface.

1. Laurent, il a pris ses **cliques et ses claques** en disant qu'y voulait jamais rev'nir!
   ☐ a. personal belongings
   ☐ b. keys

2. Tu sais pas pourquoi Irène, è s'fâche avec toi? **Ça crève les yeux**!
   ☐ a. I'm tired
   ☐ b. It's staring you in the face

3. J'ai entendu un bruit qui m'a réveillé **au plus profond d'la nuit**.
   ☐ a. in the early evening
   ☐ b. in the middle of the night

4. J'**m'en suis tiré à bon compte**!
   ☐ a. have a huge bank account
   ☐ b. got off easy

5. **Quoi d'neuf?**
   ☐ a. Is that new?
   ☐ b. What's new?

6. Le prof, il **applique toujours le règlement**. Si tu fais pas tes d'voirs, y t'puni. Il accepte pas d'excuses!
   ☐ a. always goes by the book
   ☐ b. got off easy

7. Quand j'ai vu l'cambrioleur, j'ai **crié à tue-tête**!
   ☐ a. cried for a long time
   ☐ b. screamed at the top of my lungs

8. Ma mère, è va m'rencontrer à la bibliothèque à midi. J'dois **mett' les bouts** tout d'suite si j'veux pas être en r'tard.
   ☐ a. to arrive soon
   ☐ b. to leave

9. Vite! Faut **éponger le retard**!
   ☐ a. to make up for lost time
   ☐ b. clean up this mess

10. Regarde sa bouche! Y a pas d'doute. C'est l'**portrait tout craché** d'sa mère.
    ☐ a. spitting image
    ☐ b. painting

DICTATION
Test Your Aural Comprehension.

If you are following along with your cassette, you will now hear a paragraph containing many of the idioms from this section. The paragraph will be read at normal conversational speed (which may actually seem fast to you at first). In addition, the words will be pronounced as you would actually hear them in a conversation, including many common reductions.

The first time the paragraph is presented, simply listen in order to get accustomed to the speed and heavy use of reductions. The paragraph will then be read again with a pause after each group of words to give you time to write down what you heard. The third time the paragraph is read, follow along with what you have written.

A CLOSER LOOK:
Surely You Gesture!

Most people think of the Italians as cornering the market on gestures and all the dramatics that go along with them. The French certainly hold their own in expression themselves nonverbally and seem to include a great deal of slang in many of their gestures:

A. "That person's drunk!"

As learned in lesson four, the adjective *rond(e)*, whose meaning is literally "round," is commonly used in slang to mean "drunk." As well known as this slang adjective is the gesture which conveys this condition:

- Make a fist.

- Hold it up against the tip of your nose with your little finger farthest away from you.

- Now twist your fist as if you were tightening the tip of your nose.

B. "That's crazy!"

The expression *ça ne tourne pas rond* is also used to refer to one's brain in which the "wheels" aren't turning. The gesture for this is similar to the American gesture of "crazy" in which the index finger is held a few inches away from the ear then circles the outline of the ear several times. In French, it's a little more subtle:

- Holding your index finger straight, place the very tip of your finger against your temple.

- Make sure the pad of your finger is facing slightly forward.

- Now twist the pad of your finger down and slightly back.

C. "My eye!"

In English, when someone tries to pull the wool over our eyes by recounting something ludicrous, we may respond with the expression "My foot!" However, the French decided to go in the opposite direction…up to the "eye." *Mon œil* is extremely popular in France as is its gesture:

- Put your index finger just underneath your lower eyelid.

- Now pull down slightly.

D. "What are you talking about?!"

This gesture may be used in place of the gesture for *Mon œil;* however, it is much more subtle. The gesture for *Mon œil* is used to let the other person know that what he/she has just said is absolutely and undeniably hogwash, whereas the gesture for "What are you talking about?" lets him know that if he doesn't clear up what he's talking about, he will be on the verge of getting a *Mon œil!*:

- Simply cock your head to the left or right with an expression of "Oh, brother!" on your face.

E. "Beats me!"

A gesture which is constantly encountered in France, especially when asking for directions, is the one for "I dunno" or "Beats me!" It's a lovely little number that can be accessorized beautifully:

The basic gesture

- Protrude your lower lip slightly past your upper lip to form a tight pout.
- Make sure to hold the lips tightly together as you force out a quick *"ppp"* sound.

Add one or all of the following as you do the "ppp" sound:
- Lift your eye brows.
- Push your head slightly forward.
- Lift your shoulders.

Now…go for broke!

Doing all of the above at the same time is *extremely* common, which will probably be proven by the first person who can't give you directions once in Paris. However, occasionally you will encounter the *pièce de résistance* in which all of the above ingredients will be mixed together along with one another:

- Hold the palms of your hands facing upward and level to the outside of your shoulders.
- Now, as you make the *"ppp"* sound, lift your eyebrows, push your head slightly forward, and lift your shoulders and simply push the palms of your hands upward slightly.

F. "Nothing!"

The next one is a common insulting gesture in Italy. However, in French this gesture simply means "Absolutely nothing!" For example, if someone asks you what you got for your birthday and your reply is "Zip! Zero! Not a thing!" this gesture would come in quite handy:

- Make a fist holding your thumb on the side of your index finger.

- Place the nail of your thumb behind your front teeth.

- Now quickly force the thumb forward making a clicking sound.

G. Count with your fingers like the French

"Holding up two fingers to indicate that I want two of a certain item couldn't be easier. Then why do I keep getting *three*?" Simply…your thumb is being counted as well! In France and almost all of Europe, the thumb starts off the countdown and the little finger ends it:

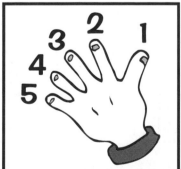

PRACTICE YOUR GESTURES

A. Write down what each gesture represents under the illustration.

1. _____

2. _____

3. _____

4. _____

5. _____

6. _____

REVIEW EXAM FOR LESSONS 6-10

(Answers to Review, p. 245)

A. Underline the appropriate word that best completes the phrase.

1. A (**un**, **deux**, **trois**) on se distrait, à (**un**, **deux**, **trois**) on s'ennuie.

2. Laurent, y m'a fait sa (**gueule**, **déclaration**, **peau neuve**)! On va s'marier dans trois mois!

3. Christine, elle a (**l'étoffe**, **le tissu**, **les vêtements**) d'un bon médecin.

4. Plus on est de fous, plus on (**pleure**, **sourit**, **rit**).

5. Paul, y m'a laissé en (**bouteille**, **verre**, **carafe**). Ça fait deux s'maines que j'l'ai pas vu.

6. C't'un secret. Motus et (**tête**, **jambe**, **bouche**) cousue!

7. J'peux pas l'croire! J'en reste comme deux ronds d'(**flan**, **gélatine**, **pains**)!

8. Pauvre Hélène. È file un mauvais (**tricot**, **coton**, **pullover**).

9. C'te robe, è coûte la peau des (**fesses**, **joues**, **yeux**)!

10. Y parle sans arrêt. Faut dire qu'il a pas la (**bouche**, **langue**, **voix**) dans sa poche.

B. Complete the following phrases by choosing the appropriate word(s) from the list below. Give the correct form of the verb.

bagages	exprès	pain
bedaine	fesses	palmées
douce	feu	pédales
envie	mal	véto

1. J'meurs d'_____ d'aller en Europe un d'ces jours.

2. C't'un très bon restaurant. Y z'ont pas _____ de desserts!

3. Tes parents, y sont millionnaires? T'as ton _____ cuit, toi!

4. J'suis épuisé après avoir fait du babysitting pour ma p'tite nièce. È pète le _____. J'ai dû courir après elle sans arrêt!

5. C't'hôtel, il est fabuleux. On s'la coule _____ ici.

6. C'était un accident. J'suis certain qu'y l'a pas fait _____.

7. Mes p'tits cousins, y voulaient jouer dans mon bureau. Là, j'y ai mis mon _____.

8. Faut être au cinéma dans vingt minutes. On plie _____?

9. Tu peux l'faire. Serres les _____!

10. Le dîner, il était excellent. Je m'suis bien rempli la _____.

11. Ce bruit, y m'rend fou! J'commence à perdre les _____!

12. È fait rien toute la journée. È les a _____, celle-là!

C. CROSSWORD PUZZLE
Fill in the crossword puzzle on page 249 by choosing from the list below.

ASPIRINE	CLIQUES	MAIN	PROFOND
ASSIETTE	COMBINE	MORT	RAB
BIERE	COMPTE	PEDALES	SYSTEME
BOITE	CULOT	PLAQUE	TETE
BOUQUET	EPONGER	POIL	VEINE
BOUTON	FIL	POMPON	YEUX
BOUTS	GAUCHE	PORTRAIT	
CHEVAL	LARGE	POUSSIERE	

ACROSS

14. _____**(être à)** *exp.* to be butt naked.

15. **mettre les** _____ *exp.* to leave.

20. **mordre la** _____ *exp.* to bite the dust.

26. _____**(de)** *exp.* *(borrowed from Arabic)* to spare.

27. **une** _____ *f.* a clever ploy or scheme.

34. **prendre pour de la petite** _____**(ne pas se)** *exp.* said of someone who is conceited.

36. **mener** _____**(ne pas en)** *exp.* to be very upset, not to know which way to turn.

40. **crier à tue-**_____ *exp.* to scream at the top of one's lungs.

46. **tirer haut la** _____**(s'en)** *exp.* to come through with flying colors.

47. **prendre ses** _____**et mes claques** *exp.* to take one's personal belongings.

51. _____**(avoir de la)** *exp.* to be lucky.

52. **perdre les** _____ *exp.* to lose it (one's sanity and patience).

58. **crever les** _____ *exp.* to be obvious.

60. **cirer toujours le même** _____ *exp*. to harp on a subject.

69. **fièvre de** _____**(avoir une)** *exp*. to have a high fever.

75. **mettre quelqu'un en** _____ *exp*. to make fun of someone.

80. **à lui le** _____ *exp*. he takes the cake.

DOWN

8. **coup de** _____ *exp*. telephone call.

11. **mourir de sa belle** _____ *exp*. to die of old age.

12. **blanc(he) comme un cachet d'**_____**(être)** *exp*. to be as white as a ghost (from shock).

13. **c'est le** _____**!** *exp*. that's the last straw!.

14. _____**tout craché de quelqu'un (être le)** *exp*. to be the spitting image of someone.

17. **dans son** _____**(ne pas être)** *exp*. to be out of it, not to be with it.

27. _____**(avoir du)** *exp*. to have nerve.

35. _____**un retard** *exp*. to make up for lost time.

37. **passer l'arme à** _____ *exp*. to die, to kick the bucket.

52. **plus** _____**de la nuit (au)** *exp*. in the dead of night.

53. **taper sur le** _____**à quelqu'un** *exp*. to bug someone, to get one someone's nerves.

67. **côté de la** _____**(être à)** *exp*. to be out of one's.

72. **tirer à bon** _____**(s'en)** *exp*. to get off easy (cheap).

CROSSWORD PUZZLE

D. Choose the correct definition of the word(s) in boldface.

1. **avoir du culot:**
   a. to be tired
   b. to have nerve
   c. to be sick
   d. to be afraid

2. **coup de fil:**
   a. headache
   b. phone call
   c. black eye
   d. a loud noise

3. **avoir un coup de pompe:**
   a. to be exhausted
   b. to be energetic
   c. to have nightmares
   d. to be amazed

4. **être cousu(e) d'or:**
   a. to be poor
   b. to be rich
   c. to be angry
   d. to be overcome with fear

5. **gagner gros:**
   a. to leave
   b. to exaggerate
   c. to make big bucks
   d. to put on weight

6. **faire peau neuve:**
   a. to sunbathe
   b. to turn over a new leaf
   c. to shave
   d. to put on makeup

7. **l'heure H:**
   a. noon
   b. midnight
   c. the big moment
   d. a boring event

8. **déguerpir:**
   a. to arrive
   b. to sleep
   c. to leave
   d. to eat

9. **y mettre son véto:**
   a. to put one's foot down
   b. to jilt
   c. to talk excessively
   d. to ski

10. **être porté(e) sur quelque chose:**
    a. to be driven by something
    b. to wear something
    c. to carry something
    d. to be in love

ANSWERS TO LESSONS 1-10

LEÇON UN - *Qu'est-ce qu'il chante-là?!*

Practice the Vocabulary

A. **CROSSWORD**

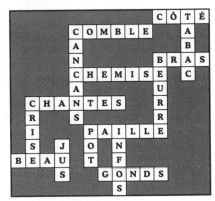

B.
1. au jus
2. paille
3. côté
4. beurre
5. bras
6. tabac
7. vingt
8. chantes
9. début
10. pommes

C.
1. jus
2. vingt
3. plaqué
4. tendre et cher
5. à côté
6. malheur
7. chantes
8. cancans
9. pot
10. salades
11. crise
12. beau
13. morceau
14. gonds
15. beurre noir
16. gênée pour
17. trois pommes
18. tabac
19. oh, là, là
20. chemise
21. tombent
22. début
23. tout flamme
24. rose
25. onde
26. petit
27. noise
28. pis
29. sidérant
30. arrivés là
31. bon
32. parfait amour
33. paille

A CLOSER LOOK I:
Practice Using the Personal Pronoun "On"

A. 1. On l'a pas vu.

2. On devrait signaler l'accident à la police.

3. Si on allait à la plage?

4. On s'voit tout l'temps.

5. J'crois qu'on s'est rencontré avant.

6. On arrive!

7. On pourra aller au cinéma si tu veux.

8. On s'amuse ici.

9. J'espère qu'on trouv'ra une belle maison.

10. On y va?

A CLOSER LOOK II:
Practice the Colloquial Usage of "En"

A. 1. Si! J'en veux, du gâteau.

2. Si! Il en a, des lunettes de soleil.

3. Si! Elle en a, des sœurs.

4. Si! J'en ai vus, des oiseaux au parc.

5. Si! J'en ai, des idées sur le sujet.

6. Si! J'en ai mangé, des chocolats belges.

7. Si! Il en a vus, des couchers d'soleils.

8. Si! Elle en a, de la chance.

9. Si! J'en ai, de l'argent sur moi.

10. Si! Il en prend, des risques.

B. 1. J'en ai huit, des chemises.

2. Elle en a trois, des enfants.

3. Il en a bu quatre, des bières.

4. J'en ai ach'té six, des pantalons.

5. Elle en a pris cinq, des aspirines.

6. Il en a huit, des chaussures.

7. J'en ai cinq, des frères.

8. J'en compte quarante, des spectateurs.

9. J'en ai rencontré dix, des vedettes.

10. Elle en a brûlé cinq, des dîners cette semaine.

11. J'en ai trouvé cinq, des erreurs.

12. J'en veux un millier, des macarons au chocolat.

LEÇON DEUX - *Une fée du logis*

Practice the Vocabulary

A.　1. c　　　　5. a　　　　9. a
　　2. a　　　　6. a　　　　10. b
　　3. c　　　　7. b
　　4. b　　　　8. a

B.　1. b　　　　5. a　　　　9. b
　　2. b　　　　6. a　　　　10. b
　　3. a　　　　7. b
　　4. b　　　　8. b

C.　1. incorrect usage　　5. correct usage　　9. incorrect usage
　　2. incorrect usage　　6. correct usage　　10. correct usage
　　3. correct usage　　　7. incorrect usage
　　4. incorrect usage　　8. incorrect usage

A CLOSER LOOK:

Fruits and Vegetables Used in Idiomatic Expressions

A.　1. G　　　　5. B　　　　9. D
　　2. I　　　　6. E　　　　10. F
　　3. H　　　　7. A
　　4. C　　　　8. J

LEÇON TROIS - *On a Piqué Ma Téloche!*

Practice the Vocabulary

A.　1. mouche　　　5. gratte　　　9. doigts
　　2. cadre　　　　6. baisse　　　10. papiers
　　3. pied　　　　7. tête
　　4. porte　　　　8. fait

B. **WORD SEARCH**

C. 1. J   3. C   5. D   7. F   9. H
   2. G   4. A   6. E   8. I   10. B

A CLOSER LOOK:

Practice Using Professions in Slang

A. 1. J   4. K   7. C   10. E
   2. L   5. I   8. F   11. B
   3. G   6. A   9. H   12. D

B. 1. a, b, d   3. b, d   5. c, e   7. a, d
   2. b, d, e   4. a, c, d, e   6. b

LEÇON QUATRE - *La Joie d'Être Bouchon*

Practice the Vocabulary

A. **CROSSWORD**

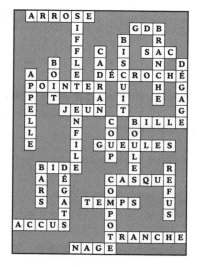

B. 1. a   3. a   5. b   7. a   9. a
    2. b   4. a   6. b   8. a   10. a

C. 1. L   4. I   7. F   10. G
    2. A   5. E   8. K   11. H
    3. J   6. C   9. B   12. D

A CLOSER LOOK:
Practice Slang Suffixes

A. 1. téloche   5. fadasse   9. richard(e)
    2. duraille   6. follasse   10. glandouiller
    3. lichailler   7. cinoche
    4. poiscaille   8. prétentiard

LEÇON CINQ - *Elle est laide à pleurer!*

Practice the Vocabulary

A. 1. correct usage   5. incorrect usage   9. correct usage
    2. incorrect usage   6. correct usage   10. correct usage
    3. correct usage   7. incorrect usage
    4. incorrect usage   8. incorrect usage

B. 1. a   3. a   5. a   7. a   9. b
    2. b   4. a   6. b   8. b   10. b

C. 1. dèche   3. disque   5. casser   7. œil   9. donné
    2. belle   4. dernier   6. lèche   8. air   10. maintes

A CLOSER LOOK:
Practice Using Fish, Insects, and Animals in Idiomatic Expressions

A. 1. C   4. H   7. F   10. K   13. N
    2. E   5. D   8. B   11. J   14. M
    3. G   6. A   9. I   12. L

B. 1. chien   4. kangourou   7. baleine   10. lapin
   2. mouches   5. chevaux   8. vers   11. rat
   3. cochon   6. cheval   9. moutons   12. lièvre

REVIEW EXAM FOR LESSONS 1-5

Practice the Vocabulary

A. 1. milieu   4. le bide   6. tranche   8. dernier
   2. cancans   5. c'est dans   7. rond comme   9. pointé
   3. boules   l'sac   une bille   10. vitrines

B. 1. pleurer   4. rien   7. casque   10. pommes
   2. œil   5. biscuit   8. matraque   11. bras
   3. maintes   6. branche   9. disque   12. vingt

C. **CROSSWORD**

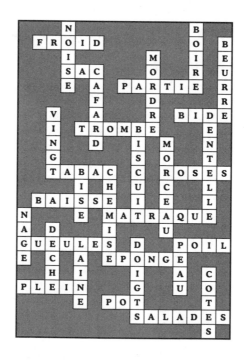

D. 1. L   4. C   7. F   10. I
   2. A   5. D   8. G   11. J
   3. B   6. E   9. H   12. K

LEÇON SIX - *On n'apprend pas à un vieux singe à faire la grimace*

Practice the Vocabulary

A. 1. c   3. a   5. a   7. a   9. b
    2. b   4. c   6. b   8. c   10. a

B. 1. dis   5. rit   9. peau
    2. faire   6. air   10. l'étoffe
    3. rentrer au bercail   7. carafe   11. trois
    4. bouche   8. m'taper   12. tissu

C. 1. G   3. C   5. A   7. E   9. F
    2. B   4. D   6. H   8. J   10. I

A CLOSER LOOK:
Practice Using Using Proper Names in Idiomatic Expressions

A. 1. c   3. a   5. b   7. c   9. c
    2. b   4. b   6. c   8. c   10. c

LEÇON SEPT - *Elle file un mauvais coton!*

Practice the Vocabulary

A. **CROSSWORD**

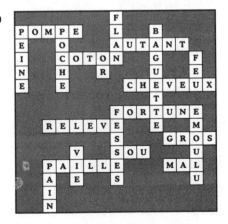

B. 1. a   3. a   5. a   7. a   9. a
    2. b   4. b   6. b   8. a   10. a

C. 1. poche   9. baguette   17. peau   25. fortune
    2. placer   10. char   18. autant   26. feu
    3. peine   11. meurs   19. frais   27. paille
    4. relève   12. vie   20. cheveux   28. touché
    5. pompe   13. or   21. sous   29. cuit
    6. coton   14. pas mal   22. gros
    7. serviette 15. remonter 23. jouent
    8. feu   16. flan   24. évidence

A CLOSER LOOK:
Practice Expressions that Contain Numbers

A. 1. b   4. b   7. a   10. a
    2. c   5. c   8. a   11. b
    3. a   6. a   9. c   12. c

LEÇON HUIT - *Je pète les plombs!*

Practice the Vocabulary

A. 1. douce   5. plier   9. rame   13. culot   17. heu
    2. bon   6. véto   10. porté   14. dents   18. intérêt
    3. ronge   7. sauter   11. grasse   15. bedaine
    4. pieds   8. pédales   12. deux   16. exprès

B. 1. porté   4. bouquet   7. fil   10. nouveau   13. mort
    2. pieds   5. ronflette 8. œuf   11. bouton   14. soupé
    3. palmées   6. compte   9. bagages   12. frein

C. 1. F   3. D   5. C   7. I   9. B
    2. G   4. E   6. H   8. A   10. J

A CLOSER LOOK 1:

Practice Using Movie and Theater Slang

A. 1. C   4. G   7. J   10. B
    2. E   5. L   8. A   11. F
    3. H   6. I   9. K   12. D

A CLOSER LOOK 2:

Practice "Verlan"

A. 1. calibre;   5. mec;   9. falzar;
       revolver   guy   pants

    2. être au parfum;   6. gonzesse;   10. femme;
       to be up-to-date   girl   woman/wife

    3. poulet;   7. baraque;   11. jobard;
       police officer   house   crazy

    4. clope;   8. être dans le coltar;   12. pourri;
       cigarette   to be exhausted   rotten/corrupt

B. 1. raquebar   5. lépou   9. péclot
    2. balpeau   6. quèm   10. zesgon
    3. fumpar   7. meuf   11. barjot
    4. brelica   8. tarcol   12. zarfal

LEÇON NEUF - *J'en ai gros sur la patate*

Practice the Vocabulary

A. **CROSSWORD**

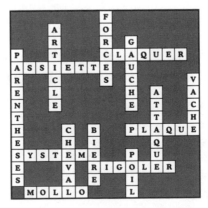

B. 1. a   3. a   5. b   7. b   9. b
    2. b   4. a   6. b   8. a   10. a

C. 1. dirait   7. forces   13. poil   19. œil
    2. assiette   8. attaque   14. système   20. plaque
    3. patate   9. mollo   15. bière   21. boîte
    4. article   10. claquer   16. parenthèses   22. gym
    5. cheval   11. rigoler   17. vache
    6. arme   12. manquerait   18. biscottos

A CLOSER LOOK 1:

Practice Slang Terms of Affection

A. 1. ma bellotte   4. ma chouchoute   7. ma mimine
    2. ma biquette   5. ma cocotte   8. ma poulette
    3. ma choute   6. ma louloute

A CLOSER LOOK 2:

Practice "Largonji"

A. 1. marteau; crazy   5. bateau; boat   9. vingt; 20,
    2. femme; woman/wife   6. beau; handsome   a 20-franc piece
    3. sac; a ten-franc   7. cher; expensive   10. bistrot; bistrot,
      piece   8. beurre; money/   café
    4. bout; end   butter

B. 1. loufoque   4. lamefé   7. listrobèm
    2. laubiche   5. loucedoc   8. lacsé
    3. loinqué   6. loucherbèm   9. lerche

LEÇON DIX - *Elle est enceinte jusqu'aux dents!*

Practice the Vocabulary

A. 1. correct usage   5. correct usage   9. incorrect usage
    2. incorrect usage   6. correct usage   10. correct usage
    3. incorrect usage   7. incorrect usage
    4. incorrect usage   8. incorrect usage

B. 1. ombre   4. H   7. mordre   10. roche
    2. rab   5. cru   8. retard   11. dents
    3. yeux   6. prune   9. déguerpir   12. yeux

C. 1. a   3. b   5. b   7. b   9. a
    2. b   4. b   6. a   8. b   10. a

A CLOSER LOOK:
Practice Your Gestures

A. 1. "Beats me!"   4. "What are you talking about?!"
    2. "My eye!"   5. "That's crazy!"
    3. "Nothing!"   6. "That person's drunk!"

REVIEW EXAM FOR LESSONS 6-10

Practice the Vocabulary

A. 1. deux; trois   3. l'étoffe   5. carafe   7. flan   9. fesses
    2. déclaration   4. rit   6. bouche   8. coton   10. langue

B. 1. envie   4. feu   7. véto   10. bedaine
    2. mal   5. douce   8. bagages   11. pédales
    3. pain   6. exprès   9. fesses   12. palmées

C. **CROSSWORD**

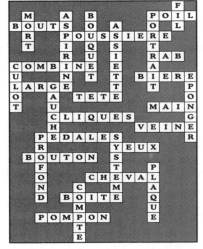

D. 1. b   3. a   5. c   7. c   9. a
    2. b   4. b   6. b   8. c   10. a

Glossary

****ORDER FORM ON BACK****

Prices subject to change

AMERICAN	BOOK	CASSETTE
STREET TALK -1 . . . . *How to Speak and Understand American Slang*	$16.95	$12.50
STREET TALK -2 . . . . *Slang Used in Popular American Television Shows*	$16.95	$12.50
STREET TALK -3 . . . . *The Best of American Idioms*	$18.95	$12.50
BIZ TALK -1 . . . . *American Business Slang & Jargon* (general office • finance • meetings & negotiations • business travel • "computerese" • marketing & advertising)	$16.95	$12.50
BIZ TALK -2 . . . . *More American Business Slang & Jargon* (international trade • hotel & tourism • hospitality • real estate • human resources • management • "bureaucratese" • legalese • politics)	$16.95	$12.50
BLEEP! . . . . *A Guide to Popular American Obscenities*	$14.95	$12.50

FRENCH		
STREET FRENCH -1 . . . . *The Best of French Slang*	$15.95	$12.50
STREET FRENCH -2 . . . . *The Best of French Idioms (available September '96)*	$15.95	$12.50
STREET FRENCH -3 . . . . *The Best of Naughty French (available September '96)*	$15.95	$12.50

SPANISH		
STREET SPANISH . . . . *How to Speak and Understand Spanish Slang*	$15.95	$12.50

GERMAN		
STREET GERMAN -1 . . . . *The Best of German Idioms*	$16.95	$12.50

— OPTIMA BOOKS Order Form —

2820 Eighth Street · Berkeley, CA 94710

For U.S. and Canada, use our TOLL FREE FAX line: 1-800-515-8737
International orders FAX line: 510-848-8737 · Publisher direct: 510-848-8708

Name _____

(School/Company) _____

Street Address _____

City _____ State/Province _____ Postal Code _____

Country _____ Phone _____

Quantity	Title	Book or Cassette?	Price Each	Total Price

Total for Merchandise _____
Sales Tax (California Residents Only) _____
Shipping (See Below) _____
ORDER TOTAL _____

METHOD OF PAYMENT (check one)

☐ Check or Money Order   ☐ VISA   ☐ Master Card   ☐ American Express   ☐ Discover
(Money orders and personal checks must be in US funds and drawn on a US bank.)

Credit Card Number: **Card Expires:**

☐☐☐☐ ☐☐☐☐ ☐☐☐☐ ☐☐☐☐ ☐☐☐☐   ☐☐ ☐☐

Signature (important!):

SHIPPING

Domestic Orders: SURFACE MAIL (delivery time 5-7 days).
Add $5 shipping/handling for the first item · $1 for each additional item.
RUSH SERVICE available at extra charge.

International Orders: OVERSEAS SURFACE (delivery time 6-8 weeks).
Add $6 shipping/handling for the first item · $2 for each additional item.
OVERSEAS AIRMAIL available at extra charge.

SF2